高等院校金融学专业系列教材

金融英语(第 2 版)

杨静宽　施　箐　徐　璐　编著

清华大学出版社
北　京

内 容 简 介

本书为金融学本科系列教材之一。全书共十五个单元，基本涵盖了金融业务的基础知识，主要包括货币与利率、汇率与外汇市场、金融市场概述、货币市场、资本市场、金融衍生品市场、金融机构、商业银行、投资银行、金融服务、信贷、国际结算、银行业监管、保险业和会计学基础知识等内容。

本书设计独特，所有单元的编排遵循了循序渐进的课堂教学规律。每个单元通过案例导入、课文预习、课后阅读理解和拓展阅读等多样练习的设计，使学生能够较为扎实地掌握与本单元主题相关的金融知识和英语语言知识。

本书可供国际经济与贸易、金融学、会计学、工商管理、商务英语和金融英语等专业的学生使用，也可作为金融英语证书考试的考前辅导教材。

本书封面贴有清华大学出版社防伪标签，无标签者不得销售。
版权所有，侵权必究。举报: 010-62782989, beiqinquan@tup.tsinghua.edu.cn。

图书在版编目(CIP)数据

金融英语/杨静宽，施箐，徐璐编著. —2版. —北京: 清华大学出版社, 2019(2023.1重印)
(高等院校金融学专业系列教材)
ISBN 978-7-302-53694-9

Ⅰ.①金… Ⅱ.①杨… ②施… ③徐… Ⅲ.①金融—英语—高等学校—教材 Ⅳ.①F83

中国版本图书馆 CIP 数据核字(2019)第 187555 号

责任编辑：孟　攀
封面设计：刘孝琼
责任校对：吴春华
责任印制：宋　林

出版发行：清华大学出版社
　　　　网　　址：http://www.tup.com.cn, http://www.wqbook.com
　　　　地　　址：北京清华大学学研大厦 A 座　　邮　编：100084
　　　　社 总 机：010-83470000　　邮　购：010-62786544
　　　　投稿与读者服务：010-62776969, c-service@tup.tsinghua.edu.cn
　　　　质量反馈：010-62772015, zhiliang@tup.tsinghua.edu.cn
　　　　课件下载：http://www.tup.com.cn, 010-62791865
印 装 者：大厂回族自治县彩虹印刷有限公司
经　　销：全国新华书店
开　　本：185mm×260mm　　印　张：17　　字　数：413
版　　次：2014 年 6 月第 1 版　2019 年 9 第 2 版　印　次：2023 年 1 月第 5 次印刷
定　　价：49.00 元

产品编号：080774-01

第2版前言

　　本书自2014年6月第1版问世以来,有幸承蒙各兄弟院校同行的厚爱,选用本书作为金融学专业学生专业英语的教材。但是,由于本书是编者在编写了一些商务英语教材后的一次新尝试,第1版中存在诸多不足和疏漏。非常感谢出版社对《金融英语》进行再版,使编者有机会对本书第1版进行修订。

　　编者根据自己对本书的使用体验和本书使用者的反馈意见,在本书第2版中依然沿用了第1版的布局和体例。考虑到每一单元的课文主要涉及的是金融学的基本理论,在第1版的编写过程中编者对课文已做了精挑细选,所以在第2版中编者基本保留了第1版每一单元的课文。本书第2版主要在以下三个方面做了修改。

　　(1) 替换了阅读理解练习这一模块中的部分练习,主要是完形填空和翻译练习。

　　(2) 替换了拓展阅读中那些已失去时效的文章,选用了一些与课文所涉及的金融学基本理论相关的报刊文章,尤其是金融科技方面的文章。一方面,编者希望通过这些报刊文章的拓展阅读,培养学生理论联系实际的能力,使学生能够用课文中学到的金融学理论知识,用英语来思考和讨论当下国内外在经济和金融领域发生的变化。另一方面,编者希望通过拓展阅读,帮助金融专业的学生养成阅读英文报刊的良好习惯,因为编者深信,这种习惯对于他们今后的职业发展大有裨益。

　　(3) 修正了本书第1版中存在的疏漏。

　　编者希望能够做到精益求精,不断完善本书。由于编者水平有限,书中难免依然存在不妥和疏漏之处,恳请本书的使用者继续不吝指正。

编　者

第1版前言

随着国际金融市场的飞速发展，需要大批既有扎实的金融知识，又有娴熟的英语交流能力的国际金融人才。本书旨在帮助培养既懂得金融学的基本理论、专业知识及操作过程，又具有国际沟通能力的金融人才。

本书中的课文基本选自英语原版教材，部分课文经过编者的重新编排，内容基本涵盖了金融业务的基础知识。每个单元围绕某一特定的金融主题进行组织编排，课文练习的设计兼顾了口头表达、阅读理解、金融知识和金融信函写作等技能的训练。

每个单元主要包括以下几个模块。

(1) 案例导入：通过一个简短的案例激活学生的背景知识，启发学生进行独立思考，从而引出单元的主题，同时训练学生口头表达的能力。

(2) 课文预习：通过略读和查读、词汇预测等练习的设计来训练学生快速阅读的能力。

(3) 课文注释：通过对课文难点的注释帮助学生正确理解课文。

(4) 阅读理解练习：通过设计课文阅读理解、词汇练习、完形填空、英汉单句翻译、汉英段落翻译等练习，帮助学生全面巩固该单元所涉及的金融知识和重点需掌握的语言知识。

(5) 金融知识自测题：通过设计10个与本单元主题相关的金融知识综合训练题，检测学生对本单元所涉及的主题金融知识的掌握情况，为学生今后参加金融英语证书考试做准备。

(6) 金融信函写作：帮助学生掌握常见的金融信函写作的要诀。

(7) 拓展阅读：该部分阅读材料基本选自最新的报纸杂志和网站的文章或演讲稿，设计该练习的目的是引导学生阅读英语报纸杂志，培养学生的探索能力和自主学习的能力。

本书是编者在编写了一些商务英语教材后的一次新尝试。由于编者水平有限，书中不妥、疏漏之处在所难免，敬请广大师生和使用者不吝指正。

编　者

目　　录

Unit 1　Money and Interest 1
　　　　Case 1
　　　　Preview 1
　　　　Text 4
　　　　Terminology 7
　　　　Notes on the Text 8
　　　　Exercises 10
　　　　Supplementary Reading 14

Unit 2　Foreign Exchange Rates and Markets 16
　　　　Case 16
　　　　Preview 16
　　　　Text 18
　　　　Terminology 23
　　　　Notes on the Text 24
　　　　Exercises 26
　　　　Supplementary Reading 30

Unit 3　An Overview of Financial Markets 33
　　　　Case 33
　　　　Preview 33
　　　　Text 36
　　　　Terminology 40
　　　　Notes on the Text 41
　　　　Exercises 42
　　　　Supplementary Reading 46

Unit 4　Money Market 49
　　　　Case 49
　　　　Preview 49
　　　　Text 51
　　　　Terminology 55
　　　　Notes on the Text 55
　　　　Exercises 57
　　　　Supplementary Reading 61

Unit 5 Capital Market 64

    Case 64
    Preview 64
    Text 66
    Terminology 70
    Notes on the Text 71
    Exercises 72
    Supplementary Reading 78

Unit 6 Derivatives Markets 80

    Case 80
    Preview 80
    Text 83
    Terminology 87
    Notes on the Text 87
    Exercises 88
    Supplementary Reading 92

Unit 7 Financial Institutions 96

    Case 96
    Preview 96
    Text 99
    Terminology 102
    Notes on the Text 103
    Exercises 104
    Supplementary Reading 109

Unit 8 Commercial Banks 112

    Case 112
    Preview 112
    Text 114
    Terminology 120
    Notes on the Text 120
    Exercises 122
    Supplementary Reading 126

Unit 9 Investment Banks 128

    Case 128
    Preview 128

		Text	130
		Terminology	134
		Notes on the Text	135
		Exercises	135
		Supplementary Reading	139
Unit 10	Financial Services		142
		Case	142
		Preview	142
		Text	145
		Terminology	149
		Notes on the Text	149
		Exercises	151
		Supplementary Reading	155
Unit 11	Loans		157
		Case	157
		Preview	157
		Text	159
		Terminology	164
		Notes on the Text	164
		Exercises	165
		Supplementary Reading	170
Unit 12	International Settlement		172
		Case	172
		Preview	172
		Text	174
		Terminology	180
		Notes on the Text	180
		Exercises	182
		Supplementary Reading	187
Unit 13	Banking Supervision		190
		Case	190
		Preview	190
		Text	192
		Terminology	198
		Notes on the Text	199

| | Exercises | 200 |
| | Supplementary Reading | 205 |

Unit 14　Basics of Insurance ... 209

Case	209
Preview	209
Text	211
Terminology	215
Notes on the Text	217
Exercises	218
Supplementary Reading	222

Unit 15　Basics of Accounting ... 226

Case	226
Preview	226
Text	228
Terminology	232
Notes on the Text	233
Exercises	234
Supplementary Reading	239

Reference Key for the Exercises in the Texts ... 241

Unit 1　Money and Interest

Case

David was offered a well-paid job but the company was twenty miles away from his home, so he decided to buy a car. Since he had been working for only two years with almost no savings, he planned to buy in installments. He went to several car dealers to find out the best loan he could get. Most car dealers would finance through a bank or through the carmaker's financial company, and the rates, just like car prices, were in competition.

David finally found a rate he was satisfied with, but in the following month, he found that the rate had declined. Though he felt satisfied with the deal he got, he wondered what factors would influence interest rates.

Questions

1. Do you know why there are different types of interest rates?
2. Can you help David figure out the factors that influence interest rates?

Preview

Previewing, which gives you an overview of the text, is mental preparation for reading. It increases both reading comprehension and speed. Efficient readers generally preview before reading a text thoroughly. Previewing can take from 30 seconds to 10 minutes, depending on the length of the reading material. In this text, previewing includes skimming, scanning and guessing the meaning of some words from the context.

Skimming

Skimming involves quickly looking over the reading material in order to gain a general idea of the text. You are supposed to glance at the title, headings (if there are any) / the first and last paragraphs, and the topic sentence of each paragraph. If there are illustrations, cartoons, graphic aids, or sources, briefly glance at them as well.

Skim the following text quickly to answer the following questions and discuss your answers with your partners.

1. What are the two essential ideas that dominate the monetary system?
   _____
   _____.

2. What are the two types of money mentioned in the text?
   _____
   _____.

3. What are the factors that affect interest rates?
_____
_____.

4. What is the relationship between interest rates and business?
_____
_____.

5. What are the goals of the Federal Reserve's monetary policy?
_____
_____.

Scanning

Scanning involves quickly looking over the reading material in order to find specific information. You should glance over each part, trying to find the key word or words for the question. After you have located the answer, read the sentence carefully.

Scan the following text quickly to find the specific information.

1. What is the oldest form of currency?
_____
_____.

2. What is the first form of paper currency in England?
_____
_____.

3. When did "modern" banking begin in England?
_____
_____.

4. What are primary reserves made up of?
_____
_____.

5. What kind of rates does the Federal Reserve control?
_____
_____.

6. How are money supply and the economy related to interest rates?
_____
_____.

7. What resources can a bank use to create money?
_____
_____.

8. How does the Federal Reserve achieve its monetary policy?
_____
_____.

Vocabulary in Context

Guessing the meaning of new or unfamiliar words by using context clues is an important reading skill. It is not necessary to guess the precise meaning; a general idea will enable you to proceed with your reading. The context includes the meanings of the individual words in the sentences as well as the overall meaning of the sentences or paragraph.

Read the following sentences and try to guess the meaning of the italicized words by using the context. Then replace the italicized words with synonyms (words or phrases that have nearly the same or similar meanings).

1. Although the monetary system has *remnants* from long ago, it is also a modern "agreement" dating from the 1930s.
   Although the monetary system has _____ from long ago, it is also a modern "agreement" dating from the 1930s.
2. If you and some friends agreed to use certificates you made for value between you, and you all abided by that *convention*, your currency system would work.
   If you and some friends agreed to use certificates you made for value between you, and you all abided by that _____, your currency system would work.
3. There is no longer silver in a *quarter*, though everyone agrees that it is worth 25 percent of a dollar.
   There is no longer silver in a _____, though everyone agrees that it is worth 25 percent of a dollar.
4. Your deposits are *liabilities* for the bank that holds them, because the bank will have to give your money back to you.
   Your deposits are _____ for the bank that holds them, because the bank will have to give your money back to you.
5. Interest rates are the primary way banks make money and the *focal* point of almost everything they do.
   Interest rates are the primary way banks make money and the _____ point of almost everything they do.
6. When rates drop, more credit is *accessible*, and the economy tends to gather speed.
   When rates drop, more credit is _____, and the economy tends to gather speed.
7. The Fed does indeed attempt to *nudge* rates up and down in the interest of its monetary policy.
   The Fed does indeed attempt to _____ rates up and down in the interest of its monetary policy.
8. Both savers and investors look for higher rates when they fear that inflation will *erode* the value of what they earn.
   Both savers and investors look for higher rates when they fear that inflation will _____ the value of what they earn.
9. Banks are constantly *monitoring* and adjusting their reserves to make sure they can cover their liabilities.
   Banks are constantly _____ and adjusting their reserves to make sure they can cover their liabilities.
10. If rates rise, it discourages borrowing, so lending activity slows. When rates fall, banks may

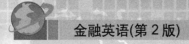

feel *sage* to lend more to earn money.

If rates rise, it discourages borrowing, so lending activity slows. When rates fall, banks may feel _____ to lend more to earn money.

Text

Money and Interest Rate

The Nature of Money

To understand where the money supply[1] comes from, how it moves, and how banks and the Federal Reserve[2] influence it, you need to understand what money in the United States really is. Although the monetary system[3] has remnants from long ago, it is also a modern "agreement" dating from the 1930s. Two essential ideas dominate the monetary system. One is the idea of fiat money, and the other is the idea of a fractional-reserve system.

Two Types of Money

Why does money have value? Money is a medium of exchange—something with an agreed-upon value used for trade. Today that agreed-upon value is strictly a convention of the government and has no necessary relationship to the value of gold, silver, bushels of grain, feathers, or any other commodity. A dollar is worth a dollar because everyone agrees that it is, not because it is backed by an amount of precious metal somewhere. Historically, there are two types of monetary systems.

Commodity money is based on some items of value, for example, gold or precious stones. Coins, the oldest form of currency, had some value because of the metal in them. Bank notes were originally issued to represent holdings of precious metal and became the first paper currency. The notes had value because they could be exchanged for an actual amount of a valuable commodity. Although many of the symbolic ideas and concepts associated with commodity money remain in play, commodity money is not generally in use today.

Fiat money is money that is deemed legal tender[4] by the government, and it is not based on or convertible into a commodity. The word "fiat" refers to any order issued by legal authority, and in the case of money, the authority is the Federal Reserve as created by Congress[5]. Take a look at a dollar bill. It announces that it is a Federal Reserve note. The cost to make a dollar bill is only a little more than four cents, and you cannot take Federal Reserve notes to the bank and exchange them for gold or silver. What makes Federal Reserve notes valuable is that they are the only kind of money the government will accept for payment of taxes and for payment of debts related to court actions. They are, in short, the official currency of the United States.

Fiat money makes sense as a medium of exchange. If you and some friends agreed to use certificates you made for value between you, and you all abided by that convention, your currency system would work. In the case of the national system, the government enforces what is acceptable currency, and the Federal Reserve, banks, and market influence its value. In any case, there is no longer silver in a quarter, though everyone agrees that it is worth 25 percent of a dollar.

The Fractional-Reserve System

One of the key concepts in understanding how money is created and manipulated arose almost a thousand years ago. Some people say "modern" banking began in England around 1200. At that time, people began to pay goldsmiths to store precious metals safely. The goldsmiths charged a fee for this service. When people left gold or silver, the goldsmiths gave them receipts, indicating that the holder of the receipts had deposited a certain quantity. Soon, people began to use these receipts as a medium of exchange, because trading them was a lot simpler than going to the goldsmiths, getting the gold, and giving it to the person owed. It was easier just to give the receipt. These receipts were the first bank notes in England, and became a form of paper currency.

The goldsmiths quickly got into the business of lending the gold and silver they had on deposit, charging interest for the loans. That business was good, so goldsmiths began to pay interest to attract deposits, and thus spread[6] was born.

The goldsmiths also noticed something else. Not everyone wanted their gold back at the same time. Therefore, the goldsmiths adopted a fractional reserve system whereby they needed to keep back, or reserve, only a fraction of the total gold that had been deposited — just enough to cover those who might want to withdraw their gold. They could also lend notes, thus making circulation eventually exceeded the reserves of gold that the goldsmiths actually held. In effect, money was "created" without changing the amount of gold.

Although what the goldsmiths noticed was based on a system of commodity money, some of the same principles apply today. First, even though Federal Reserve notes are fiat money, money is created in more or less the same way. Second, a fractional-reserve system is still in use today, and adjusting its requirements in one way that the Federal Reserve controls the money supply.

How Money is Created

How money is created and how currency is printed are two different things. The Bureau of Engraving and Printing[7] performs the task of printing currency. No matter how much the Bureau prints, it isn't actually considered part of the money supply until the Federal Reserve System calls for it. Money is actually created by the interaction of the demand for it, banks' use of it, and the Federal Reserve's supply and control of it.

Banks and other financial institutions play a key role in the creation of money by transacting their business. Banks earn much of their profit by lending. The lending function, however, does much more than earn money for the bank and its stockholders. Because of the function of the Federal Reserve and the banking system as a whole, banks actually "create" and circulate money as they do business.

Deposits and Reserves

Your deposits are liabilities for the bank that holds them, because the bank will have to give your money back to you. In order to guarantee that the bank will have money on hand to cover its liabilities, the Federal Reserve requires banks to hold money in reserve. Only a portion of the total amount of deposits is required to be reserved. Primary reserves consist of cash on hand, deposits that may be due from other banks, and the percentage required by the Federal Reserve System, either held in the vault or on deposit in the District Reserve Bank[8] for the area. A bank may have other reserves as well called secondary reserves. These include securities the bank purchases from the Federal government, usually in the form of government securities. Those reserves held by a bank beyond its reserve requirement are called excess reserves. The excess reserves are the resources a bank uses to create money through its business transactions.

The Multiplier Effect

To understand the role banks play in creating money, consider again the fractional-reserve system. Remember that a bank needs to keep on hand only part of its total liabilities, and that liabilities always exceed reserves. This fractional-reserve system works just as it did for the goldsmiths long ago. Money on deposit, minus the reserve requirement, can be loaned to customers. When it is, it creates new deposits, which also go out to customers as loans and create more deposits, thus expanding the amount of money in the system. This phenomenon is called the multiplier effect.

Interest Rates and Business

Interest rates are the primary way banks make money and the focal point of almost everything they do. Bankers are not creating money purely from the goodness of their hearts. Banks are businesses, and businesses depend on profit to survive. The money supply and the economy are linked closely to interest rates. Generally, when rates are high, money is said to be "tight" and business tends to slow, because it costs more to acquire capital. When rates drop, more credit is accessible, and the economy tends to gather speed. Interest rates play a critical role in determining what the economy is doing.

Factors Affecting Interest Rates

Contrary to what many people believe, the Federal Reserve does not decide interest rates, but its actions influence them. The Fed does indeed attempt to nudge rates up or down in the interest of its monetary policy[9], but forces that determine interest rates are not completely under the Fed's control.

Market forces determine most interest rates. Banks are free to charge whatever rates they want for most of their transactions with customers (within limits), but it is a balancing act. Setting a higher rate for a loan does bring in more income, but it also tends to drive away business. Banking is more fiercely competitive than ever, and the lower the rate banks can charge, the more customers they are likely to have.

The economic conditions at large help determine interest rates, too. If the demand for capital is high, interest rates tend to rise like any other prices. If they rise too far, demand falls off. The inflation outlook influences rates as well, as both savers and investors look for higher rates when they fear that inflation will erode the value of what they earn. Bankers are no different from any other investors in this regard.

The cost of money itself is a factor, and here the Federal Reserve's monetary policy matters. The Federal Reserve does control two rates.

- The federal funds rate is the amount of interest charged for short-term interbank loans[10].

Banks are constantly monitoring and adjusting their reserves to make sure they can cover their liabilities, both those required by the Federal Reserve and those that occur in day-to-day banking. They often borrow or lend funds to each other to make those adjustments. The Fed influences the interest rates on these loans through its open market operations[11] with Treasury securities[12].

- The discount rate is the interest rate that the Federal Reserve sets and charges for loans to member banks[13]. This rate is not to be confused with the prime rate, which is the rate that banks charge their best and most reliable customers. The prime rate is usually the same among major banks, and movement in it often follows movement of the discount rate, but they are not the same thing.

Changes in these rates affect the amount of money banks are willing to borrow to maintain reserves. If rates rise, it discourages borrowing, so lending activity slows. When rates fall, banks may feel sage to lend more to earn more. The goal of these rates is to implement monetary policy by affecting reserves, which in turn affect the money supply, which affects the economy.

Monetary Policy and Interest Rates

The goals of the Federal Reserve's monetary policy are to maintain economic growth, to stabilize prices, and to help international payments flow. Adjusting reserves, setting the discount rate, and influencing the federal funds rate are its tools for achieving policies.

The Federal Reserve sets the discount rate, but it only influences the federal funds rate. Using open market operations, the Fed buys and sells government securities, paying for them by making a deposit in the selling bank's Federal Reserve account. When it sells the securities to dealer banks, it withdraws their cost from the dealer's account at the Federal Reserve. In this way, reserves are increased or decreased, affecting the rate that banks charge each other for interbank loans. The Federal Reserve may buy or sell securities to yield a higher rate than the federal funds rate in order to achieve its goals, without taking gain or loss into consideration.

Terminology

money supply	货币供应
Federal Reserve	美国联邦储备
monetary system	货币体系
fiat money	不兑现法币
fractional-reserve system	部分准备金制度
commodity money	商品货币
primary reserves	一级准备金
secondary reserves	二级准备金
excess reserves	超额准备金
the multiplier effect	乘数效应
interest rate	利率

federal funds rate   美国联邦基金利率
discount rate   贴现率
prime rate   优惠利率
monetary policy   货币政策

Notes on the Text

1. money supply — all the money in circulation and held by banks and individuals in a given country's economy at a given time.

2. the Federal Reserve — It is the central bank for the United States banking system and the institution that holds the primary responsibility for the making and execution of American monetary policies. It is a combination of government power and private ownership and control. it is set up like a private corporation, with member banks holding stock in their district reserve bank, but the President appoints the Board of Governors. The Congress compromises on a mix of private and public interests for the Federal Reserve, and that mix is intended to serve the interest of the nation at large. The Federal government appropriates no money for the Federal Reserve. Its income is derived from financial services and interest on loans to its member banks. Any money made above the cost of providing services is turned over to the U.S. Treasury.

3. monetary system — a set of policy tools and institutions through which a government provides money and controls the money supply in an economy.

4. legal tender — It is a medium of payment allowed by law or recognized by a legal system to be valid for meeting a financial obligation. Paper currency and coins are common forms of legal tender in many countries. (法定货币)

5. Congress — the United States Congress which is the bicameral legislature of the federal government, consisting of the Senate and the House of Representatives.

6. spread — the difference between what a bank pays in interest and what it receives in interest.(利息差价幅度)

7. the Bureau of Engraving and Printing(B.E.P.) — It is a government agency within the United States Department of the Treasury that designs and produces a variety of security products for the United States government, most notable of which is paper currency for the Federal Reserve. In addition to paper currency, the B.E.P. produces Treasury securities, military commissions and award certificates, invitations and admission cards, and many different types of identification cards, forms, and other special security documents for a variety of government agencies. The B.E.P. does not produce coins; all coinage is produced by the United States Mint.

8. District Reserve Bank — The Federal Reserve consists of twelve regional District Reserve banks, located in Atlanta, Boston, Chicago, Cleveland, Dallas, Kansa City, Minneapolis, New York, Philadelphia, Richmond, San Francisco, and St. Louis, which carry out banking functions for government offices in their area, examine member banks in the district, decide whether to loan banks funds, recommend interest rates and implement policy decisions of the

Board of Governors.

9. monetary policy — It is that part of the government's economic policy which tries to control the size of the total stock of money (and other highly liquid financial assets that are close substitutes for money) available in the national economy in order to achieve policy objectives that are often partly contradictory: controlling the rate of increase in the general price level (inflation), speeding up or slowing the overall rate of economic growth (mainly by affecting the interest rates that constitute such a large share of suppliers' costs for new investment but partly by influencing consumer demand through the availability of consumer credit and mortgage money), managing the level of unemployment (stimulating or retarding total demand for goods and services by manipulating the amount of money in the hands of consumers and investors), or influencing the exchange rates at which the national currency trades for other foreign currencies (mainly by pushing domestic interest rates above or below foreign interest rates in order to attract or discourage foreign savings from entering or leaving domestic financial markets). Monetary policy is said to be "easy", "loose" or "expansionary" when the quantity of money in circulation is being rapidly increased and short-term interest rates are thus being pushed down. Monetary policy is said to be "tight" or "contractionary" when the quantity of money available is being reduced (or else allowed to grow only at a slower rate than in the recent past) and short-term interest rates are thus being pushed to higher levels.

10. interbank loans — It is loans between banking institutions, with terms ranging from overnight to one week. Interbank loans are facilitated to cover liquidity requirements set by a regulatory agency. In instances where a bank has a shortage of liquid assets, it borrows from other banks whose liquid assets are in excess than that required. (银行同业拆款)

11. open market operations — It is any of the purchases and sales of government securities and sometimes commercial paper by the Central Bank in the open market as part of its efforts to influence the size of the money supply and the levels of interest rates. The Central Bank's decision to buy up government debt instruments represents an expansionary monetary policy, while sales of government debt instruments by the Central Bank represents a contractionary monetary policy. (公开市场操作)

12. treasury securities — including Treasury bills, notes, and bonds, are debt obligations issued by the United States' Department of Treasury

13. member banks — It is any bank that is part of the Federal Reserve System. In the United States, all national banks must be member banks of the Federal Reserve System. They must purchase stock in the District Reserve Banks in their regions. This stock cannot be bought or sold, and it does not offer control of the District Reserve Bank. It does convey voting rights for directors of the District Bank, and it also pays a 6 percent dividend. State-chartered banks are not required to be member banks, although they may choose to do so if they meet the requirements.

Exercises

I. Reading Comprehension.

Read the text carefully and decide whether the following statements are true (T) or false (F).

___ 1. Fiat money is not backed by commodity reserves but it is money because the government says it is.

___ 2. Lowering the discount rate has the effect of making it less expensive for commercial banks to borrow from the central banks.

___ 3. The Federal Reserve sets both the federal funds rate and the discount rate.

___ 4. The key factor that decides how much a bank can lend is the amount of its excess reserves.

___ 5. The lending ability of a bank increases when the Fed sells government securities in the open market.

II. Vocabulary Building.

A. Match the term in Column A with the definition in Column B.

1. commodity money   a. interest rate that the Fed charges for loans to member banks

2. discount rate   b. currency based on some item of value, such as gold or precious stones

3. federal funds rate   c. interest rate banks charge their best and most reliable customers

4. fiat money   d. cash on hand, deposits due from banks, and the percentage required by the Fed

5. fractional-reserve system   e. phenomenon that creates new deposits from lending

6. multiplier effect   f. interest charged for short-term, interbank loans

7. primary reserves   g. money deemed legal tender by the government, but not based on or convertible into a commodity

8. prime rate   h. securities the bank purchased from the government

9. secondary reserves   i. practice of reserving only part of a deposited quantity

10. money supply   j. liquid assets held by banks and individuals

B. Complete the following sentences with the words given in the box and change the form of the words where necessary.

implement	access	dominate	liquidity	issue	enforce
tight	adjust	guarantee	loose	monitor	stable

1. An association of bankers has been established to _____ self-discipline of the

banking industry.

2. The establishment of a unified inter-bank money market in 1996 in China facilitated better _____ adjustment for financial institutions.

3. South Korea's economy and its stock market are _____ by dozens of financially complex, family-run multinational conglomerates that have been central to the nation's rise on the global stage.

4. The primary capital market mainly deals with the _____ of new securities.

5. The PBC relies on required reserve ratio, interest rate _____ and open market operations as its major monetary policy tools.

6. The establishment of a comprehensive risk _____ and warning system can strengthen banking supervision and enhance bank's capacity for prudential management.

7. The company has decided to intensify the _____ of penalties on those responsible for taking excessive risks and causing serious losses.

8. The banks with extensive overseas branch networks will be required to _____ the new Basel Capital Accord in due course.

9. The safety and availability of liquid funds for transactions and other purposes are essential for the _____ and efficiency of the financial system.

10. Since the late 1990s, more and more private companies in China _____ to the securities and futures markets.

III. Cloze.

There are 10 blanks in the following two passages. For each blank there are four choices marked A, B, C and D. You are supposed to choose the best answer.

Passage 1

Reserve requirements are a percentage of commercial banks' and other depository institutions' demand deposit liabilities (i.e. chequing accounts) that must be (1) _____ on deposit at the Central Bank as a requirement of Banking Regulations. Though seldom used, this percentage may be changed by the Central Bank at any time, thereby affecting the money supply and credit conditions. If the reserve requirement percentage is (2) _____, this would reduce the money supply by requiring a (3) _____ percentage of the banks, and depository institutions, demand deposits to be held by the Central Bank, thus taking them out of supply. As a result, an increase in reserve requirements would increase interest rates, as less currency is (4) _____ to borrowers. This type of action is only performed occasionally as it affects money supply in a major way. Altering reserve requirements is not merely a short-term corrective measure, (5) _____ a long-term shift in the money supply.

(1) A. put   B. stored   C. kept   D. remained
(2) A. increased   B. risen   C. decreased   D. lowered
(3) A. small   B. smaller   C. large   D. larger
(4) A. accountable B. available   C. acceptable   D. allowed
(5) A. but   B. or   C. and   D. though

Passage 2

The function of the Federal Reserve System is to regulate money and credit by buying and selling government securities, thereby influencing (6) _____ of recession and inflation. (7) _____, the Fed cooperates with the Department of the Treasury to issue new coins and paper notes to bank and (8) _____ in international financial policies through member banks overseas.

The Fed includes twelve district reserve banks and branches, all national commercial banks and credit unions, as well as several committees and councils, including the powerful Board of Governors appointed by the President.

Because of its powerful membership, the Fed has been compared (9) _____ a fourth branch of government, but the President's policies are usually (10) _____.

(6) A. stages   B. phases   C. periods   D. times
(7) A. However   B. Moreover   C. Instead   D. Therefore
(8) A. participates B. involves   C. joins   D. engages
(9) A. with   B. to   C. for   D. as
(10) A. implemented B. adapted   C. guaranteed   D. carried on

IV. Translate the following sentences into English.

1. 商业银行提高房贷利率后，通过按揭购房的人每月需还的房贷费用增加。(charge)
2. 中国人民银行是中华人民共和国的中央银行，其主要使命是制定和执行货币政策，监管规范金融业。(implement)
3. 在20世纪30年代大萧条发生之前，许多经济学家往往认为一个经济体其内部是稳定的，因为它有着很强的自我纠错的倾向。(tend to)
4. 非银行金融机构主要由信托投资公司、资产管理公司、证券公司、财务公司、保险公司和许多城市、农村的信用合作社组成。(consist of)
5. 人们普遍认为世界上最早由国家发行的纸币始于大约公元960年的中国，当时中国的宋朝因为铜材短缺限制了铜币的发行，开始发行纸币。(date from)

V. Translate the following paragraphs into Chinese.

1. The Federal Reserve System, commonly called the Fed, is an independent agency of the United States government charged with overseeing the national banking system. Since 1913, the Federal Reserve System has served as the central bank for the United States. The Fed's primary function is to control monetary policy by influencing the cost and availability of money and credit through the purchase and sale of government securities. If the Federal Reserve provides too little money, interest rates tend to be high, and borrowing is expensive, so business activity slows down. If there is too much money, interest rates decline, and borrowing can lead to excess demand, pushing up prices and fueling inflation.

2. The People's Bank of China cut interest rates last week for the first time since December 2008. Its one-year lending rate now stands at 6.31%, which still leaves room for further cuts to help soften the economic slowdown. Industrial production grew by 9.3% in the year to April, its slowest rate since 2009, but growth picked up to 9.6% in May. China's inflation rate also

leaves room for a looser monetary policy. Consumer prices rose by only 3% in the year to May, down from 3.4% in April, the slowest rate since June 2010. That is well below the 4% threshold that has traditionally worried the government.

VI. Self-Testing.

1. The primary function of money is to serve as _____.
   A. a medium of exchange B. a means of payment
   C. a unit of account D. all of the above

2. Which of the following statements about the interest rate is correct ?
   A. The interest rate is determined in the goods market and has an influence on the money market.
   B. The interest rate is determined in the goods market and has no influence on the money market.
   C. The interest rate is determined in the money market and has no influence on the goods market.
   D. The interest rate is determined in the money market and has an influence on the goods market.

3. The central bank can control the following EXCEPT _____.
   A. the discount rate B. the federal fund rate
   C. reserve requirement ratio D. prime rate

4. The main function of the PBC is to _____.
   A. conduct monetary policy B. prevent and dissolve financial risks
   C. maintain financial stability D. all of the above

5. Which of the following is NOT the indirect instrument for implementing monetary policy?
   A. Required reserve ratio. B. Credit ceilings.
   C. Interest rate adjustment. D. Open market operations.

6. A decrease in the money supply usually _____ the interest rate and _____ aggregate demand.
   A. increases…increases B. increases…decreases
   C. decreases…increases D. decreases…decreases

7. To combat inflation, central banks tend to _____ government securities and _____ the discount rate.
   A. sell … raise   B. sell … lower   C. buy … lower   D. buy … raise

8. The higher the required reserve ratio, _____.
   A. the larger the deposit expansion multiplier
   B. the smaller the deposit expansion multiplier
   C. the more excess reserves a bank can use to create money
   D. the more money a bank has to lend to its customers

9. The most flexible tool of monetary policy is _____.
   A. adjusting reserve requirement ratio B. setting the discount rate
   C. influencing open market operations D. raising taxes

10. Assume a reserve rate of 25%, the multiplier effect will be _____, and the original deposit of 20,000 can create up to _____ of new deposits.

    A. 3 … 60,000   B. 4 … 80,000   C. 5 … 100,000   D. 2 … 40,000

VII. Writing.

Please write a letter to Balek Bank in English as fallows.

1. 希望与贵行建立代理行关系。
2. 我方很高兴看到在过去几年里两国之间的贸易在快速增长。为了快速处理两国之间日益增加的银行业务，我方很乐意与贵行建立代理行关系。
3. 出于这一良好的意愿，我方随函附上我们2018年的年度报告供参考。
4. 盼佳音。

Supplementary Reading

Federal Reserve Hikes Rates for Third Time This Year

By Donna Borak
(www.cnnmoney.com, September 26, 2018)

    The decision, which was expected, is a sign of increased confidence in the US economy. Unemployment is low, economic growth is strong and inflation is relatively stable.

    Policymakers under Chairman Jerome Powell unanimously agree to raise the federal funds rate a quarter percentage point, to a range of 2% to 2.25 %. The rate helps determine rates for mortgages, credit cards and other consumer borrowing.

    "Our economy is strong," Power said at a press conference on Wednesday. "These rates remain low, and my colleagues and I believe that this gradual returning to normal is helping to sustain this strong economy."

    Central bankers raised expectations for a fourth rate hike in December, with a majority now in favor of such a move. In June, policymakers were split on whether the Fed should raise rates four times this year or three.

    Looking ahead to 2019, Fed officials expect at least three rates hikes will be necessary, and one more in 2020.

    "The Fed shows no signs of taking a breath in rate hikes," Robert Frick, corporate economist with Navy Federal Credit Union, wrote in a research note.

    The central bank also stripped the word "accommodative" from its description of monetary policy. That may be a signal that the Fed believes interest rates are finally at a neutral level, meaning they neither stimulate nor hinder the economy.

    The Fed kept rates near record lows for years to encourage growth after the financial crisis. But it has been gradually raising them over the past three years.

    Daragh Maher, the head of FX strategy for the United States at HSBC, said the change in language reflects "the reality that policy can no longer be usefully described as loose".

    The Fed wants to raise interest rates steadily to keep the economy from overheating, but avoid raising rates so quickly that it brings on could help start a recession.

For now, the chairman has maintained that gradual interest-rate increases are the best way to balance those risks.

Powell said that central bankers have heard a "rising chorus" of concerns from businesses about the US-China trade war. But he said the economic impact of US tariffs is "still relatively small".

He warned that tariffs could lead to higher consumer prices, but said policymakers don't see that in the numbers just yet.

Walmart, Gap, Coco-Cola, General Motors, Macy's and other companies have said tariffs could force them to raise prices on everyday consumer goods.

The Fed raised its expectation for economic growth this year to 3.1% from 2.8%, reflecting strength in the second and current quarters.

But for 2019, the Fed officials expect growth to slow to 2.5% amid worries about the growing trade rift between the United States and China. The revised estimate is slightly higher than what policy makers expected last quarter, at 2.4%.

The FOMC also gave its first look of what it expects for the economy in 2021. Policy makers anticipate economic growth will shrink to 1.8% in that year.

Investors and former Fed Chairman Ben Bernanke have warned of an economic slowdown in 2020.

Questions

1. Why has the Fed decided to raise the interest rate again, the third time this year?
2. Why has the Fed been raising the rate gradually in the past three years?
3. What does the Chairman think of the the impact of the trade war?
4. What are the policymakers, economists and investors expectation of the economic growth in the US in 2020 and 2021?
5. What is the background of the US interest rate cycle that began in late 2015? What were the impacts of each rate hike on the US economy as well as on China's financial market?

Unit 2　Foreign Exchange Rates and Markets

Case

Joan is the CFO of a Chinese company manufacturing chemical fertilizers. In order to enhance its competitive edge, the company has decided to upgrade its products. So they have placed an order with a French company for some advanced equipment, with payment to be made in three installments: the first to be paid within one month after signing the contract, the second within 6 months and the third within 12 months. Because of the debt crisis among the EU member states, it seems that the current Chinese yuan-to-euro exchange rate is at its record high level and Joan is not sure if the price for euro will rise again in a year's time. So she is thinking of using some financial instruments to avoid the exchange risk.

Questions

1. What methods can Joan use to avoid the exchange risk?
2. What are the factors that can affect the fluctuation of foreign exchange rate?

Preview

Skimming

Skim the following text quickly to answer the following questions and discuss your answers with your partners.

1. What are the two basic types of exchange rates?
   _____.

2. What is the main function of the foreign exchange markets?
   _____.

3. What does the portfolio balance theory attempt to explain regarding exchange rates?
   _____.

4. What are the two main exchange rate systems?
   _____
   _____.

5. What are the factors that are likely to influence changes in a country's exchange rate?
   _____
   _____.

Unit 2 Foreign Exchange Rates and Markets

Scanning

Scan the following text quickly to find the specific information.

1. How is the exchange rate of a currency determined?
   _____
   _____.

2. Where are national currencies bought and sold?
   _____
   _____.

3. When does arbitrage take place?
   _____
   _____.

4. What can importers and exporters do to avoid exchange risk?
   _____
   _____.

5. In what way are arbitrage and speculation similar?
   _____
   _____.

6. How do large experienced investors reduce overall investment risks?
   _____
   _____.

7. What is essential if the fixed exchange system is to function satisfactorily?
   _____
   _____.

8. What is the main flaw of floating rates system?
   _____
   _____.

Vocabulary in Context

Read the following sentences and try to guess the meaning of the italicized words by using the context. Then replace the italicized words with synonyms (words or phrases that have nearly the same or similar meanings).

1. Foreign exchange is the act of *converting* the currency of one country into the currency of another.
   Foreign exchange is the act of _____ the currency of one country into the currency of another.

2. The forex markets play a central role in *facilitating* international trade, and their smooth functioning is essential for the expansion of trade and investment.
   The forex markets play a central role in _____ international trade, and their smooth functioning is essential for the expansion of trade and investment.

3. Inconsistencies between exchange rates, if they appeared, would quickly be *exploited* by a process known as arbitrage.

17

Inconsistencies between exchange rates, if they appeared, would quickly be _____ by a process known as arbitrage.

4. Forward contracts can reduce or eliminate the risk of *adverse* movements in exchange rates, which may upset the profitability of importers and exporters.

   Forward contracts can reduce or eliminate the risk of _____ movements in exchange rates, which may upset the profitability of importers and exporters.

5. Like arbitrage, speculation on forex markets *hastens* the adjustments in exchange rates by anticipating changes.

   Like arbitrage, speculation on forex markets _____ the adjustments in exchange rates by anticipating changes.

6. Movements of such balances in response to anticipated changes in exchange rates in the forex markets can overcompensate for any possible degree of *non-alignment*, thereby causing much greater short-term changes in exchanges rates.

   Movements of such balances in response to anticipated changes in exchange rates in the forex markets can overcompensate for any possible degree of _____, thereby causing much greater short-term changes in exchanges rates.

7. "Dirty" floating — in which the monetary authorities *profess* to follow freely floating exchange rates policies, yet intervene, behind the scenes…

   "Dirty" floating — in which the monetary authorities _____ to follow freely floating exchange rates policies, yet intervene, behind the scenes…

8. Those countries which are unwilling or unable to *abide by* the strict discipline of fixed exchange rates will find their price levels rising above those of the countries which are adhering to such discipline.

   Those countries which are unwilling or unable to _____ the strict discipline of fixed exchange rates will find their price levels rising above those of the countries which are adhering to such discipline.

9. In *stark* contrast to the fixed exchange rate regime, there is the freely floating system.

   In _____ contrast to the fixed exchange rate regime, there is the freely floating system.

10. Even if this raises import prices and *curbs* the growth in imports, it may so stimulate domestic inflation that the "cost" of this policy is still too high, despite balance of payments equilibrium.

    Even if this raises import prices and _____ the growth in imports, it may so stimulate domestic inflation that the "cost" of this policy is still too high, despite balance of payments equilibrium.

Text

Foreign Exchange Rates and Markets

Foreign Exchange and Foreign Exchange Rates

Foreign exchange is the act of converting the currency of one country into the currency of

Unit 2 Foreign Exchange Rates and Markets

another. The term also refers to any currency other than your own. A foreign exchange rate is the price of one nation's money in terms of another nation's money. Like any other price, it is determined by the supply of and demand for the currency in the foreign exchange markets. There are two basic types of exchange rate, depending on the timing of the actual exchange of money. The spot exchange rate is the price for "immediate" exchange. The forward exchange rate is the price now for an exchange that will take place sometime in the future. Forward exchange rates are prices that are agreed today for exchange of money that will occur at a specified time in the future, such as 30, 90, or 180 days from now. Foreign exchange (forex) markets provide an international system of buying and selling claims to currencies immediately (spot) and in the future (forward) involving a world-wide group of banks, brokers, commercial companies and other financial institutions.

Operation of Foreign Exchange Markets

Traders and investors must be able to buy and sell national currencies if they are to make international payments. The forex markets have developed to allow this. Trading in these markets determines the rates at which one currency can be exchanged for others. The forex markets play a central role in facilitating international trade, and their smooth functioning is essential for the expansion of trade and investment.

National currencies are bought and sold in major financial centres, e.g. New York, Singapore, Hong Kong, Tokyo, Frankfurt, Paris and London. London is one of the largest centres of activity with several hundred institutions, mainly banks, dealing in foreign exchange, and with more currencies traded than in any other major centre. Foreign exchange dealers in forex markets do not meet in a particular location but keep in touch via telephone, telex, and other more sophisticated forms of electronic communication.

Exchange rates adjust continually, depending on the balance between orders for buying and selling currencies, and instant communications, combined with extreme competitiveness, ensure that exchange rates in different financial centres keep closely in step.

Inconsistencies between exchange rates, if they appeared, would quickly be exploited by a process known as arbitrage. This involves buying currencies in the financial centres where they are quoted more cheaply and selling them on forex markets where they are quoted at a better rate. The overall result of arbitrage is that the exchange rates soon adjust and come into line in each centre until there is no incentive for arbitrage.

There are two basic types of foreign exchange transactions: spot[1] and forward[2]. Currency is bought and sold for prompt delivery (i.e. two working days hence) in the spot market; currency is bought and sold for delivery at a specified future date in the forward market. Forward contracts[3] can reduce or eliminate the risk of adverse movements in exchange rates, which may upset the profitability of importers and exporters. The extent to which importers and exporters choose to avoid exchange risk by using the forward market, depends partly on their expectations of future movements in spot rates compared to the cost of covering forward, and partly on their own attitude to risk.

Whereas arbitrage exploits the inconsistencies between exchange rates quoted in various centres, speculation[4] aims at profit-making from the expected movements in exchange rates; for example, by

19

selling a currency on the spot market in the hope of buying it later at a lower rate of exchange, or by buying a currency on the spot market in the hope of selling it later at a higher rate. Like arbitrage, speculation on forex markets hastens the adjustments in exchange rates by anticipating changes; thus, in this sense, both arbitrage and speculation are market forces which help forex markets regain equilibrium quickly, so that it can be argued that these market forces serve an economic purpose. However, in recent years, the amount of speculative balances has increased substantially, both in volume and volatility[5]. Movements of such balances in response to anticipated changes in exchange rates in the forex markets can overcompensate for any possible degree of non-alignment, thereby causing much greater short-term changes in exchanges rates. This will place intense pressure on the central banks of the countries whose currencies are the object of speculation, whether for appreciation[6] or depreciation[7].

The Determination of Exchange Rates

Since the exchange rate of a currency is its price on the forex markets in terms of other currencies, it is determined by demand and supply conditions in the forex markets: instant communications and extreme competiveness among the forex markets make them almost perfect markets. The demand and supply of a country's currency are derived from the country's balance of payments[8] position; if it is a surplus country[9], then the demand for its currency will be rising relative to the supply. The forex market will then quote the currency at a higher exchange rate. On the other hand, if it is a deficit country[10], the supply of its currency will be rising relative to the demand and the forex markets will quote a lower exchange value for it. There are two main theories which seek to explain the determination of exchange rates: one relates to the current account[11], and the other to the capital account[12].

The Purchasing Power Parity[13] (PPP) Theory

In its original form the theory states that the equilibrium exchange rate between one currency and another is that rate which equalizes the domestic purchasing powers of the two currencies. If, for example, £1 buys the same amount of goods and services in the UK as do US$ 1.4 in America. If this were not the case, there would be strong incentives to import goods from the "cheaper" country, which would lead to a deficit on the current account for the "expensive" country; as the supply of its currency increased in settling its current account deficit, the forex markets would mark down its exchange rate. The incentive for importing goods and services from the "cheaper" country would only disappear when the sterling/US dollar exchange rate becomes equal to £1= US$ 1.4.

The PPP theory was originally developed to explain the values of exchange rates in the long run. However, there are many problems associated with this theory in its original form. For instance, the theory ignores transport and insurance costs and import duties. More importantly, it depends on the extent to which the goods and services involved may enter into international trade; there are many goods and services which are traded internally, but which cannot be traded internationally, e.g. houses, haircuts. The theory has been refined to take account of differences in patterns of consumption and levels of income of different countries. Nevertheless, the problem of devising baskets of goods and services which reflect common consumption patterns in different countries yet which only include goods which are traded internationally, has limited the usefulness of the theory in predicting exchange rates. Since the relative costs and prices of non-traded goods and services can vary between countries, a comparison of general price levels is not therefore a reliable way of determining the exchange rate equilibrium.

However, the theory has a broad relevance in times of differing inflation rates in the domestic economies of trading partners. If a country's inflation rate significantly exceeds that of its trading partners then, generally speaking, its exports will become uncompetitive at any given exchange rate; as a result it may encounter balance of payment problems, and, in a floating system, the exchange rate will fall.

The Portfolio Balance Theory

This theory emphasizes the importance of interest rate differentials in the financial centres, and their impact on international investment and speculative flows, as a major determinant of exchange rates. It is assumed that large sophisticated investors are aware of interest rate differentials and move funds to take advantage of higher yields; also that they seek to reduce overall investment risks by diversifying their portfolios. The inflow of these funds into financial centres offering higher yield increases the demand for the currencies of such centres, so that the exchange rates of these currencies rise on the forex markets.

Different Types of Exchange Rate Systems

National monetary policies of the trading partners are to some extent interdependent, on account of the exchange rate links between their currencies. Therefore, changes in national monetary policies, even if in pursuit of internal objectives, put pressure on the international exchange rate system in operation.

There are two main exchange rate systems, absolutely fixed and freely floating.

Absolutely Fixed Exchange Rates

The central bank of each country is obliged to intervene to increase or decrease the supply of its currency on the forex markets, so that its exchange rate is maintained at a predetermined exchange parity[14] with certain other currencies.

Freely Floating Exchange Rates

The exchange value of each currency is determined not only by the monetary authorities, but also by the market forces of supply and demand for each currency on the forex markets. In a "pure" float, the central banks take no action, whatever the exchange values quoted for their respective currencies.

In between these two extremes, there are a number of compromise arrangements:

(a) Fluctuation limits around parity values — the international trading community agrees that exchange rates can vary within specific bands either side of an agreed central parity; the central banks only intervene on the forex markets to ensure that the foreign exchange values of their currencies remain within the agreed bands.

(b) "Dirty" floating — in which the monetary authorities profess to follow freely floating exchange rates policies, yet intervene, behind the scenes, to limit the fluctuations in the exchange rates of their currencies to such levels as are most beneficial for their own economies. This is sometimes called a "managed" float.

(c) Crawling peg — the monetary authorities, instead of declaring and maintaining a fixed parity, allow the parities to adjust from time to time, i.e. a system of "gliding" fixed parities.

(d) Direct foreign exchange control — each central bank states the terms and conditions for the release of foreign exchange. An extreme type of direct control is "counter trading", i.e. all foreign trade transactions are undertaken as purely bilateral barter arrangements.

Fixed Versus Floating Exchange Rates

If the fixed exchange rate regime is to function satisfactorily, it is essential that all countries under this regime should ensure that they do not let their interest rates, inflation rates and monetary expansion rates move too far out of line with those prevailing elsewhere within the regime. Those countries which are unwilling or unable to abide by the strict discipline of fixed exchange rates will find their price levels rising above those of the countries which are adhering to such discipline; their exports will become less, and imports more, competitive, leading to rising balance of payments deficits year by year. In order to defend the fixed exchange rate parities, the central banks of these countries will have to continue buying their own currencies on an increasing scale, spending their foreign exchange reserves, until their reserves fall dangerously low. The monetary authorities may then be forced to devalue their currencies by declaring lower exchange parities, in order to avoid continuous intervention on the forex markets. There is a stigma attached to "devaluing" under a fixed exchange rate regime, which countries under such a regime will try to avoid at almost any cost. The strongest argument in favor of fixed exchange rates is that, since currencies will be accepted at known and fixed exchange rates, there will be certainty in international payments and receipts. Fixed exchange rates will eliminate exchange risks and thereby promote international trade and investment.

With fixed exchange rates, however, inflation in the economies of some trading partners will be "imported" into other non-inflation economies, unless the demand for imports is relatively price elastic, and cheaper domestic import substitutes are preferred.

In stark contrast to the fixed exchange rate regime, there is the freely floating system. With freely floating, the market determines exchange rates. It is claimed that there will be less need for official reserves; this follows since (a) there will be no exchange parities to defend, and (b) balance of payments' imbalances should not be automatically corrected by movements in exchange rates. Furthermore, with no fixed regime rules to obey, national governments will be able to pursue independent domestic economic policies, aimed at higher growth and employment. Individual economies will be insulated against "imported" inflation. The economies with the higher inflation rates will tend to experience an automatic fall in their exchange rates. This will reduce their export prices, making imports into the non-inflation economies somewhat cheaper.

However, these theoretical advantages of floating exchange rates do not always fully materialize.

For instance, if the adjustment of balance of payments imbalances is to be automatic, it is essential that the elasticity of demand[15] for imports and exports are sufficiently high to support the automatic adjustment process. Again, even though there is no exchange rate parity to defend, countries are not always free to follow independent monetary policies. For example, rapid growth may bring about higher imports and a fall in the exchange rate; even if this raises import prices and curbs the growth in imports, it may so stimulate domestic inflation that the "cost" of this policy is still too high, despite balance of payments equilibrium.

There will be less need for official reserves or international borrowing only if the exchange rates are truly floating. If floating is "dirty", i.e. managed, there will still be a need for official reserves so that the authorities can intervene on forex markets.

The principal weakness of floating rates is that they might discourage international trade and investment. It is not so much the flexibility in current exchange rates that discourages trade and investment; rather it is the uncertainty about future exchange rates that might have this effect. If, however, movements in exchange rates were easily predicted, then traders and investors could take them into account when planning overseas business and investment.

Terminology

foreign exchange	外汇
foreign exchange rate	汇率
foreign exchange (forex) market	外汇市场
spot exchange rate	现货汇率，即期汇率
claim	索偿权，债权
forward exchange rate	远期汇率
broker	经纪人
international payments	国际收支，国际支付
foreign exchange dealer	外汇经纪人，外汇交易商
arbitrage	套汇
speculation	投机
appreciation	升值
depreciation	贬值
balance of payments	国际收支差额表
surplus	(国际收支)顺差
deficit	(国际收支)逆差
current account	经常项目
capital account	资本项目
purchasing power parity	购买力平价
exchange rate equilibrium	均衡汇率
portfolio	投资组合
interest rate differential	利率差别
fixed exchange rate system	固定汇率制度

freely floating exchange rate system	自由浮动汇率制度
exchange (rate) parity	外汇比价
floating exchange rate	浮动汇率
parity value	比价值
central parity	中间价
dirty floating	受操纵的浮动汇率制度
managed floating	有管理的浮动汇率制度
crawling peg	爬行盯住汇率制度
fixed exchange rate regime	固定汇率制度
foreign exchange reserve	外汇储备
international payments and receipts	国际收支
price elastic	价格弹性
import substitutes	进口替代品
elasticity of demand	需求的价格弹性
volatility	波幅
counter trading	对等贸易

Notes on the Text

1. spot transaction — Spot transaction are purchases or sales of foreign currency for "immediate" delivery. In every exchange deal, there are normally two key dates involved: (1) the "transaction date", on which the respective contract is concluded, and (2) the "value date", on which settlement, i.e., the actual delivery of funds, must take place. A spot foreign exchange transaction involves the purchase of one currency at an agreed price for delivery on the value date. The value date of a spot FX transaction is usually the trade date plus two working days, or one working day in the case of North American currencies.

2. forward FX transaction — Forward exchange transactions involve the purchase or sale of foreign currency at an exchange rate established when the contract is created calling for payment and delivery at a specified future date. Many forward exchange contracts have maturities of one month, three months or six months.

3. forward contract — Forward contracts are foreign exchange transactions with a specified price, and are used to cover future foreign currency payables. To minimize the risk of the fall in the price of the currency in which the seller will be paid, a forward agreement is made between the holder of the currency and the prospective buyer. In a forward contract, the buyer and the seller agree to trade the currency at a particular rate. Forward contracts establish firm prices for exchange proceeds, and reduce transaction losses based on exchange rate fluctuations. Forward contracts are sometimes suitable tools for exporters. Forward contracts are one of the techniques frequently used by exporting companies to hedge against foreign exchange rate risk. Other techniques used to manage foreign exchange related risk include futures trading, options trading and swaps.

4. speculation — It is the act of trading in an asset or conducting a financial transaction that has

a significant risk of losing most or all of the initial outlay in expectation of a substantial gain. With speculation, the risk of loss is more than offset by the possibility of a huge gain; otherwise, there would be very little motivation to speculate. While it is often confused with gambling, the key difference is that speculation is generally tantamount to taking a calculated risk and is not dependent on pure chance, whereas gambling depends on totally random outcomes or chance.

5. volatility — the degree to which the market price of a foreign exchange moves up and down during a short period of time.
6. appreciation — an increase in the value of an asset over time. The increase can occur for a number of reasons including increased demand or weakening supply, or as a result of changes in inflation or interest rates.
7. depreciation — a decrease in an asset's value caused by unfavorable conditions.
8. balance of payments — a record of all transactions made between one particular country and all other countries during a specified period of time. Balance of payments compares the dollar difference of the amount of exports and imports, including all financial exports and imports. A negative balance of payments means that more money is flowing out of the country than coming in, and vice versa. Balance of payments provides detailed information concerning the demand and supply of a country's currency. It can also be used to evaluate the performance of a country in international economic competitiveness.
9. surplus country — a country with more exports of goods and services than imports, which represents a net inflow of domestic currency from foreign markets.
10. deficit country — a country with more imports of goods and services than exports, which means a net outflow of domestic currency to foreign markets.
11. current account — items of transactions taking place frequently in international payments, which include trade incomes and expenditures, income from and expenditures on labor services and unilateral transfers.
12. capital account — the increase and decrease of assets and liabilities in the balance of payments as a result of the inflow and outflow of capital, including direct investment, loans and portfolio investment, etc.
13. purchasing power parity — an economic theory that estimates the amount of adjustment needed on the exchange rate between countries in order for the exchange to be equivalent to each currency's purchasing power. The relative version of PPP is calculated as follows:

$$S = \frac{P_1}{P_2}$$

where:
"S" represents exchange rate of currency 1 to currency 2
"P_1" represents the cost of good "x" in currency 1
"P_2" represents the cost of good "x" in currency 2

14. exchange parity — the exchange rate between the currencies of two countries making the purchasing power of both currencies substantially equal.
15. elasticity of demand — a measure used in economics to show the responsiveness of the quantity demanded of a good or service to a change in its price.

Exercises

I. Reading Comprehension.

Read the text carefully and decide whether the following statements are true (T) or false (F).

_____ 1. Spot transactions are undertaken for an actual exchange of currencies two business days later.

_____ 2. Foreign exchange is dealt across a trading floor.

_____ 3. If the exchange rate makes foreign goods less expensive, demand will increase and imports are likely to rise.

_____ 4. The currency of a surplus country is usually quoted at a higher exchange value on the forex market.

_____ 5. Floating rates might have an adverse effect on international trade and investment because under such a system traders and investors find it difficult to plan their overseas business and investment.

II. Vocabulary Building.

A. Match the term in Column A with the definition in Column B.

1. spot exchange rate
2. forward exchange rate
3. current account
4. capital account
5. exchange parity
6. arbitrage
7. crawling peg
8. appreciation
9. fixed exchange rate
10. dirty floating

a. the difference between a nation's total exports of goods, services and transfers, and its total imports of them

b. the simultaneous buying and selling of the same foreign exchange in two or more markets to take advantage of price differentials

c. the rate of a foreign-exchange contract for immediate delivery

d. a system of floating exchange rates with central bank intervention to reduce currency fluctuations

e. the rate of a foreign-exchange contract with payment or delivery at some future date

f. the net result of public and private international investments flowing in and out of a country

g. the exchange rate between the currencies of two countries making the purchasing power of both currencies substantially equal

h. a system of exchange rate adjustment in which a currency with a fixed exchange rate is allowed to fluctuate within a band of rates

i. a foreign exchange system in which the value of a country's currency to the value of other currencies is maintained at fixed conversion rate through government intervention

j. an increase in the value of a country's currency

B. Complete the following sentences with the words given in the box and change the form of the words where necessary.

| diversify | curb | adverse | band | volatility | pursue |
| quote | regime | relevance | discourage | hasten | incentive |

1. A local economist said that continuing macro-economic risks is a main reason for the weakening of the Vietnam's competitiveness, _____ foreign investors.
2. The prime minister said China would continue to _____ the policies laid down at the APEC summit.
3. Intervention by central banks to reduce the _____ or misalignment in floating rates, or to support the central rates of the European Monetary System, has been a feature of markets for many years.
4. On July 21, 2005, RMB exchange rate _____ was changed to a managed floating system with a reference to a basket of currencies.
5. During the Asian financial crisis period, China narrowed the floating band of the RMB exchange rate so as to _____ the deterioration of the crisis.
6. At the current stage, the daily floating _____ of the exchange rate of RMB/USD in the inter-bank foreign exchange market remains +/− 0.3% of the central parity of RMB/USD publicized by the PBC.
7. We may face trade barriers that could have a material _____ effect on our results of operations and result in a loss of customers or suppliers.
8. The authorized financial institutions are allowed to open foreign exchange accounts for their clients and conduct _____ foreign exchange operations.
9. Chicago Mercantile Exchange Inc. (CME), the largest futures exchange and the world's largest regulated foreign exchange marketplace, today announced a new _____ pricing program for electronic foreign exchange trading for commercial banks that are not currently CME members.
10. One of the ways of _____ your investments within an asset category is to identify and invest in a wide range of companies and industry sectors.

III. Cloze.

There are 10 blanks in the following two passages. For each blank there are four choices marked A, B, C and D. You are supposed to choose the best answer.

Passage 1

Swap transactions (掉期业务) consist of a simultaneous sale or purchase of spot currency accompanied by a purchase or sale, (1)_____ of the same currency for forward delivery. They are also known as "double deals" as the spot is "swapped" (2)_____ the forward. If the spot part of the transaction represents a purchase of a foreign currency, the forward side will represent a sale of the foreign currency. (3)_____, if the spot part is a sale, the forward part will be a purchase. Different exchange rates are used for the contracts, the spot rate and forward rate, (4)_____ the return each party can earn on the currency held for the contract.

Swap transactions are mostly used in investments of foreign securities, in intercompany loans between parent company and (5)_____, in credit swaps, in covering the exchange risks associated with cash flow transactions and in hedging to protect the value of physical and financial assets denominated in foreign currencies.

(1) A. separately   B. respectively   C. simultaneously   D. instantly
(2) A. from   B. into   C. against   D. over
(3) A. Similarly   B. Obviously   C. Differently   D. Conversely
(4) A. representing   B. represent   C. will represent   D. represents
(5) A. departments   B. offices   C. branches   D. subsidiaries

Passage 2

The Bank of England expects to sign a final agreement to set up a three-year yuan-sterling swap line "shortly", during a meeting between Sir Mervyn and his (6)_____ Zhou Xiaochuan in Beijing.

European and US official have been pressing China for years to do more to open up the yuan to market forces, saying its (7)_____ weakness was one of the key imbalances of the global economy.

Beijing is slowly delivering, (8)_____ it still keeps a tight rein on gains for the currency for fear that it will weaken its export-powerhouse economy, (9)_____ has been the biggest engine growth for a decade.

This would be the (10)_____ in a string of bilateral currency agreements that has seen cross-border trading of the yuan expand four-fold since August 2010, and the first with a major developed economy.

(6) A. associate   B. counterpart   C. rival   D. opponent
(7) A. natural   B. innate   C. internal   D. artificial
(8) A. while   B. although   C. unless   D. if
(9) A. which   B. that   C. this   D. it
(10) A. newest   B. recent   C. latest   D. last

IV. Translate the following sentences into English.

1. 在预测外汇走势时，我们应考虑哪些因素？(take account of)
2. 为了消除汇率风险，他通过卖出三个月的美元远期来实现套期保值(hedge)。(eliminate)
3. 一些国家的外汇管制条例不允许将银行券(bank notes)转换为外汇。(conversion)
4. 中国人民银行规定在国内外汇市场从事人民币兑美元交易的银行要遵守每日交易汇率上下幅度不超过上午设定的中间价1%的限制规定。(abide by)
5. 我们应加快发展多层次资本市场，稳步推进利率和汇率市场化改革，逐步实现人民币资本项目可兑换。(take steps)

V. Translate the following paragraphs into Chinese.

1. Almost every nation has its own currency or monetary unit — its dollars, its peso, its rupee —

Unit 2 Foreign Exchange Rates and Markets

used for making and receiving payments within its own borders. But foreign currencies are usually needed for payments across national borders. Thus, in any nation whose residents conduct business abroad or engage in financial transactions with persons in other countries, there must be a mechanism for providing access to foreign currencies, so that payment can be made in a form acceptable to foreigners. In other words, there is a need for "foreign exchange" transactions — exchange of one currency for another.

2. The determinants of the size of the forward premium or discount include relative interest rates between countries. Differences in interest rates between countries move forward rates to either premium or discounts from the spot exchange rate. In addition, expected changes in macroeconomic activity, i.e., growth in gross domestic product, and expected inflation rates also will have an impact on forward exchange rates.

VI. Self-Testing.

1. If foreigners expect the future price of U.S. dollars will drop, _____.
   A. the supply of U.S. dollars will decrease and the exchange rate will rise
   B. the demand of U.S. dollars will decrease and the exchange rate will rise
   C. the supply of U.S. dollars will increase and the exchange rate will fall
   D. the demand of U.S. dollars will increase and the exchange rate will fall

2. When a country runs persistent foreign trade deficits under a floating exchange rate system, _____.
   A. its imports may increase   B. its interest rates may fall
   C. inflation may happen   D. its currency may appreciate

3. If a nation's interest rates are relatively high compared to those of other countries, its currency may _____ under a _____ exchange rate system.
   A. appreciate…floating   B. appreciate… fixed
   C. depreciate…floating   D. depreciate…fixed

4. Which of the following can be used as a technique to manage foreign exchange risk?
   A. Spot.   B. Forward.   C. Speculation.   D. Arbitrage.

5. Which of the following statement(s) is(are) true of arbitrage?
   A. Arbitrage helps keep exchange rate consistent across markets.
   B. Arbitrage is highly risky.
   C. Arbitrage is the process of taking advantage of price difference in different foreign exchange markets.
   D. Both A and C.

6. Which of the following would contribute to China's current account surplus?
   A. A Chinese company exports leather shoes to Britain.
   B. The People's Bank of China buys $100,000 American bonds.
   C. Chinese tourists go to America for a visit.
   D. A Chinese company imports kiwi fruits from New Zealand.

7. An importer will use the forward foreign exchange market when _____.
   A. it has a large payment to make on a particular date in the future

29

B. price of its home currency is stable

C. it expects to make a profit out of the foreign exchange market

D. it has a small payment to make in the future

8. Which of the following statements is (are) the determinant(s) of foreign exchange rate?

   A. Inflation.

   B. Interest rate.

   C. Trade and investment flows between countries.

   D. All of the above.

9. A spot transaction which involves the Canadian dollars traded against the U.S. dollars is settled in _____.

   A. one working day   B. two working days

   C. three working days   D. four working days

10. A possible disadvantage of freely floating exchange rates with no government intervention is that _____.

    A. it may discourage foreign trade and investment

    B. a nation may need a larger supply of foreign exchange reserves

    C. the exchange rates may experience wide and frequent fluctuations

    D. both A and C

VII. Writing.

Please writer a letter to Bank of China in English as follows.

1. 收到中国银行关于建立代理关系的信函后，进行了认真研究。
2. 同意建立代理关系的提议。
3. 随着业务量的增加，我们也觉得很有必要。
4. 根据对方要求，随函寄上 2018 财政年度的年报。

Supplementary Reading

The World's Greatest Investor

George Soros was born in Budapest in 1930. The son of a lawyer, he became a global investment superstar, with a net worth in 2012 estimated at $20 billion. In the 42 years since its founding in 1969, his investment fund earned an incredible average return of about 20 percent per year.

As a Jewish boy, he and his family struggled to evade the Nazis, and they managed to survive. In 1947 he went to England, expecting to continue his engineering studies. Instead, he enrolled in the London School of Economics and graduated in 1952. He began working at a small London brokerage, but he was frustrated by the lack of responsibilities.

In 1956, Soros moved to New York City, where he worked at two securities firms before joining the firm Arnold & Bleichroeder in 1963. In 1967, he became head of investment research, and he was successful at finding food investment opportunities in under-valued European stocks. In 1969, he founded an off-shore hedge fund, using $250,000 of his own money and about $6 million from non-American investors whom he knew. (A hedge fund is an investment partnership that is not restricted by regulations of government agencies like the U.S. Securities and Exchange Commission.

Each hedge fund can establish its own investment style and strategy, and these vary. While some hedge funds do use investment strategies that involve different kinds of hedging, others do not. The manager of a fund usually gets fees and a percentage of the profits, as well as having a substantial amount of his or her own money invested in the fund.)

Soon Soros left Arnold & Bleichroeder, taking his Soros Fund with him. While the 1970s were poor years for the U.S. stock market generally, the Soros Fund prospered. As the manager, Soros focused on finding undervalued sectors in the United States and other countries. He bought unpopular low-priced stocks and sold short popular high-priced stocks. He expected oil demand to outstrip supply, so he bought stocks of companies in oil-field services and oil drilling before the first oil shock in 1973. In the mid-1970s, he invested heavily in Japanese stocks. In 1979, he changed the name of the fund to Quantum Fund, in honor of Heisenberg's uncertainty principle in quantum mechanics. In 1980, the fund return was 103 percent. It had grown to $380 million.

In 1981, *Institutional Investor* magazine named him "the world's greatest investor". But 1981 was a difficult year. The fund lost 23 percent, and one-third of his investors withdrew their investments. This was their mistake. Spectacular returns were still to come.

In early September 1985, Soros became convinced that the U.S. dollar was overvalued relative to the Japanese yen and the German mark, and that a correction was coming soon. He decided to establish speculative investment positions to try to profit from the changes he expected. For instance, he borrowed dollars, used the dollars to buy yen and marks, and bought Japanese and German government bonds. In total, he established an $800 million position, a position larger than the entire capital of the fund. In late September the major governments announced the Plaza Agreement, in which they vowed to take coordinated actions (like intervention in the foreign exchange markets) to raise the values of other major currencies relative to the dollar. Within a month, as the dollar depreciated, Soros had profits of $150 million. The fund's total return for 1985 was 122 percent, as he had also invested in foreign stocks and long-term U.S. Treasury bonds. Of course, not all of his positions turned out so well. For instance, in 1987, the Quantum Fund lost up to $840 million when the U.S. and other stock markets crashed in October. But the fund still earned a return of 14 percent for the entire year.

In September 1992, Soros placed his most famous bet. Following German reunification in 1989, German interest rates increased, and the mark tended to appreciate. But most EU currencies were pegged to each other in the Exchange Rate Mechanism (ERM) of the European Monetary System. So the other countries had to raise their interest rates to maintain the pegged exchange rates. Soros predicted that the British government could not sustain this policy because the British economy was already weak and unemployment was high. He expected that Britain would either devalue the pound within the ERM or pull out of the ERM. In either case, the exchange rate value of the pound would decline. He established his speculative investment positions short in pounds and long in marks, using pound borrowings and mark investments, as well as futures and options. And the positions were big — $10 billion. As Soros and other speculative investors established their positions, they sold pounds, putting downward pressure on the exchange rate value of the pound. The central banks tried to defend the pegged rate, but soon the British government gave up and pulled out of the ERM. The pound depreciated against the mark. Within a month the Quantum Fund made a profit of about $1 billion on its pound positions, and a profit of up to $1 billion on other European currency positions. The *Economist* magazine called Soros "the man who broke the Bank of England".

After 1992, Soros turned over most trading decisions in the Quantum Fund to his chosen successor, Stanley Druckenmiller. The Quantum Fund continued to have some large successes and some large losses. In early 1997, Soros and Druckenmiller foresaw weakness in the Thai baht, and Quantum established short baht positions in January and February. The crisis hit in July, the Thai baht depreciated, and Quantum made money. But when the Thai baht and other Asian currencies continued to depreciate, they thought that the market had taken the rates too far. For instance, when the Indonesian rupiah fell from 2,400 per dollar to 4,000 per dollar, they established long positions in rupiah, and then lost money as the rupiah continued to fall beyond 10,000 per dollar. In 1998, the Quantum Fund lost $2 billion on investments in Russia when Russian financial markets and the ruble collapsed. But the fund still earned more than 12 percent for the entire year. In 1999, the fund was down 20 percent in the first half of the year. It then shifted to investing in tech stocks and ended up 35 percent for the year. The tech investments and long positions in the euro took revenge in early 2000. For the first four months the fund was down 22 percent. Weary of the battles, Druckenmiller resigned in April. Soros announced that the fund was shifting to investing with less risk and lower returns. The fund shrank from over $20 billion in 1998 to $11 billion in 2001.

As he reduced his role in fund management, Soros turned to writing articles and books and to philanthropy. His writing is curious. He is deeply critical of excessive capitalism and individualism — what he calls "market fundamentalism". He believes that unregulated global financial markets are inherently unstable, and he calls for greater national regulation and the establishment of new global institutions like an international credit-insurance organization to guarantee loans to developing countries.

Although Soros is not active much in investment decisions anymore, he remains the quintessential international speculative investor. His name is synonymous with hedge funds, especially those that take large speculative positions. He has been denounced by government officials, like Prime Minister Mahathir Mohamad of Malaysia in 1997, as the source of immense and unjustified speculative pressures on their countries' currencies and financial markets. Soros continues to defend his own investment activities, stating that he merely perceived changes that were going to happen in any case. But, as his writings indicate, at a broader level he has mixed feelings about the current global financial system.

Questions

1. How did Soros found Soros Hedge Fund?
2. Why is Soros regarded as "the world's greatest investor"?
3. Why did the *Economist* magazine call Soros "the man who broke the Bank of England"?
4. How is Soros related to the 1997 Asian financial crisis?
5. What does Soros often criticize in his writings?

Unit 3 An Overview of Financial Markets

Case

1. Tom wants to buy a house that costs $100,000, but he has only $20,000 in savings. How can he raise the other $80,000?

2. Carolina Power & Light (CP&L) forecasts an increase in the demand for electricity in North Carolina, and the company decides to build a new power plant. Because CP&L will almost certainly not have the hundreds of millions of dollars necessary to pay for the plant, the company will have to raise these funds in the financial markets.

Questions

1. Do you know the functions of financial markets?
2. Can you give them some suggestions to cope with their problems?

Preview

Skimming

Skim the following text quickly to answer the following questions and discuss your answers with your partners.

1. What do we generally mean when we speak of market efficiency?
   _____
   _____.

2. What are the three methods by which funds are transferred from savers (lenders) to borrowers?
   _____
   _____.

3. What are the three categories informational efficiency is classified into?
   _____
   _____.

4. What are the different types of financial markets?
   _____
   _____.

5. What is the difference between the debt market and the equity market?
   _____
   _____.

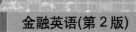

Scanning

Scan the following text quickly to find the specific information.

1. What is a financial market?

2. Why is it important to have a basic understanding of financial markets?

3. What does it mean to have economically efficient financial markets? What does it mean to have informationally efficient financial markets?

4. Why do you think that most transfers of money and securities are indirect rather than direct?

5. According to the three categories of informational efficiency, how do you think of the efficiency of the financial markets?

6. How are the financial markets differentiated?

7. What are the functions of primary markets?

8. What types of assets are traded in the derivatives market?

Vocabulary in Context

Read the following sentences and try to guess the meaning of the italicized words by using the context. Then replace the italicized words with synonyms (words or phrases that have nearly the same or similar meanings).

1. Suppose Carolina Power & Light (CP&L) *forecasts* an increase in the demand for electricity in North Carolina, and the company decides to build a new power plant.
   Suppose Carolina Power & Light (CP&L) _____ an increase in the demand for electricity in North Carolina, and the company decides to build a new power plant.

2. People and organizations that need money are brought together with those that have *surplus* funds in the financial markets.

People and organizations that need money are brought together with those that have _____ funds in the financial markets.

3. In a general sense, the term financial market refers to a conceptual *"mechanism"* rather than a physical location or a specific type of organization or structure.

   In a general sense, the term financial market refers to a conceptual "_____" rather than a physical location or a specific type of organization or structure.

4. In developed economies, financial markets help efficiently *allocate* excess funds of savers to individuals and organizations in need of funds for investment or consumption.

   In developed economies, financial markets help efficiently _____ excess funds of savers to individuals and organizations in need of funds for investment or consumption.

5. When we borrow, for example, we *sacrifice* future income to increase current income; when we save, or invest, we sacrifice current income in exchange for a greater expected income in the future.

   When we borrow, for example, we _____ future income to increase current income; when we save, or invest, we sacrifice current income in exchange for a greater expected income in the future.

6. Older adults, when they become established in their careers and reach or near their *peak* income years, generally save (invest) greater percentages of their incomes.

   Older adults, when they become established in their careers and reach or near their _____ income years, generally save (invest) greater percentages of their incomes.

7. For example, the next time IBM raises funds by issuing stock, it will probably *utilize* the services of an investment banker, such as Goldman Sachs to sell the issue in the financial markets.

   For example, the next time IBM raises funds by issuing stock, it probably will _____ the services of an investment banker, such as Goldman Sachs or Lynch, to sell the issue in the financial markets.

8. In this case, it does no good to *scrutinize* such published data as a corporation's financial statements, because market prices will have adjusted to any good or bad news contained in such reports as soon as they are made public.

   In this case, it does no good to _____ such published data as a corporation's financial statements, because market prices will have adjusted to any good or bad news contained in such reports as soon as they are made public.

9. Strong-form efficiency states that current market prices reflect all *pertinent* information, whether publicly available or privately held.

   Strong-form efficiency states that current market prices reflect all _____ information, whether publicly available or privately held.

10. That is, individuals, corporations, and governments use derivatives to *hedge* risk by offsetting exposures to uncertain price changes in the future.

    That is, individuals, corporations, and governments use derivatives to _____ risk by offsetting exposures to uncertain price changes in the future.

Text

An Overview of Financial Markets[1]

Financial markets are extremely important to the economic well-being of the United States. For this reason, it is important that both investors and financial managers understand the environment and markets within which securities are traded and businesses are operated.

What Are Financial Markets?

Businesses, individuals, and government units often need to raise capital (funds). Whereas some individuals and firms need funds, others have incomes that are greater than their current expenditures. Thus they have funds available to invest, or save. For example, Alexandre Trottier has an annual income of $50,000, but her expenses are only $40,000. Conversely, Chief Consolidated Mining Company needs funds to complete renovation projects and to explore for minerals.

People and organizations that need money are brought together with those that have surplus funds in the financial markets. Note that "markets" is plural — a greater many different financial markets exist, each of which includes many institutions and individuals in a developed economy such as that of the United States. Unlike physical asset markets, which deal with products such as wheat, cars, real estate, computers and machinery, financial asset markets deal with stocks, bonds, mortgages, and other claims on real assets with respect to the distribution of future cash flows.

In a general sense, the term financial market refers to a conceptual "mechanism" rather than a physical location or a specific type of organization or structure. We usually define the financial market[2] as a system that includes individuals and institutions, instruments, and procedures that bring together borrowers and savers, no matter where the location.

Importance of Financial Markets

The primary role of financial markets is to help bring together borrowers and savers (lenders) by facilitating the flow of funds from individuals and businesses that have surplus funds to individuals, businesses, and governments that have needs for funds in excess of their incomes.[3] In developed economies, financial markets help efficiently allocate excess funds of savers to individuals and organizations in need of funds for investment or consumption. The more efficient the process of funds flow, the more productive the economy, both in terms of manufacturing and financing.

Flow of Funds

By providing mechanisms by which borrowers and lenders get together to transfer funds, the financial markets allow us to consume amounts different than our current incomes. In this way, they provide us with the ability to transfer income through time. When we borrow, for example, we sacrifice future income to increase current income; when we save, or invest, we sacrifice current income in exchange for a greater expected income in the future. For example, young adults borrow funds to go to college or to buy such high-priced items as a house or a car, so they tend to save little or nothing. Older adults, when they become established in their careers and reach or near their peak income years, generally save (invest) greater percentages of their incomes. Finally, when adults retire, they rely on the funds accumulated from early years' savings to provide their retirement income. Consequently, adults go through three general phases that would not be possible without financial markets:

1. Young adults desire to consume more than their incomes, so they must borrow.

2. Older working adults earn more than their consumption needs, so they save.

3. Retired adults use the funds accumulated in earlier years to at least partially replace income lost due to retirement.

Without financial markets, consumption would be restricted to income earned each year plus any amounts put aside (perhaps in a coffee can) in previous years. As a result, our standard of living would be much lower than is now possible.

Funds are transferred from those with surplus (savers) to those with needs (borrowers) by the three different processes.

1. Direct Transfers. A direct transfer of money and securities occurs when a business sells its stocks or bonds directly to savers (investors) without going through any type of intermediary or financial institution. The business delivers its securities to savers, who in turn give the firm the money it needs.

2. Indirect Transfers through Investment Bankers. A transfer also can go through an investment banking house, which serves as a middleman and facilitates the issuance of securities. The company sells its stocks or bonds to the investment bank, which in turn sells these same securities to savers. The business's securities and the savers' money merely "pass through" the investment banking house. For example, the next time IBM raises funds by issuing stock, it probably will utilize the services of an investment banker, such as Goldman Sachs or sell the issue in the financial markets.

3. Indirect Transfers through a Financial Intermediary[4]**.** Transfers can also be made through a financial intermediary such as a bank or a mutual fund. In this case, the intermediary obtains funds from savers and then uses the money to lend out or to purchase another business's securities. For example, when you deposit money in a saving account at your local bank, the bank takes those funds along with other depositors' funds and creates such loans as mortgages, business loans, and automobile loans. The existence of intermediaries greatly increases the efficiency of the financial markets.

For simplicity, the classification assumes that the entity in need of capital is a business, and specifically a corporation. Nevertheless, it is easy to visualize the demander of funds as being a home purchaser or a government unit. Direct transfers of funds from savers to borrowers are possible and do occur on occasion. Generally, however, corporations and government entities use investment bankers to help them raise needed capital in the financial markets, and individual savers use such intermediaries as banks and mutual funds to help them lend their funds or borrow needed funds.

Market Efficiency

If the financial markets did not provide efficient funds transfers, the economy simply could not function as it now does. Because Carolina Power & Light would have difficulty in raising needed capital, Ralegh's citizens would pay more for electricity. Likewise, you would not be able to buy the house you want, and Alexandra Trottier would have no place to invest her savings. Clearly, the level of employment and productivity, and hence our standard of living, would be much lower. Therefore, it is absolutely essential that our financial markets function efficiently — not only quickly, but also at a low cost. When we speak of market efficiency, we generally mean either economic efficiency or informational efficiency.

Economic Efficiency

The financial markets are said to have economic efficiency[5] if funds are allocated to their optimal use at the lowest costs. In other words, in economically efficient markets, businesses and individuals invest their funds in assets that yield the highest returns, and the costs of searching for such opportunities are lower than those observed in less efficient markets. Often individuals hire brokers, who charge commissions and other costs associated with transactions, which are called transaction costs[6], are very high. Investments will not be as attractive as when transactions are low.

Informational Efficiency

The prices of investments bought and sold in the financial markets are based on available information. If these prices reflect existing information and adjust very quickly when new information becomes available, then the financial markets have achieved informational efficiency[7]. When the financial markets have a larger number of participants in search of the most profitable investments, informational efficiency generally exists. For instance, in the United States, millions of individual investors and more than 100,000 tightly trained professionals participate in the financial markets. As a consequence, you would expect investment prices to adjust almost instantaneously to new information, because a large number of the market participants will evaluate the new information as soon as possible in an effort to find more profitable investments.

Informational efficiency generally is classified into one of the following three categories.

1. Weak-form efficiency states that all information obtained in past price movements is fully reflected in current market prices. Therefore, information about recent or past trends in investment prices is of no use in selecting investments — the fact that an investment has risen for the past three days, for example, gives us no clues as to what it will do today or tomorrow.

2. Semi-strong-form efficiency states that current market prices reflect all publicly available information. In this case, it does no good to scrutinize such published data as a corporation's financial statements, because market prices will have adjusted to any good or bad news contained in such reports as soon as they are made public. Insiders (for example, the presidents of companies), even under semi-strong-form efficiency, can still make abnormal returns[8] on their own companies investments (stocks).

3. Strong-form efficiency states that current market prices reflect all pertinent information, whether publicly available or privately held. If this form of efficiency holds, even insiders would find it impossible to earn abnormal returns in the financial markets.[9]

The informational efficiency of the financial markets has received a great deal of attention. The results of most of the market efficiency studies suggest that the financial markets are highly efficient in the weak form and reasonably efficient in the semi-strong form, but strong-form efficiency does not appear to hold.

Financial markets that are informationally efficient also tend to be economically efficient. This situation arises because investors can expect prices to reflect appropriate information and thus make intelligent choices about which investments will likely provide the best returns.

Types of Financial Markets

A number of different financial markets, with a variety of investments and participants, exist today. We generally differentiate among financial markets based on the types of investments, maturities of investments, types of borrowers and lenders, locations of the markets, and types of transactions.

Money Markets Versus Capital Markets

The markets for short-term financial instruments are termed the money markets[10], and the markets for long-term financial instruments are dubbed the capital markets[11]. More specifically, the money markets include instruments that have maturities equal to one year or less when originally issued, and the capital markets include instruments with original maturities greater than one year. By definition, then, money markets include only debt instruments, because equity instruments (that is, stocks) have no specific maturities, whereas capital markets include both equity instruments and such long-term debt instruments as mortgages, corporate bonds, and government bonds.[12]

Debt Markets Versus Equity Markets

Simply stated, the debt markets[13] are where loans are traded, and the equity markets[14] are where stocks of corporations are traded. A debt instrument is a contract that specifies the amounts, as well as the time, a borrower must repay a lender. In contrast, equity represents "ownership" in a corporation; it entitles the stockholder to share in cash distributions generated from income and from liquidation of the firm.

Primary Markets Versus Secondary Markets

The primary markets[15] are where "new" securities are traded, and the secondary markets[16] are where "used" securities are traded.

Primary markets are the markets in which corporations raise new capital. If IBM were to sell a new issue of common stock to raise capital, this activity would be a primary market transaction. The corporation selling the newly created stock receives the proceeds from the sale in a primary market transaction. Secondary markets are markets in which existing, previously issued securities are traded among investors. Thus, if Jessica Rogers decided to buy 1,000 shares of existing IBM stock, the purchase would occur in the secondary market. The New York Stock Exchange is a secondary market, because it deals in outstanding, or previously issued, stocks and bonds as opposed to newly issued stocks and bonds. Secondary markets also exist for mortgages, other types of loans, and other financial assets. The corporation whose securities are traded in the secondary market is not involved in the transaction and, therefore, does not receive any funds from such a sale.

Derivatives Markets

Options, futures, and swaps are some of the securities traded in the derivatives markets[17]. These securities are called derivatives because their values are determined, or "derived", directly from other assets. For example, if an individual owns a call option written on AT&T stock, he or she has the ability to purchase shares of AT&T at a price specified in the option contract. Because the contract fixes the purchase price of the AT&T stock, the value of the call option changes as the actual market value of AT&T shares changes.

Although any investors use derivatives to speculate about the movements of the prices in the financial markets and the markets for such commodities as wheat and soybeans, these instruments are typically employed to help manage risk. That is, individuals, corporations, and governments use derivatives to hedge risk by offsetting exposures to uncertain price changes in the future.

Terminology

financial market	金融市场
securities	股票，有价证券
cash flow	现金流
stocks	股票
bonds	债券
direct transfer	直接转账
indirect transfer	间接转账
financial intermediary	金融中介
mutual funds	共同基金
savings account	储蓄账户
mortgages	按揭
loans	贷款
fund transfer	基金转换
market efficiency	市场效率
economic efficiency	经济效率
informational efficiency	信息效益
broker	(股票，外币等)经纪人
commissions	佣金
transaction costs	交易费用，交易成本
financial instrument	金融工具
money market	货币市场
capital market	资本市场
debt instrument	债务工具
equity instrument	权益工具
corporate bonds	公司债券
government bonds	政府债券
debt markets	债券市场

equity market	股票市场
liquidation	清偿；结算，清算
primary market	初级市场(证券发行机构)
secondary market	二(中，次)级市场
derivatives market	衍生品市场
options	期权
futures	期货
swaps	调期
call/ put option	看涨/看跌期权

Notes on the Text

1. In this text, we primarily refer to corporations as the users or issuers of financial assets such as debt and equity, although governments, government agencies, and individuals also issue debt in reality.
2. financial markets — a system consisting of individuals and institutions, instruments, and procedure that bring together borrowers and savers.
3. Through this text, we often refer to the parties involved in financial market transactions as borrowers or lenders, which implies that only loans are traded in the financial markets. In reality, stocks, options, and many other financial assets also are traded in the financial markets. In our general discussion, we will use the term "borrowers" to refer to parties such as individuals and government units that raise needed funds through various types of loans as well as corporations that use both loans and stock issuers to raise needed funds. We will use the term "lenders" to refer to those parties that provide funds, whether the medium is a loan or a stock.
4. financial intermediary — a financial institution that connects surplus and deficit agents.
5. economic efficiency — it refers to a situation where funds are allocated to their optimal use at the lowest costs in the financial markets.
6. transaction costs — costs associated with buying and selling investments, including commissions, search costs, taxes, and so on.
7. informational efficiency — the prices of investments reflect existing information and adjust quickly when new information enters the markets.
8. An abnormal return is one that exceeds the return justified by the riskiness of the investment.
9. Several cases of illegal insider trading have made the news headlines in the past. In a famous case, Ivan Boesky admitted making $50 million by purchasing the stocks of firms which he knew were preparing to merge. Boesky went to jail and had to pay a large fine, but he helped disprove strong-form efficiency.
10. money markets — the segments of the financial markets where the instruments that are traded have maturities equal to one year or less.
11. capital markets — the segments of the financial markets where the instruments that are traded have maturities greater than one year.

12. All these financial instruments, including both debt and equity instruments, are called financial assets.
13. debt markets — financial markets where loans are traded.
14. equity markets — financial markets where corporate stocks are traded.
15. primary markets — markets in which various organizations raise funds by issuing new securities.
16. secondary markets — markets where financial assets that have previously been issued by various organizations are traded among investors.
17. derivatives markets — financial markets where options and futures are traded.

Exercises

I. Reading Comprehension.

Read the text carefully and decide whether the following statements are true (T) or false (F).

___ 1. In a general sense, the term financial market refers to a conceptual "mechanism" rather than a physical location or a specific type of organization or structure.

___ 2. Financial markets provide us with the ability to transfer income through location.

___ 3. A transfer of money and securities cannot occur without going through any type of intermediary or financial institution.

___ 4. Weak-form efficiency states that all information obtained in past price movements cannot be fully reflected in current market prices.

___ 5. The primary markets are where "new" securities are traded, and the secondary markets are where "used" securities are traded.

II. Vocabulary Building.

A. Match the term in Column A with the definition in Column B.

1. money markets
2. capital markets
3. financial market
4. financial instrument
5. financial intermediary
6. transaction costs
7. informational efficiency

a. a system consisting of individuals and institutions, instruments, and procedure that bring together borrowers and savers

b. the segments of the financial markets where the instruments that are traded have maturities equal to one year or less

c. a financial institution that connects surplus and deficit agents

d. financial markets where options and futures are traded

e. funds are allocated to their optimal use at the lowest costs in the financial markets

f. costs associated with buying and selling investments

g. the segments of the financial markets where the instruments that are traded have maturities greater than one year

8. economic efficiency h. a tradable asset of any kind
9. primary markets i. the prices of investments reflect existing information and adjust quickly when new information enters the markets
10. derivatives markets j. markets in which various organizations raise funds by issuing new securities

B. Complete the following sentences with the words given in the box.

explore	consume	accumulate	deposit	establish
adjust	entitle	entity	facilitated	expect
well-being	distribution			

1. We are now concerned for the economic _____ of the country.
2. We signed strategic agreements with financial institutions, to _____ capital-raising channels for the company.
3. This tax reform would lead to a more efficient economy, a more equitable _____ of wealth and greater protection for the environment.
4. He argued that the economic recovery had been _____ by his tough stance.
5. Note that these activities do not produce real wealth; they only _____.
6. By definition, poorer countries lack the ability to _____ substantial stocks of financial assets.
7. In order to keep the security and stability of the financial system, some countries have established the financial security network to solve this problem, and the _____ insurance system is an important part of the financial security network.
8. Diversification is one of the reasons that make the regional economy so dynamic, but a diversified culture and different development levels have also made it very difficult to establish a regional economic _____ like European union.
9. In the wake of the international financial crisis, China has adopted a host of policy measures to boost domestic demand, _____ economic structure, promote growth and improve people's well-being.
10. A positive balance in a capital account or any other account for a person shall not bear interest; affect the allocation of income, gain, receipt, loss, deduction or credit to a person; or _____ a person to any distributions or other economic benefits.

III. Cloze.

There are 10 blanks in the following two passages. For each blank there are four choices marked A, B, C and D. You are supposed to choose the best answer.

Passage 1

In an economy without financial institutions, the level of funds flowing between suppliers of funds and users of funds through (1) _____ markets is likely to be quite low. There are several reasons for this. Once they have lent money in (2) _____ for financial claims, suppliers of funds need to (3) _____ continuously the use of their funds. They must be sure that the user of funds neither steals the funds outright nor wastes the funds on projects that have low or negative returns, since this would lower the (4) _____ of being repaid and/or earning a positive return on their investment (such as through the receipt of dividends or interest). Such monitoring is often extremely (5) _____ for any given fund supplier because it requires considerable time, expenses, and effort to collect this information relative to the size of the average fund supplier's investment.

(1) A. capital   B. financial   C. money   D. stock
(2) A. exchange   B. change   C. transfer   D. move
(3) A. supervise   B. guide   C. monitor   D. usher
(4) A. chance   B. opportunity   C. probable   D. likely
(5) A. great   B. needed   C. cheap   D. costly

Passage 2

Everyone has experienced the need for cash. The need to (6) _____ bills and other obligations of everyday life (7) _____ us all. Similarly, we are confronted with the periodicity of income flows. Most working people receive their wages in cash, either biweekly or monthly. How many times have we been confronted with the planned or unplanned need for cash just prior to payday? The opportunity to buy something at a reduced price or the emergency requiring cash always seems to present itself when there is no convenient payday to fill the need.

The typical (8) _____ to this problem is borrowing to (9) _____ the income gap between outgo and income. The loan might be an informal one from a friend or relative ("five till payday"), or it might be a formal short-term loan from the commercial banker ("sign on the dotted line"). In (10) _____ case, the short-term loan from one who is not currently using the funds (the friend, relative, or banker) to one who needs the funds (you) erases the problem.

(6) A. pay   B. repay   C. compensate   D. obtain
(7) A. challenges   B. meets   C. faces   D. confronts
(8) A. resolution   B. solution   C. reply   D. answer
(9) A. bridge   B. connect   C. link   D. fill
(10) A. either   B. both   C. neither   D. each

IV. Translate the following sentences into English.

1. 这些是私人银行，我们为什么必须为他们的错误买单？(pay for)
2. 专家指出，就金融改革而言，某些控制风险的建议获得了广泛的支持。(in terms of)
3. 有关部门将在保持适当资本账户监管的同时，努力扩大私人和外资的准入。(access)
4. 日益明显的是，市场不知道将要发生什么事情，许多金融机构选择置身事外，看管理层下一步的动作。(expect)
5. 中国在金融市场融资结构调整方面取得了巨大进展，银行信贷占金融总量的比重从10年前的90%下降到目前的60%。(with the proportion of)

Unit 3　An Overview of Financial Markets

V. Translate the following paragraphs into Chinese.

1. The primary role of financial markets is to help bring together borrowers and savers (lenders) by facilitating the flow of funds from individuals and businesses that have surplus funds to individuals, businesses, and governments that have needs for funds in excess of their incomes. In developed economies, financial markets help efficiently allocate excess funds of savers to individuals and organizations in need of funds for investment or consumption. The more efficient the process of funds flow, the more productive the economy, both in terms of manufacturing and financing.

2. The markets for short-term financial instruments are termed the money markets, and the markets for long-term financial instruments are dubbed the capital markets. More specifically, the money markets include instruments that have maturities equal to one year or less when originally issued, and the capital markets include instruments with original maturities greater than one year. By definition, then, money markets include only debt instruments, because equity instruments (that is, stocks) have no specific maturities, whereas capital markets include both equity instruments and such long-term debt instruments as mortgages, corporate bonds, and government bonds.

VI. Self-Testing.

1. _____ facilitates the lending of funds from savers to those who wish to undertake investment.
   A. Financial market　B. Capital market　　C. Money market　　D. Bond market

2. _____ are claims that those who lend their savings have on the future incomes of the borrowers who use those funds for investment.
   A. Mutual funds　　B. Debts　　　　　C. Securities　　　D. Bonds

3. Which of the following statements is NOT true?
   A. The maturity of debt instrument is the date when such instrument will become due for payment.
   B. A debt instrument is short-term if its maturity is less than a year.
   C. A debt instrument is long-term if its maturity is five years or longer.
   D. Debt instruments with a maturity between one and ten years are said to be intermediate term.

4. An important financial institution that assists in the initial sale of securities in the primary market is the _____.
   A. investment bank　　　　　　　　　B. New York Stock Exchange
   C. Federal Reserve System　　　　　　D. financial intermediary

5. All the followings are the examples of the secondary markets, EXCEPT _____.
   A. stock markets　　　　　　　　　　B. foreign exchange markets
   C. futures markets　　　　　　　　　　D. options markets

6. Sometimes, financial intermediaries by "borrowing short and lending long" find themselves in difficult financial situations because _____.
   A. short-term rates are failing

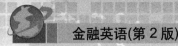

B. long-term rates are rising

C. short-term rates rise relative to rates of their holdings

D. long-term rates rise more sharply than short-term rates

7. Regulation of the money supply and financial markets is referred to as _____.

   A. fiscal policy   B. income policy

   C. monetary policy   D. budgetary policy

8. Financial markets serve to channel funds from _____.

   A. the government to contractors

   B. investors to consumers

   C. consumers to producers

   D. savers to investors

9. Open-market operations refer to _____.

   A. loans from commercial banks to corporations and consumers

   B. inter-bank loans

   C. changes in interest rates caused by the changes in commercial bank loans

   D. buying and selling governmental securities by the central bank

10. Which of the following statements is NOT true?

   A. The money market is a financial market in which only short-term debt instruments are traded.

   B. The capital market is the market in which long-term debt and equity instruments are traded.

   C. Money market securities are usually more widely traded than long-term securities.

   D. Money market securities tend to be less liquid.

VII. Writing.

Please write a letter to ××bank in English as follows.

1. 为合理使用密押协议,以减少相关费用,我们已审查了与国外银行间的密押协议。

2. 我们发现,在多数情况下,即使曾经使用过密押,也用得很少,这意味着报关这些文件要导致额外的费用,而这些费用本来是可以避免的。

3. 为此,如你行同意,我们建议废除你们××等分行的密押协议。

4. 如在2013年1月1日前未收到你行的反对意见,我们将终止与你们分行间的协议,并指示我分行停止使用该密押表。请销毁由你们的上述分行所持有的我行密押表,并将本信所附副本签字后寄还我行,以确认该文件已被销毁。

5. 感谢你们在此事中的合作。

Supplementary Reading

Oil and Tech's Crash Have Wrecked Hedge Funds

By Matt Egan

(*www.cnnbusiness.com*, November 28, 2018)

    New York (CNN Business) — It's not just average investors getting hurt by the market mayhem. Hedge funds that placed big bets on tech and oil have been rocked as well.

The tech wreck has been especially painful to hedge funds because many piled into crowded stocks like Facebook (FB), Amazon (AMZN), Alphabet (GOOGL) and Alibaba (BABA). Fears about rising interest rates and slowing growth sparked an exodus from those former tech darlings, all of which are down sharply from their peaks.

A Goldman Sachs basket of popular stocks held by hedge funds tumbled 9% between mid-June and mid-November. That's well worse than the 2% decline in the S&P 500 over that span.

October was the weakest month for hedge fund performance since 2011, according to HFR, a research firm tracking the alternative investment space. Just one in four funds gained ground in October — and market volatility only deepened in November.

"The problem with crowded trading is if anything goes wrong, the downside is extreme," said Troy Gayeski, senior portfolio manager at SkyBridge Capital, an investment firm that helps clients invest money in hedge funds. "Everyone is rushing for the door at the same time. It was a very painful month."

'Vicious downward cycle'

And that's an added problem for hedge funds because these firms charge hefty fees with the promise of delivering superior performance — especially during scary times.

"Hedge fund returns, portfolio leverage and the performance of popular stocks have entered a vicious downward cycle," Goldman Sachs strategist Ben Snider wrote in a recent note to clients.

In other words, the unwinding of those popular hedge fund trades helped deepen the market volatility.

Most hedge funds make bullish or bearish bets on stocks. But some hedge funds also invest in commodities — and crude oil was a very hot trade until recently. Outsized bets by hedge funds helped lift US oil prices to a four-year high of $76 a barrel in early October. Some analysts even believed $100 oil was on the horizon.

Oil crash doesn't help

But much like the sudden tech rout, crude abruptly collapsed into a bear market due to worries about excess supply and deteriorating demand. US oil prices have plunged by one-third in less than two months.

Gayeski said that even though hedge funds have much less exposure to commodities, the oil crash was "another kick in the teeth for hedge fund investors".

The Great Oil Crash of 2018: What's really happening

The oil plunge dragged down energy stocks, especially shale companies like Continental Resources (CLR) and Pioneer Natural Resources (PXD). The VanEck Vectors Unconventional Oil & Gas ETF (FRAK) is down 26% since early October. Not surprisingly, equity hedge funds focused on the energy and basic materials space tumbled by 8% last month, the worst performance in the group.

For the year, equity hedge funds declined nearly 3% through the end of October. That's well shy of the S&P 500's total return (including dividends) of 3% over that span.

Of course, not all hedge funds are struggling. Funds focused on healthcare, fixed income and events like mergers have outperformed. And hedge funds overall advanced 9% last year, though that is less than half of the S&P 500's gain.

Fees are 'too darn high'

Still, the recent performance will only give investors added leverage to demand hedge funds slash fees they charge with the promise of beating the market.

"The past few years have been pretty awful versus the market," said Richard "Trip" Miller, founder and managing partner of Gullane Capital Partners, a Memphis-based hedge fund.

Miller said that Gullane was up 16% through the first half of the year before a difficult third quarter. By the end of the third quarter, the firm was up 6.5% on the year.

For many years, most hedge funds charged a flat fee of 2% on total assets and an additional 20% on any profits earned. But that "two and twenty" fee structure seriously erodes returns for clients and has come under pressure due to poor performance.

For instance, Gullane doesn't charge a performance fee on the first six percentage points of gains.

"Hedge fund fees are too darn high in general," said Miller. "It's ridiculous. I think three-fourths of the hedge funds need to go away. They don't serve any purpose. Quite frankly, I don't know how they exist."

Hedge funds are going out of business

Some hedge funds are indeed going away. In recent months, a number of prominent hedge funds have reportedly announced plans to shut their doors, including Criterion Capital Management, Highfields Capital Management and Tourbillon Capital Partners.

Between 2015 and 2017, more hedge funds liquidated than launched, according to HFR. So far this year, 306 hedge funds have launched, compared with 270 that liquidated. And the total number of hedge funds stands at 8,339, down from the peak of 8,474 in 2015, according to HFR.

SkyBridge's Gayeski said he has been surprised that some poorly-performing hedge funds were able to stay in business for up to a decade.

"Sooner or later, capitalism works," said Gayeski. "If you're not adding value for your consumer, you're no longer going to have a business."

Questions

1. Why have most hedge funds been hurt especially by the tech crash?
2. What led to the panic selling of tech stocks?
3. What's the performance of the hedge funds in October?
4. What's the impact of oil market collapse on the stock market?
5. What would happen to the hedge fund fees due to the poor performance?
6. What would happen to some poorly-performing hedge funds?

Unit 4   Money Market

Case

A Two Investment Portfolio

This option uses just two investments: a 60%/40% blend of the S&P 500 (a kind of stocks) and T-bills. This portfolio would have very low fees. The S&P 500 ETF from Vanguard costs 0.06% a year, and T-bills can be purchased commission-free straight from the Treasury Direct. This results in just $36 of fees on a $100,000 portfolio. As for performance, this combination had an average return of 9.19% from 1988 to 2006. Volatility was pretty low, with a standard deviation of 8.76%.

Questions

1. Do you know what a T-bill is?
2. Why is a money market needed? What are the key features of a money market instrument?

Preview

Skimming

Skim the following text quickly to answer the following questions and discuss your answers with your partners.

1. What are the roles and functions performed by the money market in order to aid the financial system and the economy?
   _____
   _____.

2. Who are the key actors in the workings of the money market?
   _____
   _____.

3. What are the principal goals usually pursued by money market investors?
   _____
   _____.

4. What are the two forms of maturity?
   _____
   _____.

5. What are the depth and breadth of the money market?
   _____
   _____.

Scanning

Scan the following text quickly to find the specific information.

1. What exactly do we mean by the term "money market"?
   _____
   _____.

2. In what respect does money market stand in sharp contrast to the capital market?
   _____
   _____.

3. Which institution is virtually always on the demand side of the market?
   _____
   _____.

4. What do investors in the money market mainly seek?
   _____
   _____.

5. Why are money market investors especially sensitive to risk?
   _____
   _____.

6. How can we distinguish between original maturity and actual maturity?
   _____
   _____.

7. What is of the essence in the money market?
   _____
   _____.

8. Why do we say that money market is one of the most efficient markets in the world?
   _____
   _____.

Vocabulary in Context

Read the following sentences and try to guess the meaning of the italicized words by using the context. Then replace the italicized words with synonyms (words or phrases that have nearly the same or similar meanings).

1. To the *casual* observer, the financial markets appear to be one vast cauldron of borrowing and lending activities in which some individuals and institutions are seeking credit while others are supplying the funds needed to make lending possible.
   To the _____ observer, the financial markets appear to be one vast cauldron of borrowing and lending activities in which some individuals and institutions are seeking credit while others are supplying the funds needed to make lending possible.

2. When the loan is repaid, the borrower *retrieves* the securities and returns borrowed funds to the lender.
   When the loan is repaid, the borrower _____ the securities and returns borrowed funds to the lender.

3. *Disbursements* of cash must be made throughout the year, however, to cover the wages and

salaries of government employees, office suppliers, repairs, and fuel costs, as well as unexpected expenses.

_____ of cash must be made throughout the year, however, to cover the wages and salaries of government employees, office suppliers, repairs, and fuel costs, as well as unexpected expenses.

4. When taxes are collected, governments usually are *flush* with funds that far exceed their immediate cash needs.

When taxes are collected, governments usually are _____ with funds that far exceed their immediate cash needs.

5. The checking account of an active business firm *fluctuates* daily between large cash surpluses and low or nonexistent cash balances.

The checking account of an active business firm _____ daily between large cash surpluses and low or nonexistent cash balances.

6. To fully appreciate the workings of the money market, we must remember that money is one of the most *perishable* of all commodities.

To fully appreciate the workings of the money market, we must remember that money is one of the most _____ of all commodities.

7. When idle cash is not invested, the holder incurs an opportunity cost in the form of interest income that is *foregone*.

When idle cash is not invested, the holder incurs an opportunity cost in the form of interest income that is _____.

8. The strong *aversion* to risk among money market investors is especially evident when there is even a hint of trouble concerning the financial condition of a major money market borrower.

The strong _____ to risk among money market investors is especially evident when there is even a hint of trouble concerning the financial condition of a major money market borrower.

9. The *interval* of time between the issue date of a security and the date on which the borrower promises to redeem it is the security's original maturity.

The _____ of time between the issue date of a security and the date on which the borrower promises to redeem it is the security's original maturity.

10. *Overseeing* the whole market are central banks (such as the European Central Bank and the Federal Reserve System) around the globe, who try to ensure that trading is orderly and that asset prices are reasonably stable.

_____ the whole market are central banks (such as the European Central Bank and the Federal Reserve System) around the globe, who try to ensure that trading is orderly and that asset prices are reasonably stable.

Text

Introduction to the Money Market

Introduction: The Market for Short-term Credit

To the casual observer, the financial markets appear to be one vast cauldron[1] of borrowing and lending activities in which some individuals and institutions are seeking credit while others are supplying the funds needed to make lending possible. All transactions carried out in the financial markets seem to be basically the same: borrowers issue securities (financial assets) that lenders purchase. When the loan is repaid, the borrower retrieves the securities and returns borrowed funds to the lender. Closer examination of our financial system reveals, however, that beyond the simple act of exchanging financial assets and funds, there are major differences between one financial transaction and another.

For example, an individual may borrow $100,000 for 30 years to purchase a new home, whereas another's financing need may be for a six-month loan of $3,000 to cover a federal income tax obligation[2]. A corporation may enter the financial markets this week to offer a new issue of 20-year bonds to finance the construction of an office building, and next week it may find itself in need of funds for just 60 days to purchase raw materials so that production can continue.

Clearly, then, the purposes for which money is borrowed within the financial system vary greatly among individuals and institutions and from transaction to transaction. And the different purposes for which money is borrowed result in the creation of different kinds of financial assets having different maturities, risks, and other features.

In the monetary market nearly all loans have an original maturity[3] of one year or less. Money market loans are used to help corporations and governments pay the wages and salaries of their workers, make repairs, purchase inventories, pay dividends and taxes, and satisfy other short-term, working capital needs. In this respect, the money market stands in sharp contrast to the capital market. The capital market deals in long-term credit — that is, loans and securities over a year to maturity, typically used to finance markets, but there are also important differences that make each of these two markets unique.

Characteristics of the Money Market

What the Money Market Does

The money market, like all financial markets, provides a channel for the exchange of financial assets for money. However, it differs from other parts of the financial system in its emphasis on loans to meet purely short-term cash needs (i.e., current account[4], rather than capital account[5], transactions). The money market is the mechanism through which holders of temporary cash surpluses[6] meet holders of temporary cash deficits[7]. It is designed, on the one hand, to meet the short-term cash requirements of corporations, financial institutions and governments, providing a mechanism for granting loans as short as overnight and as long as one year to maturity. At the same time, the money market provides an investment outlet for those spending (also principal corporations, financial institutions and governments) that hold surplus cash for short periods of time and wish to earn at least some return on temporarily idle funds[8]. The essential function of the money market is to bring these two groups into contact with each other in order to make borrowing and lending possible.

The Need for a Money Market

Why is such a market needed? There are several reasons. First, for most individuals and institutions, inflows and outflows of cash are rarely in perfect harmony with each other. Governments, for example, collect taxes from the public only at certain times of the year, such as in April in the United States, when personal and corporate income tax payments are due. Disbursements of cash must be made throughout the year, however, to cover the wages and salaries of government employees, office suppliers, repairs, and fuel costs, as well as unexpected expenses. When taxes are collected, governments usually are flush with funds that far exceed their immediate cash needs. At these times, they frequently enter the money market as lenders and purchase Treasury bills[9], bank certificates of deposit (CDs)[10], and other attractive financial assets. Later, they, however, as once again enter the money market as borrowers of funds, issuing short-term notes attractive to money market investors.

Business firms, too, collect sales revenues from customers at one point in time and dispense cash at other points in time to cover wages and salaries, make repairs, and meet other operating expenses. The checking account of an active business firm fluctuates daily between large cash surpluses and low or nonexistent cash balances. A surplus cash position frequently brings such a firm into the money market as a net lender of funds, investing idle funds in the hope of earning at least a modest rate of return. Cash deficits force the firm onto the borrowing when current expenditures exceed receipts and providing an investment outlet to earn interest income for units whose current receipts exceed their current expenditures.

To fully appreciate the workings of the money market, we must remember that money is one of the most perishable of all commodities. The holding of idle surplus cash is expensive, because cash balances earn little or no income for their owners, when idle cash is not invested, the holder incurs an opportunity cost in the form of interest income that is foregone. Moreover, each day that idle funds are not invested is a day's income lost forever, when large amounts of funds for even 24 hours can be substantial. For example, the interest income from a loan of $10 million for one day at a 10 percent annual rate interest amounts to nearly $2,800. In a week's time, nearly $20,000 interest would be lost from not investing $10 million in idle funds. Many students of the financial system find it hard to believe that investment outlets exist for loans as short as one day or even less. However, billions of dollars in credit are extended in the money market overnight or for only a few daylight hours to securities dealers, banks, and nonfinancial corporations to cover temporary shortfalls of cash. One important money market instrument — the federal funds[11] loan — is designed mainly for extending credit within a day or less or over a weekend.

Key Borrowers and Lenders in the Money Market

Who are the principal lenders of funds in the money market? Who are the principal borrowers? These questions are difficult to answer, because the same institutions frequently operate on both sides of the money market. For example, a large commercial bank operating in the money market (such as Citibank or the Bank of Montreal) will borrow funds aggressively through CDs, federal funds, and other short-term instruments while lending short-term instruments to corporations that have temporary cash shortages. Frequently, large nonfinancial corporations borrow millions of dollars on a single day, only to come back into the money market later in the week as lender of funds due to a sudden upsurge in cash receipts. Institutions that typically play on both sides of the money market include large banks, securities dealers, finance companies, major nonfinancial corporations, and units of government. Even central banks, such as the Federal Reserve System[12], the European Central Bank (ECB)[13], the Bank of

England[14], or the Bank of Japan, may be aggressive suppliers of funds to the money market on one day and reverse themselves the following day, demanding funds through the sale of securities in the open market. One institution that is virtually always on the demand side of the market, however, is the government. The U.S. Treasury, for example, is among the largest of all money market.

The Goals of Money Market Investors

Investors in the money market seek mainly safety and liquidity, plus the opportunity to earn some interest income. This is because funds invested in the money market represent only temporary cash surpluses and are usually needed in the near future to meet tax obligations, cover wage and salary costs, pay stockholder dividends, and so on. For this reason, money market investors are especially sensitive to risk.

The strong aversion to risk among money market investors is especially evident when there is even a hint of trouble concerning the financial condition of a major money market borrower. For example, when the huge Penn Central Transportation Company[15] collapsed in 1970 and defaulted on its short-term commercial notes, the short-term commercial paper market virtually ground to a halt because many investors refused to buy even the notes offered by top-grade companies. Similarly, during the 1980s, when the huge Continental Illinois Bank[16] had to be propped up by government loans, the rates on short-term certificates of deposit (CDs) issued by other big banks surged upward due to fears on the part of money market investors that all large-bank CDs had become more risky.

Money Market Maturities

Despite the fact that money market investments cover a relatively narrow range of maturities — one year or less — there are maturities available within this range to meet just about every short-term investment need. We must distinguish here between original maturity and actual maturity[17], however. The interval of time between the issue date of a security and the date on which the borrower promises to redeem it is the security's original maturity. Actual maturity, on the other hand, refers to the number of days, months, or years between today and the date the security is actually retired.

Original maturities on money market instruments range from as short as one day or a few hours on many loans to banks and security dealers to a full year on some bank deposits and Treasury bills. Obviously, once a money market instrument is issued, it grows shorter in actual maturity every day. Because there are thousands of money market assets outstanding, some of which reach maturity each day, investors have a wide menu from which to select the precise length of time they need to invest their cash.

Depth and Breadth of the Money Market

The money market is extremely broad and deep, meaning it can absorb a large volume of transactions with only small effects on security prices and interest rates. Investors can easily sell most money market instruments on short notice, often in a matter of minutes. This is one of the most efficient markets in the world, containing a vast network of securities dealers, money-center banks, and funds brokers in constant touch with one another and alert to any bargains. The slightest hint that a financial instrument is underpriced (i.e., carries an exceptionally high yield) usually brings a flood of buy orders, but money market traders are quick to dump or avoid overpriced financial assets. This market is dominated by active traders who constantly search their video display screens for opportunities to arbitrage funds; that is, they move money from one corner of the market with relatively low yields to another where investments offer the highest returns available. Overseeing the whole market are central banks (such as the European Central Bank and the Federal Reserve System) around the globe, who try to ensure that trading is orderly and that asset prices are reasonably stable.

There is no centralized trading arena in the money market as there is on a stock exchange, for example. The money market is a telephone and computer networks and usually confirm their transactions by wire. Speed is of the essence in this market because, as we observed earlier, money is a highly perishable commodity. Each day that passes means thousands of dollars in lost interest income if newly received funds are not immediately invested. Most business between traders, therefore, is conducted in seconds or minutes, and payment is made almost instantaneously.

Terminology

money market	货币市场
capital market	资本市场
tax obligation	纳税义务
cash surpluses	现金结余
cash deficits	现金赤字
liquidity	资产流动性
idle funds	闲散资金
sales revenues	(服务企业)销售收入
original maturity	初定偿还期，原始到期期限
actual maturity	实际到期
opportunity cost	机会成本
dividends	股息，红利
checking account	支票账户
treasury bills	[经]国库券，财政短期证券
bank certificates of deposits	银行存款证明

Notes on the Text

1. cauldron — a large round metal pot for boiling liquids over a fire.
2. tax obligation — the amount of tax that a person, business, or organization owes.
3. original maturity — the interval of time between the issue date of a security and the date on which the borrower promises to redeem it.
4. current account — a component of a nation's balance-of-payments accounts that tracks purchases and sales of goods and services (trade) and gifts made to foreigners.
5. capital account — a record of short-term and long-term funds flowing into and out of a nation and included in its balance-of-payments accounts.

6. surplus — the amount of an asset or resource that exceeds the portion that is utilized. A surplus is used to describe many excess assets including income, profits, capital and goods. A surplus often occurs in a budget, when expenses are less than the income taken in, or in inventory when fewer supplies are used than were retained.

7. deficit — the amount by which expenses exceed income or costs outstrip revenues. Deficit essentially refers to the difference between cash inflows and outflows. It is generally prefixed by another term to refer to a specific situation — trade deficit or budget deficit, for example. Deficit is the opposite of "surplus" and is synonymous with shortfall or loss.

8. idle fund — money that is not invested and, therefore, earning no interest or investment income. Idle funds are simply funds that are not deposited in an interest bearing or investment tracking vehicle, that is, not participating in the economic markets.

9. treasury bills — Treasury bills, or T-bills, are sold in terms ranging from a few days to 52 weeks. Bills are typically sold at a discount from the par amount (also called face value). For instance, you might pay $990 for a $1,000 bill. When the bill matures, you would be paid $1,000. The difference between the purchase price and face value is interest. It is possible for a bill auction to result in a price equal to par, which means that Treasury will issue and redeem the securities at par value.

10. bank certificates of deposit (CDs) — a time deposit, a financial product commonly offered to consumers in the United States by banks, thrift institutions, and credit unions. CDs are similar to savings accounts in that they are insured and thus virtually risk free; they are "money in the bank". CDs are insured by the Federal Deposit Insurance Corporation (FDIC) for banks and by the National Credit Union Administration (NCUA) for credit unions. They are different from savings accounts in that the CD has a specific, fixed term (often monthly, three months, six months, or one to five years), and, usually, a fixed interest rate.

11. the federal fund — in the United States, federal funds are overnight borrowings by banks to maintain their bank reserves at the Federal Reserve. Banks keep reserves at Federal Reserve Banks to meet their reserve requirements and to clear financial transactions.

12. the Federal Reserve System — any bank that is part of the Federal Reserve System. In the United States, all national banks must be member banks of the Federal Reserve System. They must purchase stock in the District Reserve Banks in their regions. This stock cannot be bought or sold, and it does not offer control of the District Reserve Bank. It does convey voting rights for directors of the District Reserve Bank, and it also pays a 6 percent dividend. State-chartered banks are not required to be member banks, although they may choose to do so if they meet requirements.

13. the European Central Bank — the sixth of the seven institutions of the European Union (EU) as listed in the Treaty on European Union (TEU). It is the central bank for the euro and administers the monetary policy of the 17 EU member states which constitute the Eurozone, one of the largest currency areas in the world. It is thus one of the world's most important central banks.

14. the Bank of England — formally the Governor and Company of the Bank of England, is the

central bank of the United Kingdom and the model on which most modern central banks have been based. Established in 1694, it is the second oldest central bank in the world, after the Sveriges Riksbank, and the world's 8th oldest bank. It was established to act as the English Government's banker, and to this day it still acts as the banker for HM Government. The Bank was privately owned and operated from its foundation in 1694. It was nationalized in 1946.

15. the Penn Central Transportation Company — commonly abbreviated to Penn Central, was an American railroad company headquartered in Philadelphia that operated from 1968 until 1976. It was created by the merger on February 1, 1968, of the Pennsylvania Railroad (PRR) and the New York Central Railroad (NYC). The New Haven Railroad (NH) was added to the merger at the insistence of the Interstate Commerce Commission (ICC) on January 1, 1969.

16. the Continental Illinois Bank — The Continental Illinois National Bank and Trust Company was at one time the seventh-largest bank in the United States as measured by deposits with approximately $40 billion in assets. In 1984, Continental Illinois became the largest ever bank failure in U.S. history, when a run on the bank led to its seizure by the Federal Deposit Insurance Corporation (FDIC). Continental Illinois retained this dubious distinction until the failure of Washington Mutual in 2008 during the financial crisis of 2008, which ended up being over seven times larger than the failure of Continental Illinois.

17. actual maturity — the number of days, months, or years between today and the date a loan or security is redeemed or retired.

Exercises

I. Reading Comprehension.

Read the text carefully and decide whether the following statements are true (T) or false (F).

___ 1. Beyond the simple act of exchanging financial assets and funds, there are no major differences between one financial transaction and another.

___ 2. Money market differs from other parts of the financial system in its emphasis on loans to meet purely short-term cash needs.

___ 3. Money is one of the most perishable of all commodities.

___ 4. There is one institution that is virtually always on the demand side of the market, which is the government.

___ 5. Original maturities on money market instruments can only be as short as one day or a few hours on many loans to banks and security dealers.

II. Vocabulary Building.

A. Match the term in Column A with the definition in Column B.

1. tax obligation   a. the amount of tax that a person, business or organization owes

2. original maturity   b. a record of short-term and long-term funds flowing into and out of a nation and included in its balance-of-payments accounts

3. current account   c. the amount of an asset or resource that exceeds the portion that is utilized

4. capital account   d. the interval of time between the issue date of a security and the date on which the borrower promises to redeem it

5. opportunity cost   e. money that is not invested and, therefore, earning no interest or investment income

6. surplus   f. overnight borrowings by banks to maintain their bank reserves at the Federal Reserve

7. idle funds   g. a component of a nation's balance-of-payments accounts that tracks purchases and sales of goods and services (trade) and gifts made to foreigners

8. the Federal Funds   h. they are sold in terms ranging from a few days to 52 weeks. Bills are typically sold at a discount from the par amount (also called face value)

9. liquidity   i. the cost of an alternative that must be forgone in order to pursue a certain action. Put another way, the benefits you could have received by taking an alternative action

10. Treasury Bills   j. the degree to which an asset or security can be bought or sold in the market without affecting the asset's price

B. Complete the following sentences with the words given in the box.

exceed	repay	incur	collapsed
surge	redeem	dump	confirm
default	upsurge	channel	assume

1. He advanced funds of his own to his company, which was unable to _____ him.
2. Jacques Delors wants a system set up to _____ funds to the poor countries.
3. A nation's balance of trade is favorable when its exports _____ its imports.
4. Otherwise, the principal will _____ a certain loss, and the loss increases as the risk and the agent's risk-aversion increase.
5. Saudi bankers say there's been an _____ of business confidence since the end of the war.
6. His business empire _____ under a massive burden of debt.
7. I would rather pay the individuals than let the money go to the States by _____.
8. Instead of having thinly capitalized entities taking risks on the lending side of the balance sheet while promising to _____ fixed obligations, financial institutions would become mutual funds.
9. Abroad, that could provoke trade conflicts as China tries to _____ an even greater supply of cheap goods on a world only beginning to recover from a disastrous credit binge.
10. While France and Germany were initially hit hard by the global financial crisis, both have officially exited their recessions, while Britain has yet to _____ this has happened.

Unit 4 Money Market

III. Cloze.

There are 10 blanks in the following two passages. For each blank there are four choices marked A, B, C and D. You are supposed to choose the best answer.

Passage 1

In developing countries, money markets are typically (1)_____ by large banks because their securities markets usually are not well developed. Bank-dominated money markets have a potential weakness, (2)_____, as economic problems experienced in Asia during the late 1990s suggest. They can (3)_____ more easily to government pressure, resulting (4)_____ many bad loans, and they may slow the development of long-term capital markets, which promote greater economic stability. Central banks, are usually the single most important institution in money markets, regardless of (5)_____ they are security dominated or bank dominated.

(1) A. controlled   B. dominated   C. led   D. guided
(2) A. therefore   B. yet   C. but   D. however
(3) A. yield   B. lead   C. give   D. take
(4) A. to   B. from   C. in   D. into
(5) A. what   B. how   C. whether   D. when

Passage 2

The money market has not always been as important a source of funds for banks and other depository institutions as it is today. Prior (6)_____ the 1960s, even many of the largest money-center banks (7)_____ borrowings from the money market as only a secondary source of funds. Bankers were aware that heavy (8)_____ on money market borrowing would make their earnings more (9)_____ to fluctuations in interest rates. However, the force of competition intervened in the 1960s and 1970s. Major corporations began to seek out (10)_____ investments for their short-term funds rather than holding most of their money in bank deposits. Bankers were forced to turn to the money market for additional funds.

(6) A. to   B. from   C. before   D. as
(7) A. thought   B. regarded   C. treated   D. supposed
(8) A. link   B. relevance   C. dependence   D. independence
(9) A. adaptable   B. reasonable   C. sensible   D. sensitive
(10) A. alternative   B. replaceable   C. alternate   D. changeable

IV. Translate the following sentences into English.

1. 因各国的偏好与各自的发展水平不同，每个国家的理想金融监管结构也各有不同。(differ)
2. 货币供给的增加使我国资金流动性增强，造成物价上涨，通货膨胀的压力越来越大。(result in)
3. 实际上，出价最高的交易商面临着真正的赢家诅咒，他们试图将拍卖中赢得的证券转售给客户。(in effect)
4. 因此，就其计划向政府下单的规模和他们希望出价的价格，经销商有强烈的动机彼此分享信息。(incentive)

5. 货币市场交易是批发的，这意味着它们的规模很大，并且这些交易主要发生在金融机构和公司之间，而不是个人之间。(wholesale)

V. Translate the following paragraphs into Chinese.

1. Money markets around the world share several common characteristics. They reconcile cash imbalances for public and private individuals and institutions and do so at low levels of risk for both borrowers and lenders. Money markets transmit government economic policies, aiding governments in financing their deficits (fiscal policy) and in managing the growth of money and credit (monetary policy).

2. In developing countries, money markets are typically dominated by large banks because their securities markets usually are not well developed. Bank-dominated money markets have a potential weakness, however, as economic problems experienced in Asia during the late 1990s suggest. They can yield more easily to government pressure, resulting in many bad loans, and they may slow the development of long-term capital markets, which promote greater economic stability.

VI. Self-Testing.

1. Money-market securities have three basic characteristics in common EXCEPT _____.

   A. they are usually sold in large denominations

   B. they have low default risk

   C. they mature in one year or less from their original issue date

   D. they are less liquid

2. Most investors are using the _____ as an interim investment that provides a higher return than holding cash or money in banks.

   A. financial market   B. money market

   C. capital market   D. debt market

3. _____ is the single most influential participant in the money market.

   A. Government   B. The Central Bank

   C. Business   D. Commercial Bank

4. A variety of money market instruments are available to meet the diverse needs of market participants. The more popular money market instruments include the following EXCEPT _____.

   A. treasury bills   B. commercial paper

   C. negotiable certificates of deposit   D. securities

5. Which of the following statements about treasury bills are not true?

   A. It is the most widely held liquid security.

   B. They are backed by the government and therefore are virtually free of default risk.

   C. They will probably suffer from the unexpected changes in inflation.

   D. The markets for treasury bills in most developed countries are deep and liquid.

6. Which of the following statements about commercial paper is NOT true?

   A. Commercial paper is a short-term debt instrument issued by any corporation.

B. It is typically unsecured, and the interest rate placed on it reflects the firm's level of risk.

C. It is normally issued to provide liquidity or finance a firm's investment and accounts receivable.

D. The issuance of commercial paper is an alternative to short-term bank loan.

7. A negotiable certificate of deposit is a bank-issued security that documents a deposit and specifies the interest rate and the maturity date. It was firstly issued in 1961 by _____.

   A. Citi-bank   B. the Bank of England
   C. the Continental Illinois Bank D. HSBC

8. Banker's acceptances were not major money market securities until the volume of international trade ballooned in the _____.

   A. 1950s   B. 1960s   C. 1970s   D. 1980s

9. Banker's acceptances are crucial to international trade, and there are several advantages EXCEPT_____.

   A. the exporter is paid immediately
   B. the exporter is shielded from foreign exchange risk
   C. the exporter does not have to assess the creditworthiness of the importer
   D. the exporter can enjoy a relatively low foreign exchange rate

10. It is rare for the money market of a country to allow _____ to participate in directly.

    A. the government   B. the central bank   C. the individual   D. businesses

VII. Writing.

Please write a letter to ××bank in English as follows.

我行欲与标题行中国银行达成一份代理协议。希望贵行提供有关标题行经营方式、信贷状况以及可信度的资料。针对对方2018年4月3日的来信写一封回信，介绍中国银行的情况。

① 中国银行是国际化程度最高的中资商业银行，也是唯一一家在亚、欧、澳、非、南美、北美六大洲均设有机构的银行，有强大的外币资金实力，基本形成了商业银行、投资银行和保险业三大业务协同发展的格局，成为真正的全能银行。

② 在承担国家引进外资任务的过程中，具备多年外汇专业银行的丰富经验，在中国银行业培养和造就了一批精通国内及涉外业务的专业人才，并建立起了有高度竞争力的客户服务管理模式。

③ 上述资料应该严格保密，我们对其中的任何不实之处不负责任。

Supplementary Reading

Ethics in the Money and Capital Markets
—— Scandal Rocks the Market for Government Securities

Due in part to competition and the nature of auction methods used by the U.S. Treasury Department prior to November 1998 to sell T-bills and other U.S. Government securities, the primary dealers for many years had significant incentive to "corner" the government securities market and to "collude" and place common bids, so that all dealers received some share of all new securities issued and made a profit. In such a huge and competitive market, dealers could easily overbid, eliminating potential profits by either posting bid prices that were too high or by underbidding, receiving no securities from the government to meet their obligations to their customers. Thus, the dealers had a strong incentive to share information with each other on the size of the orders they planned to place with the government and on the prices they hoped to bid. In 1991, rumors swept through the financial markets that collusion was rampant. After several weeks of investigation, officials at the Federal Reserve and the Securities and Exchange Commission alleged that they had evidence of improper trading practices on the part of the old-line primary dealer, Salomon Brothers (now part of Citigroup Global Markets, Inc.).

It was alleged that Salomon cornered a $12-billion-plus auction of U.S. Treasury notes in May 1991, inflating the amount of its bid to the Treasury well beyond the 35 percent maximum share of a new issue normally allowed. When Salomon wound up with nearly 90 percent of the new Treasury notes, other dealers filed complaints that they were being "squeezed" by Salomon — forced to pay exorbitant prices to purchase the new notes in order to fill their own customers' orders. Subsequently, government investigators found evidence of manipulation of at least seven other government auctions. Moreover, the government wound up paying higher borrowing costs as a result of manipulation of the market.

In the wake of the Salomon Scandal, the U.S. Treasury and the Federal Reserve Bank of New York quickly set up new rules by which government securities would be auctioned in the future. For one thing, customers purchasing large amounts of government securities through dealers were thereafter required to verify in writing the amounts they bid before they could receive any new securities. Any security dealer or broker registered with the SEC, not just primary dealers, could file bids on behalf of its customers without putting up a deposit or guarantee. The U.S. Treasury promised that it would move swiftly to automate the bidding process for government securities rather than relying on traditional handwritten bids. These steps were reinforced by the U.S. Congress when it enacted the Government Securities Act Amendments of 1993, broadening the U.S. Treasury's authority to regulate the government securities market.

In 1997 the Treasury Department set up large position-reporting rules and, from time to time, has conducted "test calls" in which major dealers whose net position in a particular Treasury instrument exceeds $2 billion have been required to report the extent of their holdings. The goal has been to discourage market manipulation and prevent one or a few dealers from putting a "squeeze" on other traders in government securities who may need to buy or borrow selected Treasury securities on behalf of themselves or their customers.

Perhaps the most important outcome of the Salomon Scandal was a fundamental change in the way the Treasury auction method then in use was called a first-price sealed-bid auction, or English auction. Although it possessed the advantage of allowing the market to set the prices of Treasury securities, the English auction had definite weaknesses. It encouraged dealers to bid high to increase their probability of winning some of the auctioned securities won in the auction were sold in the secondary market, because the highest bidders had to follow through on their commitment and pay the Treasury what they had bid even though other successful bidders were paying a lower amount for the same securities. Moreover, the high bidders could sell their securities for no more later in the resale market than those who bid less. In effect, dealers bidding the highest prices faced a real "winner's curse", they attempted to resell the securities won in the auction to their customers. The first-price sealed-bid auction probably reduced the aggressiveness of competitive bidding by dealers and resulted in the Treasury getting a lower price for its securities.

Several experts suggest changes in the design of Treasury auctions. The winning recommendation was to set up a Dutch or uniform-price auction, in which bids are arrayed by price from highest to lowest but all the securities in the auction are sold for just one price — the highest bid just sufficient to sell out the whole issue, sometimes referred to as the "market clearing" or "stop-out" price. Thus, the price paid by every successful participant in a Dutch auction is identical and usually comes fairly close to the market consensus price, meaning less of a winner's curse. Dutch auctions tend to incite more aggressive bidding and to encourage more individuals and institutions to participate in Treasury auction.

Questions

1. What is the Salomon Scandal?
2. To what extent do you think of the importance of ethics in the money and capital markets?
3. What are the possible harms of the manipulation of government auctions?
4. How do the U.S. Treasury and the Federal Reserve Bank of New York react to the Salomon Scandal?
5. What are the pros and cons of a first-price sealed-bid auction, or English auction?
6. What are your suggestions on how to combat such scandals?

Unit 5   Capital Market

Case

Below are a series of financial-market transactions.
1. You purchase 100 shares of common stock from a member of a welling group.
2. You buy a Treasury bill, which has 29 days to maturity, from a Treasury-bill dealer.
3. A direct placement of an entire issue of short-term notes is negotiated between a sales finance company (seller) and a pension fund (buyer).
4. You sell 100 shares of preferred stock, using the facilities of a member of the NYSE.
5. You borrow $10,000 for 90 days from your bank.

Questions

1. Do you know what the differences between capital market and money market are?
2. Classify them as either the primary or secondary market transactions.

Preview

Skimming

Skim the following text quickly to answer the following questions and discuss your answers with your partners.

1. What are the two characteristics of capital goods?
   _____
   _____.

2. What are the two ground rules for capital markets?
   _____
   _____.

3. What are the major institutions involved in the distribution of securities in capital markets?
   _____
   _____.

4. What are the two subdivisions of the secondary market?
   _____
   _____.

5. What is the New York Stock Exchange?
   _____
   _____.

Unit 5 Capital Market

Scanning

Scan the following text quickly to find the specific information.
1. What would the economic activity be like if there were no capital market?
   _____
   _____.

2. In what way do the Securities Act of 1933 and the Securities Exchange Act of 1934 complement each other?
   _____
   _____.

3. To what extent does the distribution of new securities vary from the distribution of any other product?
   _____
   _____.

4. What is the distinguishing characteristic of the broker?
   _____
   _____.

5. What is the difference between the broker and the dealer?
   _____
   _____.

6. Please describe the underwriting function.
   _____
   _____.

7. Why is the Over-the-Counter market so named?
   _____
   _____.

8. How is the secondary market differentiated from the primary market?
   _____
   _____.

Vocabulary in Context

Read the following sentences and try to guess the meaning of the italicized words by using the context. Then replace the italicized words with synonyms (words or phrases that have nearly the same or similar meanings).

1. He can stuff it in a mattress to shoe box, but this would be "*sterilizing*" income, since it would produce no income for its owner.
   He can stuff it in a mattress to shoe box, but this would be "_____" income, since it would produce no income for its owner.

2. They *accrue* income streams beyond the current income period — that is, they have relatively long lives.
   They _____ income streams beyond the current income period — that is, they have

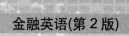

relatively long lives.

3. It should be clear that if no *conduit* for the transfer of savings into economic investment existed, the business firm would be limited to only one source of funds for capital goods.

It should be clear that if no _____ for the transfer of savings into economic investment existed, the business firm would be limited to only one source of funds for capital goods.

4. It could not issue *perpetual* claims (common stock) on its own income in order to attract funds now.

It could not issue _____ claims (common stock) on its own income in order to attract funds now.

5. We shall, in the remainder of this text, outline and discuss the terms, conditions, rules, and *constraints* under which the long-term financial markets operate.

We shall, in the remainder of this text, outline and discuss the terms, conditions, rules, and _____ under which the long-term financial markets operate.

6. As a reaction to the excesses *perpetuated* in capital markets in the 1920s, Congress passed two acts that remain the bases of regulation of the capital markets today.

As a reaction to the excesses _____ in capital markets in the 1920s, Congress passed two acts that remain the bases of regulation of the capital markets today.

7. The two laws *complement* each other in providing regulation of capital markets.

The two laws _____ each other in providing regulation of capital markets.

8. Although the titles of the transactors as well as the product line are different, there are many *parallels* between distribution in securities markets and the distribution in retail markets.

Although the titles of the transactors as well as the product line are different, there are many _____ between distribution in securities markets and the distribution in retail markets.

9. The securities broker is *analogous* to the real estate broker.

The securities broker is _____ to the real estate broker.

10. The report is read and *digested* by both the officers and the board of directors of the corporation, and the decision to undertake the new project and its financing is made.

The report is read and _____ by both the officers and the board of directors of the corporation, and the decision to undertake the new project and its financing is made.

Text

Financial Markets: Long-term Obligation

The Savings-Investment Relationship

Recall our frequent references to the saver. He is the non-consumer who decides not to consume a portion of his current income. What to do with this income that he does not use for current consumption becomes a problem. He can stuff it in a mattress or in a shoe box, but this would be "sterilizing" income, since it would produce no income for its owner. It would also be unavailable for use by those who require the funds to purchase capital goods.

Capital goods are those goods that have two characteristics: (1) They accrue income streams beyond the current income period — that is, they have relatively long lives; and (2) they are used in the production of consumer goods or other capital goods. We are speaking of such things as machine tools, buildings, transportation systems, typewriters, and indeed anything that is used in the further production of goods and services.

If there were no capital markets — that is, if there were no orderly, reliable means of smoothly transmitting funds from savers to capital accumulators — the level of economic activity would be significantly smaller. Why? It should be clear that if no conduit for the transfer of savings into economic investment existed, the business firm would be limited to only one source of funds for capital goods. That source would be savings out of its own current income. It could not borrow long-term funds from savers. It could not issue perpetual claims (common stock) on its own income in order to attract funds now. Conversely, savers who desired not to spend their entire current income would have no investment outlet for their savings.

Which brings us to our conceptualization of the capital market? The capital market is the series of institutional friendships that exist for the purpose of trading claims (bonds, common stock, preferred stock, and other claims) on those firms that want to accumulate capital stocks. Financial investment is the purchase of claims on firms that accumulates goods. Economic investment is the purchase of newly-created capital goods by those firms issuing the claims. It is clear, we hope that every dollar that is used to purchase a new claim in capital markets is channeled into capital goods. Even though the objects being traded in capital markets are financial claims, they represent real, tangible capital goods.

We shall, in the remainder of this text, outline and discuss the terms, conditions, rules, and constraints under which the long-term financial markets operate. Keep in mind that we are discussing the market for saving on the one hand, and the market for capital goods on the other.

The Ground Rules for Capital Markets: The Two Basic Acts

Probably no other area of finance has caught the attention of the general public as the capital market has. Most members of the reading public associate the trading of stocks and bonds with "high finance". It is in the trading of these securities that highly publicized excesses have taken place.

As a reaction to the excesses perpetuated in capital markets in the 1920s, Congress passed two acts that remain the bases of regulation of the capital markets today, and whose provisions help explain many activities in capital markets. The two laws are the Securities Act of 1933[1] and the Securities Exchange Act of 1934[2].

The two laws complement each other in providing regulation of capital markets: the act of 1933 providing for disclosure of information on primary issues, and the act of 1934 requiring the same for secondary issues, as well as providing the enforcement machinery, the Securities and Exchange Commission[3].

Given this treatment of the basic regulation of capital markets by the federal government, we turn to a discussion of the market for new securities, the primary market.

The Primary Market

Definition

The primary market is defined simply as the market for new securities issues. It can also be defined as the process by which new securities are distributed from their issuer to the eventual financial investor. The process is alternatively described as investment banking and underwriting. We shall look at the process by viewing the participants in it as well as the process in which they engage.

The Participants

Conceptually, the distribution of new securities varies little from the distribution of any product. The typical manufactured product goes from the manufacturer to wholesalers and in turn to retailers and the consuming public. At each step along the conduit, bulk shipments are broken down into smaller lots for resale to the next level of transactions. The wholesaler, for example, breaks down the carload shipment of candies into cartons for sale and distribution to retailers. The retailer, in turn, breaks the cartons down into packages for sale to the consuming public. Although the titles of the transactors as well as the product line are different, there are many parallels between distribution in securities markets and the distribution in retail markets.

The major institutions involved in the distribution of securities in capital markets are securities brokers and securities dealers. (The same individual, or firm may function at different times as broker and as dealer.) They operate in both the primary and the secondary markets. However, we are concerned in this section with their roles only in the primary market.

Broker. The distinguishing characteristic of the broker is his function of bringing buyer and seller together. The broker is an agent. He never takes title, but can take possession of the commodity being traded. Therefore, he does not bear the risk of price change. The real estate broker, for example, is a well-known type of broker. His function is to bring the home buyer and seller together. He may, in the course of the transaction, take possession of the property of either the buyer or seller. He never, though, takes title to the property — in other words, he never trades for his own account. The securities broker is analogous to the real estate broker. The broker handles the public's orders to buy and sell securities or commodities. For this service, a commission is charged.

Salesman, or customers' representatives, as they are sometimes called, frequently refer to themselves as "stockbrokers", even though they may perform a variety of other functions for the securities firms for which they work.

Dealer. A securities dealer acts as principal rather than an agent. Typically, a dealer buys for his own account and sells to a customer from his own inventory. The dealer's profit or loss is the difference between the price he pays and the price he receives for the same security — that is, the "spread" between the bid and the asked price of the security being traded. The dealer's confirmation must disclose to his customer that he has acted as principal.

The role of the dealer is contrasted sharply with that of the broker. The dealer buys and sells for his own account. In contrast to the broker, the dealer does not get paid a commission. As an entrepreneur, and as the principal in the transaction, he receives the difference between the purchase price and the sales price. In this respect, the securities dealer is no different from the car dealer, the shoe dealer, or indeed, any other merchant acting as principal in the sale of goods or services.

Securities Wholesaling: The Underwriting Process

The underwriting process[4] starts with the need for new capital assets by a corporation. The need for the assets is recognized by the board of directors, which authorizes the officers of the corporation to enter into preliminary discussions with an investment banking firm for the purpose of determining the feasibility of a new securities issue to finance the needed asset expansion.

The Underwriting Function. The investment banking function is conducted by securities firms that wear many hats and perform many functions for the investing public. They are simultaneously investment bankers, securities brokers, and securities dealers. From now on, we shall use the term securities dealer to describe the investment banking firm's activities. At this point, the securities dealer is acting as agent of the issuing corporation. The corporation retains the dealer to examine all facets of the proposed new issue. Economic, marketing, engineering, legal, and accounting experts, and any other kind required, are consulted to try to predict the success of the proposed new productive activity as well as the current financial health of the firm. The agent/securities dealer completes its study on the feasibility of the new projects and gives its estimate of the probability of success of such an issue at that time.

Let's assume the report is positive in all aspects, that it suggests that both the proposed project and its financing will be successful. The report is submitted to the corporation, and the securities firm is paid for its services. The principal — agent relationship[5] between the corporation and the securities dealer is ended at this point. The report is read and digested by both the officers and the board of directors of the corporation, and the decision to undertake the new project and its financing is made.

Summary

The primary market is the market for new issues of securities. It is characterized by the underwriting process, in which investment banking firms, organized into syndicates[6], purchase entire issues and then either wholesale them to securities dealers in selling groups, or retail them themselves.

The underwriting of new issues by this method provides an efficient and readily available means of feeding new securities into the capital market.

The Secondary Market

The secondary market is the national market for "used" securities. It is the market in common stock, preferred stock, and debt that have passed through the primary market, either through the underwriting process or through direct placements, and found their way into investor portfolios.

This national market in used securities is extremely important to financial investors. It permits them to make adjustments in their holdings quickly, efficiently, and economically.

The secondary market has two subdivisions. These two subdivisions involve trading on organized exchanges, and trading "over the counter" (OTC)[7]. During the following discussion, keep in mind that the commodity being traded is corporate securities, which include common, preferred, and debt.

The Over-the-Counter Market (OTC)

All securities that are not sold on one of the organized exchanges are traded in the over-the-counter market. The over-the-counter market is defined as the trading in securities between dealers and members of the investing public. This market is so named because dealers carrying inventories of securities stand willing and able to sell them "over the counter" to the financial investor.

Viewed in this light, the dealer in over-the-counter securities is no different from the dealer in over-the-counter shoes, or over-the-counter groceries, or over-the-counter anything. There should be no mystery attached to the over-the-counter market: The securities dealer, like any merchant, buys low and hopes to sell high. The spread is his margin and represents his income. Almost all corporate bonds and a very large volume of common stocks are traded "over the counter".

Organized Exchanges: The New York Stock Exchange

Although most securities issues, stocks and bonds, are traded over the counter, it is the stock exchange that the general public tends to associate with trading in the secondary market. The organized exchanges do provide the focal point for securities trading, and because it is the largest and best known of them, we shall confine our discussion to the "Big Board", or the New York Stock Exchange[8].

The New York Stock Exchange is an association of securities traders and brokers organized together for the purpose of providing trading facilities for members of the association. The organization has been in existence since 1792 when a group of New York securities dealers agreed to band together to give each other preference in their trading.

The New York Stock Exchange has been reorganized several times in its history. It stands today as an organization that provides two principal services: (1) It provides the resources and space for a continuous auction market in corporate securities, and (2) it serves as the regulatory agency for policing its members' practices.

Summary

We have spoken of the primary market, the market for new issues, and the secondary market, the market for "used" securities traded over the counter and on the organized exchanges. These transactions are normally between the securities issuer and investing public as in the case of the primary market, or between members of the investing public as in the case of the secondary market.

Terminology

underwriting	承销
long-term funds	长期资金
stock	股票
common stock	普通股，普通股股本
preferred stock	优先股

primary market	初级市场(即证券发行机构)
secondary market	二[中，次]级市场
bonds	债券
securities	股票；有价证券
OTC	场外交易
broker	(股票、外币等)经纪人
dealer	交易员
commission	佣金
principal	委托人
agent	代理人，代理商

Notes on the Text

1. the Securities Act of 1933 — the first major federal legislation to regulate the offer and sale of securities. Prior to the Act, regulation of securities was chiefly governed by state laws, commonly referred to as blue sky laws. When Congress enacted the 1933 Act, it left existing state securities laws ("blue sky laws") in place. The 1933 Act is based upon a philosophy of disclosure, meaning that the goal of the law is to require issuers to fully disclose all material information that a reasonable shareholder would require in order to make up his or her mind about the potential investment.

2. the Securities Exchange Act of 1934 — a law governing the secondary trading of securities (stocks, bonds, and debentures) in the United States. It was a sweeping piece of legislation. The Act and related statutes form the basis of regulation of the financial markets and their participants in the United States. The 1934 Act also established the Securities and Exchange Commission (SEC), the agency primarily responsible for enforcement of the United States federal securities law.

3. Securities and Exchange Commission (SEC) — a federal agency which holds primary responsibility for enforcing the federal securities laws and regulating the securities industry, the nation's stock and options exchanges, and other electronic securities markets in the United States.

4. underwriting — the process by which investment bankers raise investment capital from investors on behalf of corporations and governments that are issuing securities (both equity and debt).

5. principal-agent relationship — in political science and economics, the principal-agent problem or agency dilemma concerns the difficulties in motivating one party (the "agent"), to act in the best interests of another (the "principal") rather than in his or her own interests. Common examples of this relationship include corporate management (agent) and shareholders (principal), or politicians (agent) and voters (principal). In fact the problem potentially arises in almost any context where one party is being paid by another to do something, whether in formal employment or a negotiated deal such as paying for household jobs or car repairs. The two parties have different interests and asymmetric information (the

agent having more information), such that the principal cannot directly ensure that the agent is always acting in its (the principal's) best interests, particularly when activities that are useful to the principal are costly to the agent, and where elements of what the agent does are costly for the principal to observe. Moral hazard and conflict of interest may arise. The deviation from the principal's interest by the agent is called "agency costs". Various mechanisms may be used to align the interests of the agent with those of the principal.

6. syndicate — a self-organizing group of individuals, companies, corporations or entities formed to transact some specific business, or to promote a common interest. In most cases' formed groups aim to scale up their profits. Although there are many legal syndicates formed around the world, people tend to link the term syndicate to various criminal activities. In the case of criminal activity, the syndicate is there to promote, and engage in, organized crime. The term is also associated with anarchist theory, specifically anarcho-syndicalism, in which it forms an alternative to both the nation state and capitalist corporations.

7. over the counter — a security traded in some context other than on a formal exchange such as the NYSE, TSX, AMEX, etc. The phrase "over the counter" can be used to refer to stocks that are traded via a dealer network as opposed to on a centralized exchange. It also refers to debt securities and other financial instruments such as derivatives, which are traded through a dealer network.

8. the New York Stock Exchange — A stock exchange based in New York City, which is considered the largest equities exchange in the world based on total market capitalization of its listed securities. Formerly run as a private organization, the NYSE became a public entity in 2005 following the acquisition of electronic trading exchange Archipelago. The parent company of the New York Stock Exchange is now called NYSE Euronext, following a merger with the European exchange in 2007. Also known as the "Big Board", the NYSE relied for many years on floor trading only, using the open outcry system. Today, more than half of all NYSE trades are conducted electronically, although floor traders are still used to set pricing and deal in high volume institutional trading.

Exercises

I. Reading Comprehension.

Read the text carefully and decide whether the following statements are true (T) or false (F).

___ 1. Without capital markets, savers who desired not to spend their entire current income would have no investment outlet for their savings.

___ 2. The broker does not bear the risk of price change.

___ 3. A securities dealer acts as an agent rather than a principal.

___ 4. We can use the term securities dealer to describe the investment banking firm's activities.

___ 5. All securities that are not sold on one of the organized exchanges are traded in the over-the-counter market.

Unit 5   Capital Market

II. Vocabulary Building.

A. Match the term in Column A with the definition in Column B.

1. common stock
2. preferred stocks
3. bonds
4. security
5. broker
6. dealer
7. commission
8. principal
9. agent
10. long-term funds

a. a debt security, under which the issuer owes the holders a debt and, depending on the terms of the bond, is obliged to pay them interest (the coupon) and/or to repay the principal at a later date, termed the maturity.

b. a form of corporate equity ownership, a type of security, so its holders cannot be paid dividends until all preferred stock dividends (including payments in arrears) are paid in full.

c. an individual or party (brokerage firm) that arranges transactions between a buyer and a seller, and gets a commission when the deal is executed.

d. remuneration for services rendered or products sold is a common way to reward sales people.

e. a person buys for his own account and sells to a customer from his own inventory.

f. a financial instrument that represents: an ownership position in a publicly-traded corporation (stock), a creditor relationship with governmental body or a corporation (bond), or rights to ownership as represented by an option.

g. the person who authorizes an agent.

h. a person who is authorized to act on behalf of another (called the principal).

i. it usually carries no voting rights, but may carry a dividend and may have priority over common stock in the payment of dividends and upon liquidation.

j. an investment vehicle for a long time.

B. Complete the following sentences with the words given in the box.

reliable	principal	tangible	commission	transmit
recall	purchase	focal	associate	feasibility
disclosure	eventual	common	estimate	

1. Readers will _____ short-term interest rates being pushed to very high levels in 1997 when the Asian financial crisis began.
2. The immediate priority is for Athens to demonstrate that it is serious about cutting public expenditure, improving tax collection, publishing _____ financial statistics and tackling corruption, the officials said.

3. But the Fed needed a functioning financial system to _____ the benefits of such actions to the broader economy.

4. The simultaneous _____ and sale of identical or equivalent financial instruments or commodity futures in order to benefit from a discrepancy in their price relationship.

5. As developed economies switch from manufacturing to services and _____ to intangible products, brands make up a growing proportion of financial value.

6. Stock exchanges vary in terms of content, quantity and depth of trading information _____, given different economic and cultural background, trading system, market structure, technical model and investor location.

7. The broker was paid _____ by the buyer and the seller for executing their orders.

8. The _____ is not obligated to pay the agent for authorized services performed, unless otherwise agreed.

9. This two-year stimulus program has gone through scientific _____ studies and is supported by a detailed financial arrangement RMB 1.18 trillion *yuan* will come from central government's budget, which is expected to generate funds from local governments and other sources.

10. Because a shareholder is equal to holding a call option, we can use the stock price to _____ the market value of a company.

III. Cloze.

There are 10 blanks in the following two passages. For each blank there are four choices marked A, B, C and D. You are supposed to choose the best answer.

Passage 1

Modern capital markets are almost invariably hosted on computer-based electronic trading systems; most can be (1)_____ only by entities within the financial sector or the treasury departments of governments and corporations, but some can be accessed directly by the (2)_____. There are many thousands of such systems, most serving only small parts of the (3)_____ capital markets. Entities hosting the systems include stock exchanges, investment banks, and government departments. Physically, the systems are hosted all over the world, though they tend to be (4)_____ in financial (5)_____ like London, New York, and Hong Kong. Capital markets are defined as markets in which money is provided for periods longer than a year.

  (1) A. accessed   B. got   C. reached   D. approached
  (2) A. people   B. private   C. public   D. folk
  (3) A. whole   B. overall   C. all-round   D. all
  (4) A. appearing   B. present   C. gathered   D. concentrated
  (5) A. districts   B. cities   C. centers   D. circles

Passage 2

There is a strong relationship between the efficiency of an economy's securities markets and its (6)_____ national product. Efficient markets are necessary for the (7)_____ of saved income into capital goods and equipment. The (8)_____ of capital goods is in turn strongly related to the economy's efficiency in turning resources into goods and services. There are two types of efficiency to be measured in securities markets: operational efficiency and allocational efficiency. (9)_____ efficiency has to do with the relative efficiency of the institutions that conduct the flow of savings into investment goods. Allocational efficiency, on the other hand, (10)_____ with the efficiency of moving funds to high-return and socially desirably uses.

(6) A. great   B. whole   C. gross   D. all
(7) A. channeling   B. passing   C. changing   D. moving
(8) A. size   B. volume   C. sort   D. capacity
(9) A. Informational   B. Economic   C. Allocational   D. Operational
(10) A. deals   B. handles   C. solves   D. resolves

IV. Translate the following sentences into English.

1. 自去年10月底上任以来，这位部长宣布了一系列高调的政策，以促进股市的健康发展。(take office)
2. 新华社评论说，目前清理股市的努力还远远不够。(far from adequate)
3. 为保存和增加资产，养老基金、企业年金和其他形式的社会保险基金，需要证券公司提供专业服务。(preserve)
4. 就此前有关官员谈到了将中国庞大的养老基金投入股市的可能性的问题时，分析人士昨日敦促有关部门对股市实施更严格的监管。(impose)
5. 人力资源和社会保障部规定，在政府发布任何其他形式的投资规定之前，社会保险基金只能存入指定银行或用于购买国债。(stipulate)

V. Translate the following paragraphs into Chinese.

1. A key division within the capital markets is between the primary markets and secondary markets. In primary markets, new stock or bond issues are sold to investors, often via a mechanism known as underwriting. The main entities seeking to raise long-term funds on the primary capital markets are governments (which may be municipal, local or national) and business enterprises (companies). Governments tend to issue only bonds, whereas companies often issue either equity or bonds. The main entities purchasing the bonds or stock include pension funds, hedge funds, sovereign wealth funds, and less commonly wealthy individuals and investment banks trading on their own behalf. In the secondary markets, existing securities are sold and bought among investors or traders, usually on a securities exchange, over the counter, or elsewhere.

2. When a government wants to raise long-term finance, it will often sell bonds to the capital markets. For developing countries, a multilateral development bank would sometimes provide an additional layer of underwriting, resulting in risks being shared between the investment bank(s), the multilateral organization, and the end investors. However, since 1997, it has been increasingly common for governments of the larger nations to bypass investment banks by making their bonds directly available for purchase over the Internet. Many governments now sell most of their bonds by computerized auction. Typically, large volumes are put up for sale

in one go; a government may only hold a small number of auctions each year. Some governments will also sell a continuous stream of bonds through other channels.

VI. Self-Testing.

1. _____ refers to the total value at market prices of the shares in issue for a company (or a stock market, or a sector of the stock market).
   A. Market capitalization   B. Capital goods
   C. Market capital   D. Market liquidation

2. In December _____, China launched the Qualified Foreign Institutional Investor (QFII) scheme, which opened up China's domestic A-share market to international investors at a time when there was the non-convertibility of Renminbi under the capital account.
   A. 2000   B. 2002   C. 2003   D. 2004

3. Listed companies can issue additional shares to the public by placing them to their existing shareholders or to the general public. The following statements about the review and approval procedures are true EXCEPT_____.
   A. the issuers are required to make public their application documents before being accepted by the CSRC
   B. the Public Offering Supervision Department of the CSRC conducts preliminary reviews on the application documents
   C. the application documents are subject to the review and examination of the Public Offering Review Committee, which comprises both the CSRC staff and external experts. The Review Committee members vote by majority
   D. after taking into consideration the recommendation of the Review Committee, the CSRC finally decides whether to approve it or not

4. Investors purchase or sell securities through the brokerage of securities companies which charge commissions no higher than _____ of the trading value (but no less than the total amount of the trading regulatory fee and the charges by the stock exchanges). Furthermore, both buyers and sellers are levied a stamp duty of _____ of the trading value.
   A. 3‰, 2‰   B. 3‰, 1‰   C. 2‰, 1‰   D. 1‰, 3‰

5. _____ is the centralized process whereby transacted business is recorded and positions are maintained while _____ refers to the completion of a transaction.
   A. Settlement…clearing   B. Underwriting…settlement
   C. Clearing…resolution   D. Clearing…settlement

6. Where a listed company is under any of the following circumstances, the stock exchange shall terminate the listing of its stocks, EXCEPT _____.
   A. the total share capital or shareholding structure of the company changes and thus fails to meet the listing requirements, and is still unable to meet the listing requirements following the rectification period set by the stock exchange
   B. the company fails to disclose its financial statements or provides false information in its statements, and yet refuses to rectify
   C. the company has been making losses for the latest two consecutive years with a failure to

make profits in the third year

  D. the company is disbanded or declared bankrupt

7. The information disclosed by issuers and listed companies shall be _____.
  A. authentic   B. accurate   C. complete   D. all of the above

8. An investment consulting institution and its practitioners shall not have any of the following acts EXCEPT _____.
  A. engaging in any securities investment on behalf of its entrusting party
  B. signing with any party an agreement on sharing the gains or bearing the loss of securities investment
  C. purchasing or selling any share of a listed company, for which the consulting institution provides services
  D. providing true and useful information to investors

9. The following requirements shall be met in order to establish a fund management company EXCEPT _____.
  A. the company must have sufficient foreign exchange resources for individuals
  B. the company must have a registered capital of no less than RMB 100 million
  C. principal shareholders demonstrate a good track record and reputation in the securities business, securities investment consultation, trust assets management or other financial assets management, committing no violation of law within the preceding three years, and having a registered capital of no less than RMB 300 million *yuan*
  D. the company must meet the statutory requirement for the number of licensed fund professionals

10. _____ was launched in 2005 with a paid-up capital of RMB 6.3 billion *yuan* in order to protect the interests of securities investors against losses from failing securities companies.
  A. The Qualified Foreign Institutional Investors (QFII) scheme
  B. China Securities Regulatory Commission (CSRC)
  C. The Securities Law of China
  D. The Securities Investor Protection Fund (SIPF)

VII. Writing.

请用英文以建设银行信贷部的名义起草一封信给要求贷款的客户，表示你行同意按下列条件向其贷款：
  1. 贷款用途：建筑融资。
  2. 贷款金额：50万元人民币。
  3. 贷款方式：合约生效后一次性直接支付给贷款人。
  4. 偿还期：10年。
  5. 利率：优惠利率加1%。
  6. 担保品：贷款人提交担保物。

同时表明如果对方同意该条件，就在随附的复印件上签名并于2018年1月30日前寄回你行。

Supplementary Reading

Capital Market to Open Further

By Wang Yu and Li Xiang
(*China Daily* February 12, 2018)

China will accelerate the opening of its capital market to foreign asset managers and the market will likely see a surge in new investment products offered by foreign funds in the first quarter of this year, according to a senior official of the Asset Management Association of China.

Recent stock market volatility and intensified regulation to curb financial risks will not derail China's effort to reform and open its capital markets, and foreign fund managers have expressed optimism regarding the Chinese market's long-term prospects, the AMAC official said.

"They will come with their mature investment strategies and business models, which will bring healthy competition and benefit the long-term development of the domestic sector," the official said.

The growing affluence of Chinese investors and their growing demand for increasingly sophisticated investment products have attracted many global investment firms to China's multi-trillion dollar asset management market.

So far, 10 foreign asset managers including Fidelity International, BlackRock, UBS, Man Group, and Schroders are qualified to sell onshore funds to Chinese clients, according to the AMAC.

Despite last week's 9.6 percent fall in the Chinese mainland's A-share market, Lynda Zhou, a portfolio manager at Fidelity International, said a greater opening of China's financial market was likely this year as foreign participation helps it become increasingly mature.

"My long-term view on China is not changed. … The recent market correction is a healthy one as the valuation of blue chips was very expensive. When value re-emerges, I believe foreign investors will come in again," Zhou said.

China opened its asset management industry to international players in 2016 by allowing them to set up wholly foreign-owned enterprises to raise onshore funds and invest in the mainland's securities market. Previously, they could only enter the market by owning a minority stake in a joint venture with a local Chinese partner.

Foreign fund managers have expressed great interest in raising onshore funds to invest in the Chinese interbank bond market, which is currently unavailable to them, as they see fixed-income products as an important asset class in their portfolios and a necessary tool to hedge against risks in the equities market for their clients.

Many of them have also been seeking regulatory approval to raise onshore funds and invest in overseas markets with a certain quota under the pilot program known as the Qualified Domestic Limited Partnership.

"The QDLP program has allowed us to further understand the risk preference of Chinese investors and the existing regulatory environment in China. We will continue to use our global advantage to create value for our Chinese clients," BlackRock said in a written response to

China Daily.

China suspended the program in 2015 as the country faced mounting pressure from capital outflows. But the renewed foreign interest indicates that the authorities may lift the suspension in the near future.

The recent market correction is not expected to detract from China's effort to reform its capital market or boost the attractiveness of A-shares to domestic and foreign investors.

The Shenzhen Stock Exchange said on Friday in its 2018-20 development plan that it will reform the current listing requirements for its startup board and will make the exchange more inclusive for high-tech and innovative companies.

Questions

1. According to the passage, what will happen to the market after China's acceleration of the opening of its capital market?
2. What attitude do foreign fund managers hold toward the Chinese market's long-term prospect?
3. How did China open its asset management industry to international players in 2016?
4. Why have foreign fund managers expressed great interests in raising onshore funds to invest in the Chinese interbank bond market?
5. What have you learned about the QDLP program from this passage?
6. According to the Shenzhen Stock Exchange, what is the 2018-20 development plan about?

Unit 6   Derivatives Markets

Case

Mary Craft is expecting large-capitalization to rally close to the end of the year. She is pessimistic, however, about the performance of small-capitalization stocks. She decides to go long one December futures contract on the Dow Jones Industrial Average at a price of $9,020 and go short one December futures contract on the S&P Midcap 400 index at a price of $369.40. The multiplier for a futures contract on the Dow is $10, and the multiplier for a futures contract on the S&P Midcap 400 is $500. When Craft closes her position toward the end of the year, the Dow and S&P Midcap 400 futures prices are $9,086 and $370.20, respectively.

Questions

1. Do you know what a futures market is?
2. How much is the net gain or loss to Craft?

Preview

Skimming

Skim the following text quickly to answer the following questions and discuss your answers with your partners.

1. What is a derivative?

2. What are the two uses of derivatives?

3. Who are the major users of derivatives?

4. What are the three dimensions along which derivatives can be differentiated?

5. How can the derivatives value chain be divided?

Unit 6 Derivatives Markets

Scanning

Scan the following text quickly to find the specific information.

1. What is the relationship between derivatives market and financial market?
   _____
   _____.

2. What is the main factor that has caused the financial crisis?
   _____
   _____.

3. How can derivatives be differentiated from securities?
   _____
   _____.

4. Where can derivatives contracts be traded?
   _____
   _____.

5. What is the main distinguishing feature of derivatives trading and clearing between OTC and on-exchange derivatives?
   _____
   _____.

6. What are the two functions of derivatives market?
   _____
   _____.

7. Why has the exchange segment grown faster than the OTC segment?
   _____
   _____.

8. What suggestions does the author make to improve the OTC segments on the derivatives market?
   _____
   _____.

Vocabulary in Context

Read the following sentences and try to guess the meaning of the italicized words by using the context. Then replace the italicized words with synonyms (words or phrases that have nearly the same or similar meanings).

1. The financial market is, of course, far broader, *encompassing* bonds, foreign exchange, real estate, commodities, and numerous other asset classes and financial instruments.
   The financial market is, of course, far broader, _____ bonds, foreign exchange, real estate, commodities, and numerous other asset classes and financial instruments.

2. The derivatives market has recently attracted more attention against the backdrop of the financial crisis, *fraud* cases and the near failure of some market participants.
   The derivatives market has recently attracted more attention against the backdrop of the

financial crisis, _____ cases and the near failure of some market participants.

3. A derivative is a contract between a buyer and a seller entered into today regarding a transaction to be *fulfilled* at a future point in time, for example, the transfer of a certain amount of U.S. dollars at a specified USD-EUR exchange rate at a future date.

   A derivative is a contract between a buyer and a seller entered into today regarding a transaction to be _____ at a future point in time, for example, the transfer of a certain amount of U.S. dollars at a specified USD-EUR exchange rate at a future date.

4. The *fundamentals* explained in this document mostly apply to both wholesale and retail markets, although the share of retail users is negligible in most markets.

   The _____ explained in this document mostly apply to both wholesale and retail markets, although the share of retail users is negligible in most markets.

5. They serve as insurance against unwanted price movements and reduce the *volatility* of companies' cash flows, which in turn results in more reliable forecasting, lower capital requirements, and higher capital productivity.

   They serve as insurance against unwanted price movements and reduce the _____ of companies' cash flows, which in turn results in more reliable forecasting, lower capital requirements, and higher capital productivity.

6. Examples include credit derivatives that provide compensation payments if a creditor *defaults* on its bonds, or weather derivatives offering compensation if temperatures at a specified location exceed or fall below a predefined reference temperature.

   Examples include credit derivatives that provide compensation payments if a creditor _____ on its bonds, or weather derivatives offering compensation if temperatures at a specified location exceed or fall below a predefined reference temperature.

7. As long as local market regulation does not impose access barriers, participants can connect and trade remotely and *seamlessly* from around the world.

   As long as local market regulation does not impose access barriers, participants can connect and trade remotely and _____ from around the world.

8. Most of these contracts are held to maturity by the original counterparties, but some are *altered* during their life or offset before termination.

   Most of these contracts are held to maturity by the original counterparties, but some are _____ during their life or offset before termination.

9. However, the estimated gross market values of all derivatives outstanding total only €10 trillion, which is *markedly* lower than the equity and bond markets with a market capitalization of €43 trillion and €55 trillion, respectively.

   However, the estimated gross market values of all derivatives outstanding total only €10 trillion, which is _____ lower than the equity and bond markets with a market capitalization of €43 trillion and €55 trillion, respectively.

10. Other contributing factors are a number of advantages of on-exchange trading: price transparency, risk *mitigation* and transaction costs are among the most important.

    Other contributing factors are a number of advantages of on-exchange trading: price transparency, risk _____ and transaction costs are among the most important.

Text

An Introduction to the Global Derivatives Market

Introduction

Many associate the financial market mostly with the equity market. The financial market is, of course, far broader, encompassing bonds, foreign exchange, real estate, commodities, and numerous other asset classes and financial instruments. A segment of the market has fast become its most important one: derivatives[1]. The derivatives market has seen the highest growth of all financial market segments in recent years. It has become a central contributor to the stability of the financial system and an important factor in the functioning of the real economy.

Despite the importance of the derivatives market, few outsiders have a comprehensive perspective on its size, structure, role and segments and on how it works.

The derivatives market has recently attracted more attention against the backdrop of the financial crisis, fraud cases and the near failure of some market participants. Although the financial crisis has primarily been caused by structured credit-linked securities that are not derivatives, policy makers and regulators have started to think about strengthening regulation to increase transparency and safety both for derivatives and other financial instruments.

Basics of Derivatives

Derivatives are totally different from securities. They are financial instruments that are mainly used to protect against and manage risks, and very often also serve arbitrage[2] or investment purposes, providing various advantages compared to securities. Derivatives come in many varieties and can be differentiated by how they are traded, the underlying they refer to, and the product type.

Definition of Derivatives

A derivative is a contract between a buyer and a seller entered into today regarding a transaction to be fulfilled at a future point in time, for example, the transfer of a certain amount of U.S. dollars at a specified USD-EUR exchange rate at a future date. Over the life of the contract, the value of the derivative fluctuates with the price of the so-called "underlying[3]" of the contract — in our example, the USD-EUR exchange rate. The life of a derivative contract, that is, the time between entering into the contract and the ultimate fulfillment or termination of the contract, can be very long — in some cases more than ten years. Given the possible price fluctuations of the underlying and thus of the derivative contract itself, risk management[4] is of particular importance.

Derivatives must be distinguished from securities, where transactions are fulfilled within a few days. Some securities have derivative-like characteristics — such as certificates, warrants, or structured credit-linked securities — but they are not derivatives. This white paper focuses on the largest segment of the derivatives market: derivatives contracts for wholesale and professional users. The fundamentals explained in this document mostly apply to both wholesale and retail markets, although the share of retail users is negligible in most markets. Derivatives contracts can be traded on derivatives exchanges but also bilaterally between market participants. The latter segment — i.e. the

OTC segment — currently accounts for around 84 percent of the derivatives market.

Uses and Users of Derivatives

Derivatives make future risks tradable, which gives rise to two main uses for them. The first is to eliminate uncertainty by exchanging market risks, commonly known as hedging. Corporates and financial institutions, for example, use derivatives to protect themselves against changes in raw material prices, exchange rates, interest rates etc. They serve as insurance against unwanted price movements and reduce the volatility of companies' cash flows, which in turn results in more reliable forecasting, lower capital requirements, and higher capital productivity. These benefits have led to the widespread use of derivatives: 92 percent of the world's 500 largest companies manage their price risks using derivatives.

The second use of derivatives is as an investment. Derivatives are an alternative to investing directly in assets without buying and holding the asset itself. They also allow investments into underlyings and risks that cannot be purchased directly. Examples include credit derivatives that provide compensation payments if a creditor defaults on its bonds, or weather derivatives offering compensation if temperatures at a specified location exceed or fall below a predefined reference temperature.

Derivatives have not only widened the investment universe, they have also significantly lowered the cost of investing. The total transaction cost of buying a derivatives contract on a major European stock index is around 60 percent lower than that of buying the portfolio of underlying shares. If one compares the cost of gaining exposure to less liquid assets such as real estate, the cost differential between the derivative and the direct investment in the underlying is even significantly higher.

Derivatives also allow investors to take positions against the market if they expect the underlying as set to fall in value. Typically, investors would enter into a derivatives contract to sell an asset (such as a single stock) that they believe is overvalued, at a specified future point in time. This investment is successfully provided the asset falls in value. Such strategies are extremely important for an efficientlly functioning price discovery in financial markets as they reduce the risk of assets becoming excessively under - or overvalued.

Derivatives contracts are mainly designed for professional users. Exchange-traded derivatives contracts are typically in the range of €20,000 to €1 million financial institutions and corporates therefore make up the majority of derivatives users — more than 90 percent for some underlyings.

Types of Derivatives

Derivatives can be traded OTC or on exchanges. OTC derivatives are created by an agreement between two individual counterparties. OTC derivatives cover a range from highly standardized (so-called "exchange look-alike") to tailor-made contracts with individualized terms regarding underlying, contract size, maturity and other features. Most of these contracts are held to maturity by the original counterparties, but some are altered during their life or offset before termination.

Exchange-traded derivatives, on the other hand, are fully standardized and their contract terms are designed by derivatives exchanges. Most derivatives products are initially developed as OTC derivatives. Once a product matures, exchanges "industrialize" it, creating a liquid market for a standardized and refined form of the new derivatives product. The OTC and exchange-traded derivatives then coexist side by side.

The number of OTC-traded derivatives is unlimited in principle as they are customized and new contracts are created continuously. A broad universe of exchange-traded derivatives exists as well: for example, over 1,700 different derivatives are listed on the three major global derivatives exchanges (Chicago Mercantile Exchange[5], Eurex[6] and Euronext[7]. LIFFE[8]).

Derivatives can be differentiated along three main dimensions.

Type of derivative and market place: Derivatives can be traded bilaterally OTC (mostly individually customized contracts) or multilaterally on exchanges (standardized contracts).

Type of underlying: Underlyings can be financial instruments themselves, physical assets, or any risk factors that can be measured. Common examples are fixed-income, foreign exchange, credit risk, equities and equity indices or commodities. Exotic underlyings are, for example, weather, freight rates, or economic indicators.

Type of product: The three main types are forwards (or futures), options and swaps. They differ in terms of their dependence on the price of the underlying.

Development of the Market

The derivatives market has grown rapidly in recent years as the benefits of using derivatives, such as effective risk mitigation and risk transfer, have become increasingly important. Europe is by far the most important region for derivatives that have become a major part of the European financial services sector and a major direct and indirect contributor to economic growth.

Size and Growth of the Market

The derivatives market is the largest single segment of the financial market. As of June 2007, the global derivatives market amounted to €457 trillion in terms of notional amount outstanding. By this measure, the derivatives market is more than four times larger than the combined global equity and bond markets measured by market capitalization. However, the estimated gross market values of all derivatives outstanding total only €10 trillion, which is markedly lower than the equity and bond markets with a market capitalization of €43 trillion and €55 trillion, respectively. The derivatives market is the fastest growing segment of the financial sector: since 1995, its size has increased by around 24 percent per year in terms of notional amount outstanding, far outpacing other financial instruments such as equities (11 percent) and bonds (9 percent).

As described, the OTC segment accounts for almost 84 percent of the market with around €383 trillion of notional amount outstanding. Recently, however, the exchange segment has grown faster than the OTC segment. This is widely perceived to be a result of the increasing standardization of derivatives contracts which facilitates exchange trading. Other contributing factors are a number of advantages of on-exchange trading: price transparency, risk mitigation and transaction costs are among the most important.

Global Nature of the Market

The OTC segment operates with almost complete disregard of national borders. Derivatives exchanges themselves provide equal access to customers worldwide. As long as local market regulation does not impose access barriers, participants can connect and trade remotely and seamlessly from around the world (e.g. from their London trading desk to the Eurex exchange in Frankfurt). The fully integrated, single derivatives market is clearly a reality within the European Union[9]. Taken as a whole, the derivatives market is truly global. For example, today almost 80 percent of the turnover at Eurex, one of Europe's major derivatives exchanges, is generated outside its home markets of Germany and Switzerland, up from only 18 percent ten years ago.

The Derivatives Trading Value Chain

Derivatives trading and clearing is organized differently for OTC and on-exchange derivatives. The main distinguishing feature is the multilateral market organization with the use of safe and efficient central counterparty clearing[10] for derivatives being traded on exchanges.

The derivatives value chain can be broken down into derivatives pre-trading, derivatives trading and clearing (including the rare exercise of derivatives), and (also rare) payment and delivery. These functions are organized differently for OTC and exchange-traded derivatives. Broker-dealers (large investment or universal banks), exchanges and clearing houses are the main service providers along the value chain.

Conclusion

The derivatives market is very dynamic and has quickly developed into the most important segment of the financial market. Competing for business, both derivatives exchanges and OTC providers, which by far account for the largest part of the market, have fuelled growth by constant product and technology innovation. The competitive landscape has been especially dynamic in Europe, which has seen numerous market entries in the last decades. In the process, strong European players have emerged that today account for around 44 percent of the global market in terms of notional amount outstanding.

The derivatives market functions very well and is constantly improving. It effectively fulfills its economic functions of price efficiency and risk allocation. The imperatives for a well-functioning market are clearly fulfilled:

- The exchange segment, in particular, has put in place very effective risk mitigation mechanisms — mostly through the use of automation and CCPs[11].
- For its users, the derivatives market is highly efficient. Transaction costs for exchange-traded derivatives are particularly low.
- Innovation has been the market's strongest growth driver and has been supported by a beneficial regulatory framework especially in Europe.

Overall, it is clearly desirable to preserve the environment that has contributed to the impressive development of the derivatives market and the success of European players in it. There is thus no need for any structural changes in the framework under which OTC players and exchanges operate today. However, some aspects of the OTC segment in particular can still be improved further. Safety and transparency, and operational efficiency could be enhanced along proven and successful models helping the global derivatives market to become even safer and more efficient.

Unit 6 Derivatives Markets

Terminology

derivatives	金融衍生品
derivatives market	金融衍生品市场
certificate	凭证
warrant	认购权证
credit-linked securities	信用(风险)联结证券
credit risk	信贷风险
equity indices	股价指数
forwards	远期合约
futures	期货
options	期权
swaps	掉期，互换
clearing	票据交换，汇划结算
derivatives value chain	衍生品价值链
underlying	标的资产
clearing house	结算行；票据交换所

Notes on the Text

1. derivative — a financial instrument whose value depends on the value of some underlying asset or factor (e.g., a stock price, an interest rate, or exchange rate).
2. arbitrage — a strategy designed to generate a guaranteed profit from a transaction that requires no capital commitment or risk bearing on the part of the trader. A simple example of arbitrage trade would be the simultaneous purchase and sale of the same security in different markets at different prices.
3. underlying — an asset that trades in a market in which buyers and sellers meet, decide on a price, and the seller then delivers the asset to the buyer and receives payment. The underlying is the asset or other derivative on which a particular derivative is based. The market for the underlying is also referred to as spot market.
4. risk management — the process of identifying the level of risk an entity wants, measuring the level of risk the entity currently has, taking actions that bring the actual level of risk to the desired level of risk, and monitoring the new actual level of risk so that it continues to be aligned with the desired level of risk.
5. Chicago Mercantile Exchange (CME)— an American financial and commodity derivative exchange based in Chicago and located at 20 S. Wacker Drive. The CME was founded in 1898 as the Chicago Butter and Egg Board, an agricultural commodities exchange. Originally, the exchange was a non-profit organization.
6. Eurex — one of the world's leading derivatives exchanges, providing European benchmark derivatives featuring open and low-cost electronic access globally. Its electronic trading and clearing platform offers a broad range of products, and amongst others operates the most

liquid fixed income markets. Eurex was established in 1998 with the merger of Deutsche Terminbörse (DTB, the German derivatives exchange) and SOFFEX (Swiss Options and Financial Futures). Eurex is considered one of the "big three" derivative exchanges, along with NYSE Euronext Liffe and the Chicago Mercantile Exchange. It is owned by Deutsche Börse.

7. euronext — Euronext was formed on September 22, 2000 following a merger of the Amsterdam Stock Exchange, Brussels Stock Exchange, and Paris Bourse, in order to take advantage of the harmonization of the European Union financial markets. In December 2001, Euronext acquired the shares of the London International Financial Futures and Options Exchange (LIFFE), which continues to operate under its own governance. Beginning in early 2003, all derivatives products traded on its affiliated exchanges trade on LIFFECONNECT, LIFFE's electronic trading platform. In 2002, the group merged with the Portuguese stock exchange Bolsa de Valores de Lisboa e Porto (BVLP), renamed Euronext Lisbon. Hours of operation on non-holidays are 9:00–17:30 CET.

8. LIFFE — The London International Financial Futures and Options Exchange (LIFFE, pronounced "life") is a futures exchange based in London. LIFFE is now part of NYSE Euronext following its takeover by Euronext in January 2002 and Euronext's merger with New York Stock Exchange in April 2007.

9. European Union — an economic and political union of 27 member states that are located primarily in Europe. The EU operates through a system of supranational independent institutions and intergovernmental negotiated decisions by the member states.

10. clearing — In the case of derivatives, the management of open derivatives positions including their netting. Termination of derivatives contracts is also part of derivatives clearing involving the establishment of final positions for settlement. Mitigating the counterparty risks on open derivatives positions is the most important aspect of derivatives clearing. As derivatives contracts can have very long lives, clearing plays a crucial role in the derivatives value chain and is considerably more complex than e.g. the clearing of cash equities.

11. CCPs — an acronym for the central counterparty, a financial institution that acts as an intermediary between the buyer and seller. The CCP steps in and insures the buyer will receive possession of what was purchased, and the seller will be paid on time. When many buyers and sellers use the same CCP, it may also simplify multiple settlements by netting out transactions.

Exercises

I. Reading Comprehension.

Read the text carefully and decide whether the following statements are true (T) or false (F).

____ 1. Derivatives share some similarities with securities.

____ 2. Derivatives are an alternative to investing directly in assets without buying and holding the asset itself.

____ 3. Exchange-traded derivatives cover a range from highly standardized to tailor-made contract with individual terms.

____ 4. The OTC segment operates with almost complete disregard of national borders.

Unit 6   Derivatives Markets

___ 5. The derivatives market is the largest single segment of the financial market.

II. Vocabulary Building.

A. Match the term in Column A with the definition in Column B.

1. derivative — a. a structured and securitized product, e.g. in the form of a bearer bond, allowing an investor to participate in the performance of an underlying. As securities, certificates have to be differentiated from non-securitized derivatives.

2. warrants — b. a financial instrument whose value depends on the value of some underlying asset or factor (e.g., a stock price, an interest rate, or an exchange rate)

3. certificate — c. a security that entitles the holder to buy the underlying stock of the issuing company at a fixed price called exercise price until the expiry date

4. forwards — d. the management of open derivatives positions including their netting

5. clearing — e. a derivatives contract for the delivery or receipt of a specific amount of an underlying, at a set price, on a certain date in the future

6. arbitrage — f. an asset that trades in a market in which buyers and sellers meet, decide on a price, and the seller then delivers the asset to the buyer and receives payment

7. credit risk — g. a strategy designed to generate a guaranteed profit from a transaction that requires no capital commitment or risk bearing on the part of the trader

8. underlying — h. the risk of loss caused by a counterparty's or debtor's failure to make a promised payment

9. pre-trading — i. the value of the U.S. dollar in terms of other currencies in the foreign exchange market

10. exchange rate — j. the gathering of orders from trading parties and the channeling of these orders to the market. In both the OTC and the exchange segment this function is mostly fulfilled by brokers and broker-dealers.

B. Complete the following sentences with the words given in the box.

termination	forecast	dynamic	disregard	negligible
fluctuate	specified	perceive	predefined	segment
transparency	eliminate	underlying		

1. They require greater _____ in derivatives markets and demand greater disclosure from hedge funds.

2. Distribution to shareholders are limited by the amount of retained earnings and other capital _____ by state law.

3. Those under "basically normal" have a decrease in their business revenue and profits, or tend to have an insufficient fluidity and some of their financial indices _____ abnormally.

89

4. Contract _____, also called contract elimination, means that the financial claim and debt caused by the contract are actually no longer existed because of some reasons.
5. We can never _____ financial crises, but we can reduce their likelihood and severity.
6. If selling off those bonds caused their price to plummet, the financial losses to the U.S. would be _____.
7. The Asian Development Bank has raised its _____ economic growth for Asia's developing nations this year because of strong exports and consumption.
8. In debt rescheduling agreement, clause which states that if economic conditions improve beyond a _____ threshold, creditors will be entitled to increased reimbursement.
9. Most economic systems are reflexive — what happens is influenced by how we _____ what will happen.
10. History has shown that a vibrant, _____ financial system is at the heart of a vibrant, dynamic economy.

III. Cloze.

There are 10 blanks in the following two passages. For each blank there are four choices marked A, B, C and D. You are supposed to choose the best answer.

Passage 1

This choice among multiple OTC dealers is (1)_____ to all professional users of OTC derivatives across all product categories. According to the Bank of England 95 percent of the total transaction volume is (2)_____ among 20 different OTC derivatives broker-dealers. (3)_____, for many OTC products there are standardized alternatives available on-exchange that (4)_____ the same economic purposes. For example, both an interest rate swap with a maturity of five years — a classic OTC product — and an exchange-traded future on a five-year government bond offer (5)_____ against interest rate changes over a time horizon of five years.

(1) A. accessible   B. available   C. exclusive   D. approachable
(2) A. split   B. separated   C. divided   D. cut
(3) A. Therefore   B. However   C. Moreover   D. Rather
(4) A. complete   B. fulfill   C. meet   D. satisfy
(5) A. guidance   B. shelter   C. harbor   D. protection

Passage 2

Product innovation can (6)_____ many different forms, for example, the creation of a derivative on a new underlying or a new product type with different pay-off characteristics. New derivatives are usually first (7)_____ for OTC trading. Here, the liberal regulatory environment and new business opportunities (8)_____ product innovations. Lead times to introduce a new product in the OTC segment are comparably short (9)_____ the low set-up costs in the OTC segment and the fact that there is no need to register and issue securities. European players are especially renowned (10)_____ their innovativeness. They constantly score high in user rankings. Examples of recent OTC product innovations are exotic interest rate and credit derivatives.

(6) A. take	B. have	C. get	D. embody
(7) A. led	B. introduced	C. generated	D. recommended
(8) A. begin	B. start	C. foster	D. usher
(9) A. due to	B. leading to	C. thanks to	D. resulting from
(10) A. by	B. of	C. as	D. for

IV. Translate the following sentences into English.

1. "新规则"将允许金融机构交易信贷和大宗商品衍生品,并鼓励市场活动。(as well as)
2. 全球衍生品交易额约为 600 万亿美元,而中国的交易量却不到 1/600。(volume)
3. 考虑到中国的经济规模,中国的衍生品市场规模小得不成比例。(disproportionately)
4. 中国证监会已经就衍生品市场改革达成共识,将进一步扩大和开放衍生品市场。(consensus)
5. 随着新法规和新方案的通过,中国正在采取另一项重大措施来控制金融风险。(with the approval)

V. Translate the following paragraphs into Chinese.

1. The different risks that market participants face can ultimately lead to systemic risk, that is, the failure of one counterparty having adverse effects on other market participants, potentially destabilizing the entire financial market. A primary concern of all stakeholders, including regulators, is to limit systemic risk to the greatest extent possible.

2. The derivatives market has arrangements in place to mitigate unwanted risks that arise from conducting derivatives transactions. From a practical point of view, these arrangements have proven successful — the unwanted risks in the derivatives market have been reduced to a tolerable level. Even when failures of market participants have occurred, they have not seriously affected other market participants.

VI. Self-Testing.

1. In October 1990, as the first commodity futures market in China, _____ introduced its first futures contract.
   A. Zhengzhou Grain Wholesale Market   B. Shenzhen Metal Exchange
   C. Shanghai Metal Exchange   D. Dalian Commodity Exchange
2. Shanghai Futures Exchange (SHFE) offers futures contracts on the following commodities EXCEPT _____.
   A. copper   B. aluminum   C. rubber   D. grain
3. Futures brokage companies are the leading _____ in the futures market.
   A. principals   B. agents   C. intermediaries D. regulators
4. The regulatory requirements concern a future brokerage company's _____.
   A. establishment   B. business scope   C. risk control   D. all of the above
5. A futures brokerage company may engage in the following business activities EXCEPT _____.
   A. future brokerage   B. consultation services in relation to futures
   C. futures proprietary trading   D. training services in relation to futures

6. Besides the relevant provisions in the Company Law, which of the following statements about the requirements an applicant shall fulfill in order to establish a future brokerage company is NOT true.

   A. With a registered capital of no less than RMB 20 million.

   B. Qualified senior executives and principal employees for futures business.

   C. A physical business venue and sufficient trading facilities.

   D. A well-functioning management system.

7. The revised Company Law and Securities Law came into effect on _____.

   A. October 1, 2008   B. January 1, 2006
   C. January 1, 1996   D. January 30, 2007

8. The followings are some of the rules and regulations for corporate governance, mergers and acquisitions of listed companies, EXCEPT _____.

   A. The Guidelines for Establishing Independent Directors of Listed Companies

   B. Measures on the Administration of Stock Exchanges

   C. Code of Corporate Governance for Listed Companies

   D. Measures on the Merger and Acquisition of Listed Companies

9. The Provisional Regulations on Futures Trading enacted on September 1, 1999 for governing the futures brokerage houses in the areas of their establishment criteria, EXCEPT _____.

   A. establishment   B. approval procedure
   C. business scope   D. liquidation

10. The Securities Law, Company Law, Securities Investment Fund Law and Criminal Law expressly lay out the civil, administrative and criminal liabilities of a party guilty of securities and futures offenses and crimes, including _____.

    A. fraudulent practices   B. insider dealing
    C. market manipulations   D. all of the above

VII. Writing.

Please write a letter to ×× bank in English as follows.

1. 招商银行上海分行给××银行写一封正式信函,要求开即期美元汇票以代替由其储户 Mr. Johnson 所开支票。
2. 要求同时将该汇票寄来。
3. 确认支票上受票人签名等。

Supplementary Reading

Asia Market for Liquefied Natural Gas Derivatives Catches Alight

By Emiko Terazono
(*Financial Times*, September 7, 2017)

The derivatives market in Asian liquefied natural gas is finally taking off, as the world's largest importers look to diversify the pricing structures of their purchases by increasing short-term agreements.

LNG is one of the few remaining commodities where buyers and sellers are locked into multiyear contracts, and the long-awaited development comes as new supply projects have come online and the LNG price has fallen.

Tobias Davis, head of LNG broking at Tullett Prebon, says: "The Asian derivatives market is becoming more liquid, enough to become a fair price indicator."

Historically, a large portion of LNG sold to north-east Asia, the world's largest buyer of the commodity, has been traded under long-term, fixed destination contracts linked to oil. However, an increasing number of Japanese and Korean buyers are signing full or partial short-term contracts linked to LNG price indices.

The shifts in the prized Asian market come amid wider changes in the LNG industry. Long the preserve of the largest energy groups such as Shell and Exxon, independent energy traders including Vitol, Gunvor and Trafigura are entering the sector, agreeing on relatively short-term deals with new pricing mechanism.

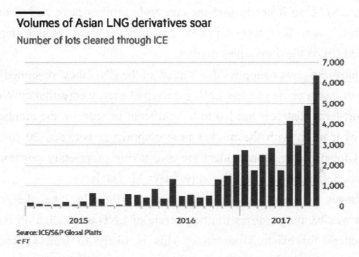

Trading volumes of LNG derivatives linked to the Asian benchmark have soared as more LNG dealers and companies look to hedge their short-term agreements. Spot and short-term trade in 2016 rose 9 percent to 74.6m tonnes from the previous year, accounting for 28 percent of all LNG trades, according to the International Group of Liquefied Natural Gas Importers.

Volumes in August cleared through ICE linked to the east Asian spot LNG index Japan-Korea Marker, assessed by S&P Global Platts, reached over 21 cargoes — a new monthly high. After more than quadrupling in 2016, volumes in 2017 overtook that of the previous year in the first five months of the year.

The short-term trades have risen as LNG supply has grown with the launch of new LNG plants, which chill and condense gas so it can be shipped on tankers overseas. New projects in Papua New Guinea and Australia have come online over the past few years, increasing the amount of LNG on the world market.

The LNG price has been in decline since 2014, when the JKM hit a record high of $20.20 per million British thermal units. It is currently trading just above $6 per mBtu.

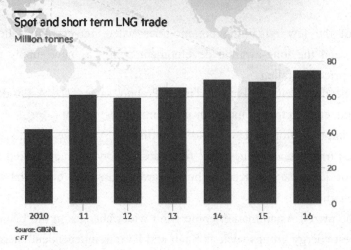

On the demand side, energy saving practices and the restart of nuclear plants in Japan led to a fall in LNG consumption over recent years in the world's largest importer. Moreover, Japan has contracted far more LNG than it needs, and the country's utilities have had to turn themselves into traders in order to resell some long-term supplies. This has increased the short-term contracts, which in turn need to be hedged on the derivatives market.

"Some of the Japanese power supplies don't need all the LNG they've signed up for," says Kerry Anne Shanks, head of Asia Pacific gas and LNG research at energy consultancy Wood Mackenzie.

The rise in short-term contracts has led to a significant increase in the number of participants in the LNG derivatives market, with the market now comprising between 20 to 30 counter parties, according to S&P Global Platts. More traders are also taking proprietary positions, adding depth to the market. "They are helping to pull [in] liquidity," says Mr Davis.

Additional changes in Japan could boost liquidity further. In June, the Japanese Fair Trade Commission said it was banning clauses limiting resale of LNG and called on companies to change their business practices for existing contracts. This is likely to lead to some contracts bring renegotiated.

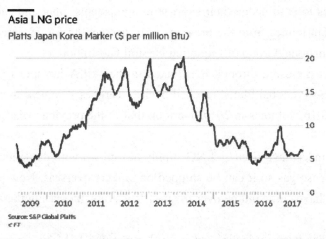

In addition, a bulk of the Japanese utilities' long-term contracts are expiring in 2019 to 2020, and are likely to be replaced with more diverse maturities and flexibility on destination.

Unit 6　Derivatives Markets

"After 2019 many existing long-term contracts will expire. They want to allocate a certain portion of that to short-term contracts," says Tomoko Hosoe, at consultants FG Energy.

But despite the rise in trading liquidity, the LNG derivatives market is still a small portion of the whole physical market.

"The futures market in oil is multiples of the physical market. JKM [derivatives] is only 1-2 percent of the LNG physical market if you assume spot trade to be around 40 percent of production," says Mr Davis.

Some industry executives warn that the liquidity in the derivatives market could dry up as the market tightens beyond 2020. Industry experts see the growth in new demand and the slowing of new production capacity growth leading to a supply dearth in 2022-2023.

"The LNG market is going to tighten driven by [demand] growth in Asia," says Eric Bensaude, in charge of LNG Commercial Operations and Asset Optimisation at Cheniere Energy.

He warns: "Yes, the spot market is in favor but I'm not sure that the market liquidity is here to stay."

Questions

1. According to Tobia David, what is the development trend of the Asia derivatives market?
2. What are the changes in the LNG industry?
3. Give a brief summary of the chart "Volumes of Asian LNG derivatives soar".
4. According to the chart "Volumes of Asian LNG derivatives soar", what is the consequence of the rise in short-term contracts?
5. What has led to the fall in LNG consumption over recent years in the world's largest importer on the demand side?
6. Do all executives and experts hold positive attitudes toward the market liquidity?

Unit 7　Financial Institutions

Case

Emma, who majored in finance, took a course in financial institutions. One of her assignments was to conduct a survey on a course-related topic, so Emma decided to survey the local financial institutions, trying to find out the services they provided and the roles they played in the financial system. She visited many local institutions and searched voraciously on the Internet, hoping to collect as much information as she could. Emma worked very hard on the survey and finally got a good mark.

Questions
1. What are the different types of financial institutions?
2. What are the roles played by financial institutions in the financial system?

Preview

Skimming

Skim the following text quickly to answer the following questions and discuss your answers with your partners.

1. What is the primary business of financial intermediaries?
   _____
   _____.

2. List at least three types of financial intermediaries.
   _____
   _____.

3. What are the largest and oldest financial intermediaries today?
   _____
   _____.

4. What are the roles played by governmental organizations in the financial system?
   _____
   _____.

5. List at least two types of governmental or quasi-governmental organizations in the financial system.
   _____
   _____.

Scanning

Scan the following text quickly to find the specific information.

1. When and where did the earliest banks appear?
   _____
   _____ .

2. Which country has a universal banking system?
   _____
   _____ .

3. What are the two types of pension plans?
   _____
   _____ .

4. What does NAV stand for?
   _____
   _____ .

5. How do venture capital firms differ from investment banks?
   _____
   _____ .

6. List at least three information service firms.
   _____
   _____ .

7. What is the central bank called in Sweden?
   _____
   _____ .

8. Which international financial institution establishes rules for international finance?
   _____
   _____ .

Vocabulary in Context

Read the following sentences and try to guess the meaning of the italicized words by using the context. Then replace the italicized words with synonyms (words or phrases that have nearly the same or similar meanings).

1. The mutual fund has substantial economies of scale in record keeping and in *executing* purchases and sales of securities and, therefore, offers its customers a more efficient way of investing in securities than the direct purchase and sale of securities in the markets.
   The mutual fund has substantial economies of scale in record keeping and in _____ purchases and sales of securities and, therefore, offers its customers a more efficient way of investing in securities than the direct purchase and sale of securities in the markets.

2. Their main function was to serve as a mechanism for clearing and settling payments, thereby facilitating the trade in goods and services that had started to *flourish* in Italy at that time.
   Their main function was to serve as a mechanism for clearing and settling payments, thereby facilitating the trade in goods and services that had started to _____ in Italy

at that time.

3. The early banks *evolved* from money changers.
   The early banks _____ from money changers.

4. In some countries banks are *virtually* all-purpose financial intermediaries, offering customers not just transaction services and loans, but also mutual funds and insurance of every kind.
   In some countries banks are _____ all-purpose financial intermediaries, offering customers not just transaction services and loans, but also mutual funds and insurance of every kind.

5. Depository savings institutions, thrift institutions, or simply thrifts are the terms used to refer *collectively* to savings banks, savings and loan associations (S&Ls), and credit unions.
   Depository savings institutions, thrift institutions, or simply thrifts are the terms used to refer _____ to savings banks, savings and loan associations (S&Ls), and credit unions.

6. Insurance companies are intermediaries whose primary function is to allow households and businesses to *shed* specific risks by buying contracts called insurance policies that pay cash compensation if certain specified events occur.
   Insurance companies are intermediaries whose primary function is to allow households and businesses to _____ specific risks by buying contracts called insurance policies that pay cash compensation if certain specified events occur.

7. In some countries, such as Germany, Japan, and the United States, a government or quasi-governmental agency *backs* the sponsor's guarantee of pension benefits up to specified limits.
   In some countries, such as Germany, Japan, and the United States, a government or quasi-governmental agency _____ the sponsor's guarantee of pension benefits up to specified limits.

8. In the case of securities, underwriting means *committing* to buy them at a guaranteed future price.
   In the case of securities, underwriting means _____ to buy them at a guaranteed future price.

9. Venture capitalists invest their funds in new businesses and help the management team get the firm to the point at which it is ready to "*go public*" — that is, sell shares of stock to the investing public.
   Venture capitalists invest their funds in new businesses and help the management team get the firm to the point at which it is ready to "_____" — that is, sell shares of stock to the investing public.

10. Central banks are intermediaries whose primary function is to promote public policy objectives by influencing certain financial market *parameters* such as the supply of the local currency.
    Central banks are intermediaries whose primary function is to promote public policy objectives by influencing certain financial market _____ such as the supply of the local currency.

Text

Financial Institutions

In financial economics, a financial institution is an institution that provides financial services for its clients or members. Probably the most important financial service provided by financial institutions is acting as financial intermediaries. Most financial institutions are regulated by the government.

Financial Intermediaries

Financial intermediaries are firms whose primary business is to provide customers with financial products and services that cannot be obtained more efficiently by transacting directly in securities markets. Among the main types of intermediaries are banks, investment companies, and insurance companies. Their products include checking accounts, loans, mortgages, mutual funds, and a wide range of insurance contracts.

Perhaps the simplest example of a financial intermediary is a mutual fund, which pools the financial resources of many small savers and invests their money in securities. The mutual fund has substantial economies of scale in record keeping and in executing purchases and sales of securities and, therefore, offers its customers a more efficient way of investing in securities than the direct purchase and sale of securities in the markets.

Banks

Banks are today the largest (in terms of assets) and oldest of all financial intermediaries. The earliest banks appeared hundreds of years ago in the towns of Renaissance[1] Italy. Their main function was to serve as a mechanism for clearing and settling payments, thereby facilitating the trade in goods and services that had started to flourish in Italy at that time. The early banks evolved from money changers. Indeed, the word *bank* comes from *banca*, the Italian word for "bench", because money changers worked at benches in converting currencies.

Most firms called banks today, however, perform at least two functions: They take deposits and make loans. They are called commercial banks.

In some countries banks are virtually all-purpose financial intermediaries, offering customers not just transaction services and loans, but also mutual funds and insurance of every kind. In Germany, for example, universal banks[2] fulfill virtually all of the functions performed by specialized intermediaries.

Indeed, it is becoming increasingly difficult to differentiate among the various financial firms doing business around the world on the basis of what type of intermediary or financial service provider they are. Thus, although Deutsche Bank[3] is classified as a universal bank, it performs pretty much the same set of functions around the world as does Merrill Lynch[4], which is usually classified as a broker-dealer[5].

Other Depository Savings Institutions

Depository savings institutions, thrift institutions, or simply thrifts are the terms used to refer collectively to savings banks[6], savings and loan associations (S&Ls)[7], and credit unions. In the United

States, they compete with commercial banks in both their deposit and lending activities. U.S. thrifts specialize in making home mortgage and consumer loans. In other countries, there is a variety of special-purpose savings institutions that are similar to the thrifts and credit unions in the United States.

Insurance Companies

Insurance companies are intermediaries whose primary function is to allow households and businesses to shed specific risks by buying contracts called insurance policies that pay cash compensation if certain specified events occur.

Insurance policies are assets of the households and businesses that buy them, and they are liabilities of the insurance companies that sell them. Payments made to insurance companies for the insurance they provide are called premiums. Because customers pay insurance premiums before benefits are received, insurance companies have the use of the funds for periods of time ranging from less than a year to several decades. Insurance companies invest the premiums they collect in assets such as stocks, bonds, and real estate.

Pension and Retirement Funds

The function of a pension plan is to replace a person's preretirement earnings combined with social security retirement benefits and private savings. A pension plan can be sponsored by an employer, a labor union, or an individual.

Pension plans are classified into two types: defined contribution and defined benefit. In a defined-contribution pension plan, each employee has an account into which the employer and usually the employee make regular contributions. At retirement, the employee receives a benefit whose size depends on the accumulated value of the funds in the retirement account. In a defined-benefit pension plan, the employee's pension benefit is determined by a formula that takes into account years of service to the employer and, in most cases, wages or salary. The sponsor of a defined-benefit plan or an insurance company hired by the sponsor guarantees the benefits and, thus, absorbs the investment risk. In some countries, such as Germany, Japan, and the United States, a government or quasi-governmental agency backs the sponsor's guarantee of pension benefits up to specified limits.

Mutual Funds

A mutual fund is a portfolio of stocks, bonds, or other assets purchased in the name of a group of investors and managed by a professional investment company or other financial institution. Each customer is entitled to a pro rata[8] share of any distributions and can redeem his or her share of the fund at any time at its then current market value.

The company that manages the fund keeps track of how much each investor has and reinvests all distributions received according to the rules of the fund. In addition to divisibility, record keeping, and reinvestment of receipts, mutual funds provide an efficient means of diversification.

There are two types of mutual funds: open end and closed end. Open-end mutual funds stand ready to redeem or issue shares at their net asset value (NAV), which is the market value of all securities held divided by the number of shares outstanding. The number of shares outstanding of an open-end fund changes daily as investors buy new or redeem old shares. Close-end mutual funds do not redeem or issue shares at NAV. Shares of closed-end funds are traded through brokers just like other common stocks, and their prices can, therefore, differ from NAV.

Investment Banks

Investment banks are firms whose primary function is to help businesses, governments, and other entities raise funds to finance their activities by issuing securities. Investment banks also facilitate and sometimes initiate mergers of firms or acquisitions of one firm by another.

Investment banks often underwrite the securities they distribute. Underwriting means insuring. In the case of securities, underwriting means committing to buy them at a guaranteed future price.

Venture Capital Firms

Venture capital firms are similar to investment banks, except their clients are startup firms rather than large corporations. Young firms with inexperienced managers often need considerable advice in running their business in addition to financing. Venture capital firms provide both.

Venture capitalists invest their funds in new businesses and help the management team get the firm to the point at which it is ready to "go public" — that is, sell shares of stock to the investing public. Once that point is reached, the venture capital firm will typically sell its stake in the corporation and move on to the next new venture.

Asset Management Firms

Asset management firms are also called investment management firms. They advise and often administer mutual funds, pension funds, and other asset pools for individuals, firms, and governments. They may be separate firms or they may be a division within a firm, such as a trust company that is part of a bank, insurance company, or brokerage firm[9].

Information Services

Many financial service firms provide information as a by-product of their main activities, but there are firms that specialize in providing information. The oldest information service firms are rating agencies, such as Moody's[10] and Standard & Poor's[11] for the securities business and Best's for the insurance industry. A more recent growth sector is the firms or divisions within firms offering analysis of financial data (such as Bloomberg and Reuters) or performance statistics on mutual funds (such as Lipper, Morningstar, and SEI).

Governmental and Quasi-Governmental Organizations

As the maker and enforcer of a society's laws, governments are ultimately responsible to regulate the financial system. In addition, governments use the financial system to achieve other public policy goals. An example is the use of monetary policy to achieve national targets for economic growth or employment. Some governmental organizations either seek to regulate the operation of some part of the financial system or use the financial system as the principal means of achieving other economic goals.

Central Banks

Central banks are intermediaries whose primary function is to promote public policy objectives by influencing certain financial market parameters such as the supply of the local currency. In some countries the central bank is subject to the direct control of the executive body of government; in others, it is semiautonomous.

In many countries, the central bank is identifiable through its title, such as the Bank of England, the Bank of Japan, and so on. But in the United States the central bank is called the Federal Reserve System, and in Sweden the Riksbank.

A central bank is usually at the heart of a country's payments system. It provides the supply of local currency and operates the clearing system for the banks. An efficient payments system requires at least a moderate degree of price stability. Central banks, therefore, usually view this as their primary goal. But central banks in many countries are also expected to promote the goals of full employment[12] and economic growth. In these countries, central banks must balance the sometimes conflicting goals of price stability and full employment.

Special-Purpose Intermediaries

This group of organizations includes entities that are set up to encourage specific economic activities by making financing more readily available or by guaranteeing debt instruments of various sorts. Examples are government agencies that make loans or guarantee loans to farmers, students, small businesses, new home buyers, and so on.

A different class of governmental organization is the agencies that are designed to insure bank deposits. Their main function is to promote economic stability by preventing a breakdown in part or all of the financial system.

Regional and World Organizations

Several international bodies currently exist for the purpose of coordinating the financial policies of national governments. Perhaps the most important is the Bank for International Settlements (BIS)[13] in Basel, Switzerland, whose objective is to promote uniformity of banking regulations.

In addition, two official international agencies operate in the international financial markets to promote growth in trade and finance: the International Monetary Fund (IMF)[14] and the International Bank for Reconstruction and Development (World Bank)[15]. The IMF monitors economic and financial conditions in member countries, provides technical assistance, establishes rules for international trade and finance, provides a forum for international consultation, and most importantly, provides resources that permit lengthening the time necessary for individual members to correct imbalances in their payments to other countries. The World Bank finances investment projects in developing countries. It raises funds primarily by selling bonds in developed countries and then makes loans for projects that must meet certain criteria designed to encourage economic development.

Terminology

financial institution	金融机构
financial intermediary	金融中介
bank	银行
commercial bank	商业银行

depository savings institution	存款储蓄机构
thrift institution	储蓄机构；节俭机构
savings bank	储蓄银行
credit union	信用合作社
savings institution	储蓄机构
insurance company	保险公司
retirement fund(pension fund)	养老基金，退休基金
mutual fund	共同基金
open-end mutual fund	开放式共同基金
close-end mutual fund	封闭式共同基金
investment bank	投资银行
venture capital firm	风险投资公司
asset management firm	资产管理公司
investment management firm	投资管理公司
trust company	信托公司
brokerage firm	经纪公司
central bank	中央银行

Notes on the Text

1. Renaissance — a cultural movement that spanned the period roughly from the 14th to the 17th centuries, beginning in Italy in the Late Middle Ages and later spreading to the rest of Europe. (文艺复兴)

2. universal bank — a bank which participates in many kinds of banking activities and is both a commercial bank and an investment bank. Universal banks are also called full-service financial firms. They are common in some European countries. (全能银行)

3. Deutsche Bank — a German global banking and financial services company with its headquarters in Frankfurt, Germany. Deutsche bank offers financial products and services to corporate and institutional clients along with private and business clients. (德意志银行)

4. Merrill Lynch — a financial management and advisory company, providing financial advisory and investment banking services. (美林公司)

5. broker-dealer — A broker is an individual or firm that charges a fee or commission for executing buy and sell orders submitted by an investor. A dealer is an individual or firm willing to buy or sell securities for their own account. A broker-dealer is an individual or firm in the business of buying and selling securities, operating as both a broker and a dealer, depending on the transaction. Broker-dealers fulfill several important functions in the financial industry; these include providing investment advice to customers, supplying liquidity through market-making activities, facilitating trading activities, publishing investment research, and raising capital for companies. Broker-dealers may range in size from small independent boutiques to large subsidiaries of giant commercial and investment banks. (证券经纪自营商)

6. savings bank — a depository financial institution that primarily accepts consumer deposits

and makes home mortgage loan.

7. savings and loan association (S&L) — a deposit financial institution that obtains the bulk of its deposits from consumers and holds the majority of its assets as home mortgage loans. (存贷协会)

8. pro rata — a method of assigning an amount to a fraction, according to its share of the whole. For example, a pro-rata dividend means that every shareholder gets an equal proportion for each share he or she owns.

9. brokerage firm — a financial institution that facilitates the buying and selling of securities between a buyer and a seller.

10. Moody's — Moody's Investors Service, a bond credit rating business of Moody's Corporation. (穆迪投资者服务公司)

11. Standard & Poor's — a subsidiary of the McGraw-Hill Companies that provides a broad range of investment services. (标准普尔公司)

12. full employment — the full utilization of all available labor (and capital) resources so that the economy is able to produce at the limits of its potential gross national product. Full employment is one of the main objectives of macroeconomics policy. In practice, 100% employment cannot be achieved. Accordingly, a more realistic interpretation of full employment is that full employment is achieved when the number of registered unemployment is equal to the number of job vacancies. (充分就业)

13. Bank for International Settlements (BIS) — an international financial organization to serve central banks in their pursuit of monetary and financial stability, foster international cooperation in those areas and act as a bank for central banks. The BIS was established in 1930 and it is the world's oldest international financial organization. As its customers are central banks and international organizations, the BIS does not accept deposits from, or provide financial services to, private individuals or corporate entities. (国际清算银行)

14. International Monetary Fund (IMF) — an international financial organization to foster global monetary cooperation, secure financial stability, facilitate international trade, promote high employment and sustainable economic growth, and reduce poverty around the world. (国际货币基金组织)

15. International Bank for Reconstruction and Development (World Bank) — an international financial organization to reduce poverty in middle-income countries and creditworthy poorer countries by promoting sustainable development through loans, guarantees, risk management products, and analytical and advisory services. (国际复兴开发银行/世界银行)

Exercises

I. Reading Comprehension.

Read the text carefully and decide whether the following statements are true (T) or false (F).

___ 1. Banks and other financial intermediaries are financial service providers.

___ 2. Loans are provided exclusively by commercial banks.

___ 3. Close-end mutual funds are "closed" because they are not allowed to trade through brokers.

Unit 7   Financial Institutions

___ 4. An investment management firm advises and often administers asset pools for individuals, firms and governments.

___ 5. Some governmental organizations are designed to encourage specific economic activities and promote financial stability.

II. Vocabulary Building.

A. Match the term in Column A with the definition in Column B.

1. asset management firm
2. bank
3. central bank
4. credit union
5. depository savings institution
6. financial intermediary
7. mutual fund
8. pension fund
9. trust company

a. organization that is engaged as a trustee or fiduciary for individuals or businesses in the administration of trust funds, estates, and other related services

b. financial institution that smoothes the flow of funds between surplus units and deficit units

c. organization that advises and often administers pooled funds for individuals, businesses or governments

d. organization that is legally allowed to accept monetary deposits

e. organization that invests its funds in startup firms and other risky but potentially profitable ventures

f. organization that does most or all of the following: receiving demand deposits and time deposits, honoring instruments drawn on them, and paying interest on them; discounting notes, making loans, and investing in securities; collecting checks, drafts, and notes; certifying depositor's checks; and issuing drafts and cashier's checks

g. plan, fund, or scheme that provides retirement income

h. member-owned financial cooperative, democratically controlled by its members, and operated for the purpose of promoting thrift, providing credit at competitive rates, and providing other financial services to its members

i. professionally managed collective investment vehicle that pools the financial resources of individuals and businesses to invest in diversified portfolio of assets

10. venture capital firm   j. public institution that issues money, administers monetary policy, holds deposits representing the reserves of other banks, and engages in transactions designed to facilitate the conduct of business and protect public interest

B. Complete the following sentences with the words given in the box and change the form of the words where necessary.

coordinate	diversification	efficient	facilitate	fulfill
initiate	mechanism	moderate	perform	promote
raise	stake			

1. The financial market is composed of a number of financial institutions that _____ a variety of functions.
2. Smooth functioning of financial institutions is very important for a(an) _____ financial market and for the conduct of fiscal and monetary policies.
3. Financial intermediaries _____ transactions between suppliers of capital and users of capital.
4. Venture capital is popular among new companies or ventures with limited operating history, which cannot _____ funds by issuing debt.
5. International financial institutions provide _____ for international cooperation in managing the global financial system.
6. _____ reduces the risk of a portfolio, but it does not necessarily reduce the returns.
7. Maintaining an orderly and stable international monetary system requires all participants in that system to _____ their financial obligations to other participants.
8. HSBC sold a 4.73% _____ in India's third-largest nongovernment bank, Axis Bank Ltd., for around $329 million, as the disposal of non-core investments.
9. The International Monetary Fund _____ exchange stability and orderly exchange relations among its member countries.
10. Several central banks _____ to provide liquidity to the global financial system.

III. Cloze.

There are 10 blanks in the following two passages. For each blank, there are four choices marked A, B, C and D. You are supposed to choose the best answer.

Passage 1

Banks, (1)_____ with insurance companies, mutual funds, and similar financial-service providers, are financial intermediaries. The term financial intermediary simply means a business that interacts (2)_____ two types of individuals and institutions in the economy: (a) deficit-spending units which need to raise funds (3)_____ through borrowing or issuing stock; and (b) surplus-spending units which have surplus funds that can be saved and invested. Intermediaries perform the indispensable task of acting as a bridge between these two groups, (4)_____ convenient financial services to surplus-spending units in order to attract funds and then allocating those funds to deficit spenders. In so doing, intermediaries accelerate economic growth by expanding the available pool of savings, (5)_____ the risk of investments through diversification, and increasing the productivity of savings and investment.

(1) A. among   B. along   C. adding   D. attending
(2) A. for   B. with   C. in   D. by
(3) A. externally   B. exterior   C. internally   D. interior
(4) A. offered   B. to offer   C. offering   D. having offered
(5) A. ascending   B. increasing   C. descending   D. lowering

Passage 2

The People's Bank of China (PBC) was established on December 1, 1948 (6)_____ on the consolidation of the Huabei Bank, the Beihai Bank and the Xibei Farmer Bank. Its headquarters were originally in the Hebei Province, but were soon moved to Beijing. Between 1949 and 1978, the PBC was responsible for both central banking and commercial banking (7)_____. Commercial banking operations were separated from the PBC in the 1980s and divided among four state-owned banks. In the mid 1990s, the Law of the People's Republic of China on the People's Bank of China (8)_____. The PBC (9)_____ currency, monitors money supply, and formulates monetary policy. The central bank is (10)_____ greater importance in the 21st century than in the past.

(6) A. relied   B. focused   C. depended   D. based
(7) A. operations   B. works   C. issues   D. things
(8) A. passed   B. had passed   C. was passed   D. was passing
(9) A. distributes   B. circulates   C. spreads   D. issues
(10) A. gaining   B. going   C. making   D. becoming

IV. Translate the following sentences into English.

1. 信用卡的免息期长短不一，通常是 20 至 50 天。(range)
2. 一些专家认为，所有的金融机构都必须受到严格的监管。(be subject to)
3. 根据协议，银行有权决定是否向客户收取手续费。(entitle)
4. 国家开发银行是一家政策性银行，专为重大基础设施项目融通资金。(specialize in)
5. 智力资本将取代金融资本成为知识密集型企业最重要的资本。(replace)

V. Translate the following paragraphs into Chinese.

1. The financial institutions are currently undergoing sweeping changes in functions and forms. In fact, the changes affecting the financial-services business today are so important that many industry analyses refer to these trends as a revolution, one that may well leave financial institutions of the next generation almost unrecognizable. Major trends affecting the performance of financial institutions today include: widening service menus, the globalization of the financial marketplace, the growing rivalry among financial institutions, and the increasing automation of financial-service production and delivery.

2. The People's Bank of China used to exercise the functions and powers of a central bank, as

well as handling industrial and commercial credits and savings business. However, since the reform and opening-up began in 1978, China has carried out a series of significant reforms in its banking system. Consequently, the financial industry has made steady development. Now China has basically formed a financial system under the regulation, control and supervision of the central bank, with the state-owned banks as the mainstay, featuring the separation of policy-related finance and commercial finance, and the cooperation of various financial institutions with mutually complementary functions.

VI. Self-Testing.

1. A central bank _____.
   A. is responsible for overseeing the monetary system of a nation or a group of nations
   B. generally issues currency
   C. is the banker's bank
   D. all of the above
2. Which of the following statements concerning banks is NOT true?
   A. Commercial banks sell deposits and make loans to businesses and individuals.
   B. Investment banks underwrite issues of new securities.
   C. Merchant banks sell deposits and make loans to merchants.
   D. Universal banks offer virtually all financial services available in today's marketplace.
3. _____ sell the public shares representing an interest in a professionally managed pool of stocks, bonds, and other securities.
   A. Credit unions   B. Mutual funds
   C. Asset management firms   D. Pension funds
4. Which of the following is a nonbank financial institution?
   A. An asset management firm.   B. A trust company.
   C. A finance company.   D. All of the above.
5. According to the revised edition of the Law of the People's Republic of China on the People's Bank of China, which of the following is NOT a key function the PBC performs?
   A. To conduct monetary policy.
   B. To prevent and dissolve financial risks.
   C. To finance major infrastructural projects.
   D. To maintain financial stability under the leadership of the State Council.
6. Which of the following is NOT a policy bank in China?
   A. China Development Bank.   B. The Export-Import Bank of China.
   C. China Merchants Bank.   D. Agricultural Development Bank of China.
7. _____ plays a critical role in financing major infrastructural projects.
   A. China Development Bank   B. The Export-Import Bank of China
   C. The People's Bank of China D. Agricultural Development Bank of China
8. The mission of _____ is to help reduce poverty.
   A. the World Bank   B. the WTO
   C. the IMF   D. the BIS

9. _____ oversees the international monetary system.
   A. The World Bank   B. The WTO   C. The IMF   D. The BIS
10. _____ serves as a bank for central banks.
   A. The World Bank   B. The WTO   C. The IMF   D. The BIS

VII. Writing.

Please write a letter to JPMorgan Chase Bank in English as follows.
1. 希望对方能够提供有关××公司的资本构成、资信状况和经营状况的资料。
2. 我行会对对方提供的资料严格保密，对方对此不承担任何责任。
3. 感谢对方的帮助。

Supplementary Reading

Interview: AIIB Operating to the Highest International Standards

By Zhang Jianhua
(*Xinhuanet* November 24, 2017)

The mission of the Asian Infrastructure Investment Bank (AIIB) to support infrastructure investment is good for the world's economy, and the institution is operating "to the highest international standards", according to Sir Danny Alexander, the bank's vice president and corporate secretary.

Alexander was a cabinet minister in the British Treasury from 2010 to 2015. He was appointed as vice president and corporate secretary of the AIIB in February 2016.

In an interview with Xinhua, Alexander said he was one of the senior ministers in the British government at the time "who advocated strongly that the UK should join the AIIB".

In March 2015, Britain became the first major western country to announce its intention to join the new multilateral development bank, which started operations in January 2016 and has grown to 80 approved members from around the world.

"The AIIB seems to us to be a very good initiative to create a new framework for countries to work together and to further that common interest in infrastructure investment," he told Xinhua in Shenzhen, Guangdong Province.

He noted that there had been more than 20 countries choosing to join the AIIB since the founding of the bank.

The fact shows that "they [members] can see that the bank is developing in the right way and to the highest international standards," said the former British politician.

Great Responsibility

In the interview, Alexander said that it is "a great responsibility" to work for the AIIB.

"It is very rare for new multilateral development banks to be set up. Ours is the first in the 21st century, and it is the first ever to be headquartered in China, so it is a great responsibility to do that well and to get it right," he explained.

As vice president, he is responsible for the bank's relations with its members, the board of governors, the board of directors and other aspects of governance, including the admission of new members.

"I have a role as part of the senior management team in the bank, with a particular responsibility for the governors of the bank, making sure the board of directors, the board of governors and so on operate in the right way," he said.

"We have a very good team ably led by President Jin Liqun. And I think together we are helping to ensure that the AIIB is built in a way that fulfills the vision that our institution is lean, clean and green," he said.

Highest Standards

In the interview, Alexander repeatedly stressed that the AIIB is committed to "operating to the highest international standards".

The bank is focused on its work "to ensure high standards in everything that we do: high standards of governance, high standards of environmental and social management and high standards of project development," the AIIB vice president said.

By focusing on investing in "good projects" that have strong safeguards on environmental and community impact, the AIIB "can help to ensure through those investments that we spread the high standards and that we share better practice," he noted. "That helps to ensure that there is a good business environment, so I think that is the main way in which the AIIB can make that contribution."

Priorities

In January, the AIIB unveiled its three priorities for the year ahead, namely sustainable infrastructure, cross-country connectivity and the mobilization of private capital, according to a statement on its website.

Alexander said sustainable infrastructure helped to support the transition for Asian countries to be "more environmentally sustainable", which requires renewable energy and sustainable cities.

On connectivity, the vice president said it meant "improving the connectivity between Asian countries, and through Asia, and other parts of the world".

"That means transport projects, like roads, railways, airports and ports, but also things like electricity transmission and energy pipelines," he said.

"The scale of the need for infrastructure in Asia is so huge that all of the national government resources and all of the international financial resources are too small," he said, highlighting the need to mobilize private capital.

"We must mobilize more private capital, so we also have a role to play in helping to make infrastructure more attractive for private sector investors as well as institutions like ours," he urged.

Shared Aim

In the interview, Alexander also shared his views on the links between the AIIB and the Belt and Road Initiative, proposed by China in 2013 with the aim of building a trade, investment and infrastructure network connecting Asia with Europe and Africa along ancient trade routes.

He said that though the AIIB and the initiative are two separate initiatives, they also overlap at certain intersections and share a similar goal.

"There is overlap and there is mutual interest and mutual benefit in terms of their shared aim to promote productivity within the Asian region," he told Xinhua.

The AIIB, together with five other major multilateral development banks, including the World Bank and the Asian Development Bank, signed a memorandum of understanding with the Chinese Ministry of Finance at the Belt and Road Forum for International Cooperation held in May this year.

"That created a framework for all of the major international financial institutions to work with the Belt and Road Initiative," Alexander said.

He stressed, however, the AIIB would invest in good projects, "according to its own strategy" and would apply the same high standards and tests to its investment projects.

Questions

1. Why did Alexander advocate strongly that the UK should join the AIIB?
2. What is Alexander's responsibility as the vice president and corporate secretary of AIIB?
3. How does the AIIB operate to the highest international standards?
4. What are the three priorities of the AIIB for the year ahead?
5. What are the links between AIIB and the Belt and Road Initiative?

Unit 8   Commercial Banks

Case

Lin finished high school in China and went to the United States to further her education. She wanted to open an account, so she went to several local banks. At the local banks, she saw a bewildering array of accounts which seemed to be too complicated for her to choose from. Also, she found that similar accounts at different banks might have different names. She made a list of questions and went to the local banks again. After collecting information from various banks, she found an account which would best meet her needs.

Questions

1. What kind of questions should Lin include in her list?
2. What are the different types of accounts and their account features?

Preview

Skimming

Skim the following text quickly to answer the following questions and discuss your answers with your partners.

1. What is the most important function of commercial banks?

2. What are the common sources of commercial bank funds?

3. What is the main use of commercial bank funds?

4. What kind of activities generate fee income without requiring an investment of funds?

5. List five popular off-balance sheet activities.

Unit 8 Commercial Banks

Scanning

Scan the following text quickly to find the specific information.

1. When were the interstate banking regulations changed?
   _____
   _____.

2. What is a bank holding company?
   _____
   _____.

3. Which deposit account permits checking writing and pays no interest?
   _____
   _____.

4. List two alternatives a commercial bank has if it needs temporary funds.
   _____
   _____.

5. Why is bank capital different from all the other sources of commercial bank funds?
   _____
   _____.

6. What are the common types of loans offered by a bank?
   _____
   _____.

7. In the case of SLC, what will the bank do if the customer fails to meet its obligation?
   _____
   _____.

8. How long is a typical term of a credit default swap?
   _____
   _____.

Vocabulary in Context

Read the following sentences and try to guess the meaning of the italicized words by using the context. Then replace the italicized words with synonyms (words or phrases that have nearly the same or similar meanings).

1. They *repackage* the funds received from deposits to provide loans of the size and maturity desired by deficit units.
   They _____ the funds received from deposits to provide loans of the size and maturity desired by deficit units.

2. One reason is that interstate banking regulations were changed in 1994 to allow banks more freedom to acquire other banks across state lines. Consequently, banks in a particular region are now subject to competition not only from other local banks but also from any bank that may *penetrate* that market.
   One reason is that interstate banking regulations were changed in 1994 to allow banks more

freedom to acquire other banks across state lines. Consequently, banks in a particular region are now subject to competition not only from other local banks but also from any bank that may _____ that market.

3. From the bank's *perspective*, demand deposit accounts are classified as transaction accounts that provide a source of funds that can be used until withdrawn by customers (as checks are written).

   From the bank's _____, demand deposit accounts are classified as transaction accounts that provide a source of funds that can be used until withdrawn by customers (as checks are written).

4. NCDs are similar to CDs *in that* they have a specified maturity date and require a minimum deposit.

   NCDs are similar to CDs _____ they have a specified maturity date and require a minimum deposit.

5. The federal funds market allows depository institutions to *accommodate* the short-term liquidity needs of other financial institutions.

   The federal funds market allows depository institutions to _____ the short-term liquidity needs of other financial institutions.

6. Bank capital generally represents funds *attained* through the issuance of stock or through retained earnings.

   Bank capital generally represents funds _____ through the issuance of stock or through retained earnings.

7. In addition, banks can easily invest in securities, *whereas* they need more resources to assess loan applicants and service loans.

   In addition, banks can easily invest in securities, _____ they need more resources to assess loan applicants and service loans.

8. Banks commonly engage in off-balance sheet activities, which generate fee income without requiring an investment of funds. These activities do create a *contingent* obligation for banks, however.

   Banks commonly engage in off-balance sheet activities, which generate fee income without requiring an investment of funds. These activities do create a _____ obligation for banks, however.

9. Banks engage in forward contracts with customers that desire to *hedge* their exchange rate risk.

   Banks engage in forward contracts with customers that desire to _____ their exchange rate risk.

10. *In essence*, the sellers of credit default swaps are providing insurance against default.

    _____, the sellers of credit default swaps are providing insurance against default.

Text

Commercial Bank Operations in the United States

Measured by total assets, commercial banks are the most important type of financial intermediary. Like other financial intermediaries, they perform a critical function of facilitating the flow of funds from surplus units to deficit units.

Background on Commercial Banks

Financial institutions commonly facilitate the flow of funds between surplus units and deficit units. Commercial banks represent a key financial intermediary because they serve all types of surplus and deficit units. They offer deposit accounts with the size and maturity[1] characteristics desired by surplus units. They repackage the funds received from deposits to provide loans of the size and maturity desired by deficit units. They have the ability to assess the creditworthiness[2] of deficit units that apply for loans, so that they can limit their exposure to credit risk[3] on the loans they provide.

Bank Market Structure

In 1985, more than 14,000 banks were located in the United States. Since then, the market structure has changed dramatically. Banks have been consolidating for several reasons. One reason is that interstate banking regulations were changed in 1994 to allow banks more freedom to acquire other banks across state lines. Consequently, banks in a particular region are now subject to competition not only from other local banks but also from any bank that may penetrate that market. This has prompted banks to become more efficient in order to survive. They have pursued growth as a means of capitalizing on economies of scale[4] and enhanced efficiency. Acquisitions have been a convenient way to grow rapidly.

As a result of this trend, there are only about half as many banks today as there were in 1985, and consolidation is still occurring. The largest banks have increased their market share of total commercial and industrial loans. Banks have also acquired many other types of financial service firms in recent years.

Many banks are owned by bank holding companies, which are companies that own at least 10 percent of a bank. The holding company structure allows more flexibility to borrow funds, issue stock, repurchase the company's own stock, and acquire other firms. Bank holding companies may also avoid some state banking regulations.

The operation, management, and regulation of a commercial bank vary with the types of service offered. The primary operations of commercial banks can be most easily identified by reviewing their main source of funds, their main uses of funds, and the off-balance sheet activities that they provide.

Bank Sources of Funds

To understand how any financial institution obtains funds and uses funds, its balance sheet can be reviewed. Its reported liabilities and equity indicate its sources of funds, while its reported assets indicate its uses of funds. The major sources of commercial bank funds are summarized as follows:

- Deposit Accounts
  - Transaction deposits
  - Savings deposits
  - Time deposits
  - Money market deposit accounts
- Borrowed Funds
  - Federal funds purchased

- Borrowing from the Federal Reserve banks
- Repurchase agreements
- Eurodollar[5] borrowings
- Long-Term Sources of Funds
  - Bonds issued by the bank
  - Bank capital

Transaction Deposits

A demand deposit account, or checking account, is offered to customers who desire to write checks against their account. A conventional demand deposit account requires a small minimum balance and pays no interest. From the bank's perspective, demand deposit accounts are classified as transaction accounts that provide a source of funds that can be used until withdrawn by customers (as checks are written).

Another type of transaction deposit[6] is the negotiable order of withdrawal (NOW) account[7], which pays interest as well as providing checking services. Because NOW accounts at most financial institutions require a larger minimum balance than some consumers are willing to maintain in a transaction account, traditional demand deposit accounts are still popular.

Savings Deposits

The traditional savings account is the passbook[8] savings account, which does not permit check writing. Passbook savings accounts continue to attract savers with a small amount of funds, as such accounts often have no required minimum balance.

Time Deposits

Time deposits are deposits that cannot be withdrawn until a specified maturity date. The two most common types of time deposits are certificates of deposit (CDs)[9] and negotiable certificates of deposit (NCDs)[10].

Certificates of deposit require a specified minimum amount of funds to be deposited for a specified period of time. Banks offer a wide variety of CDs to satisfy depositors' needs. Annualized interest rates offered on CDs vary among banks, and even among maturity types at a single bank.

Negotiable certificates of deposit are offered by some large banks to corporations. NCDs are similar to CDs in that they have a specified maturity date and require a minimum deposit. Their maturities are typically short term, and their minimum deposit requirement is $100,000.

Money Market Deposit Account

Money market deposit accounts (MMDAs)[11] differ from conventional time deposits in that they do not specify a maturity. MMDAs are more liquid than CDs from the depositor's point of view. However, they offer a lower interest than CDs. MMDAs differ from NOW accounts in that they provide limited check-writing ability, require a larger minimum balance, and offer a higher yield.

The remaining sources of funds are of a nondepository nature. Such sources are necessary when a bank temporarily needs more funds than are being deposited. Some banks use nondepository funds as a permanent source of funds.

Federal Funds Purchased

The federal funds[12] market allows depository institutions to accommodate the short-term liquidity needs of other financial institutions. Federal funds purchased (or borrowed) represent a liability to the borrowing bank and an asset to the lending bank that sells them. Loans in the federal funds market are typically for one to seven days. The intent of federal funds transactions is to correct short-term fund imbalances experienced by banks.

Borrowing from the Federal Reserve Banks

Another temporary source of funds for banks is the Federal Reserve System, which serves as the U.S. central bank. Along with other bank regulators, the Federal Reserve district banks regulate certain activities of banks. They also provide short-term loans to banks. This form of borrowing by banks is often referred to as borrowing at the discount window[13]. The interest rate charged on these loans is known as the primary credit lending rate.

Repurchase Agreements

A repurchase agreement (repo) represents the sale of securities by one party to another with an agreement to repurchase the securities at a specified date and price. Banks often use a repo as a source of funds when they expect to need funds for just a few days. The bank simply sells some of its government securities to a corporation with a temporary excess of funds and buys those securities back shortly thereafter.

Eurodollar Borrowings

If a U.S. bank is in need of short-term fund, it may borrow dollars from those banks outside the United States (typically in Europe) that accept dollar-denominated deposits, or Eurodollars. Some foreign banks or foreign branches of U.S. banks accept large short-term deposits and make short-term loans in dollars. Because U.S. dollars are widely used as an international medium of exchange, the Eurodollar market is very active.

Bonds Issued by the Bank

Like other corporations, banks own some fixed assets such as land, buildings, and equipment. These assets often have an expected life of 20 years or more and are usually financed with long-term sources of funds, such as through the issuance of bonds. Banks do not finance with bonds as much as most other corporations, because they have fewer fixed assets than corporations that use industrial equipment and machinery for production.

Bank Capital

Bank capital generally represents funds attained through the issuance of stock or through retaining earnings. With either form, the bank has no obligation to pay out funds in the future. This distinguishes bank capital from all the other sources of funds, which represent a future obligation by the bank to pay out funds. Bank capital as defined here represents the equity or net worth of the bank.

Uses of Funds by Banks

The common uses of funds by banks include the following:
- Cash
- Bank loans
- Investment in securities
- Federal funds sold
- Repurchase agreements
- Eurodollar loans
- Fixed assets

Cash

Banks must hold some cash as reserves to meet the reserve requirements enforced by the Federal Reserve. Banks also hold cash to maintain some liquidity and accommodate any withdrawal requests by depositors. Because banks do not earn income from cash, they hold only as much cash as necessary to maintain a sufficient degree of liquidity.

Banks Loans

The main use of bank funds is for loans. Banks usually offer business loans, consumer loans, and real estate loans. The loan amount and maturity can be tailored to the borrower's needs.

Investment in Securities

Banks purchase various types of securities. One advantage of investing funds in securities rather than loans is that the securities tend to be more liquid. In addition, banks can easily invest in securities, whereas they need more resources to assess loan applicants and service loans. However, they normally expect to generate higher rates of return on funds used to provide loans.

Federal Funds Sold

Some banks often lend funds to other banks in the federal funds market. The funds sold, or lent out, will be returned at the time specified in the loan agreement, with interest. The loan period is typically very short, such as a day or a few days.

Repurchase Agreements

From the borrower's perspective, a repurchase agreement (repo) transaction involves repurchasing the securities it had previously sold. From a lender's perspective, the repo represents a sale of securities that it had previously purchased. Banks can act as the lender by purchasing a corporation's holding of Treasury securities and selling them back at a later date.

Eurodollar Loans

Branches of U.S. banks located outside the United States and some foreign-owned banks provide dollar-denominated loans to corporations and governments. Eurodollar loans are short term and denominated in large amount, such as $1 million or more.

Fixed Assets

Banks must maintain some amount of fixed assets, such as office buildings and land, so that they can conduct their business operations.

Off-balance Sheet Activities

Banks commonly engage in off-balance sheet activities, which generate fee income without requiring an investment of funds. These activities do create a contingent obligation for banks, however. The following are some of the popular off-balance sheet activities:

- Loan commitments
- Standby letters of credit[14]
- Forward contracts on currencies
- Interest rate swap contracts
- Credit default swap[15] contracts

Loan Commitments

A loan commitment is an obligation by a bank to provide a specified loan amount to a particular firm upon the firm's request. The interest rate and purpose of the loan may also be specified. The bank charges a fee for offering the commitment.

Standby Letters of Credit

A standby letter of credit (SLC) backs a customer's obligation to a third party. If the customer does not meet its obligation, the bank will. The third party may require that the customer obtain an SLC to complete a business transaction.

Forward Contracts on Currencies

A forward contract on currency is an arrangement between a customer and a bank to exchange one currency for another on a particular future date at a specified exchange rate. Banks engage in forward contracts with customers that desire to hedge their exchange rate risk.

Interest Rate Swap Contracts

Banks also serve as intermediaries for interest rate swaps, whereby two parties agree to periodically exchange interest payments on a specified notional amount of principal. Once again, the bank receives a transaction fee for its services. If it guarantees payments to both parties, it is exposed to the possibility that one of the parities will default on its obligation. In that event, the bank must assume the role of the party and fulfill the obligation to the other party.

Credit Default Swap Contracts

Credit default swaps are privately negotiated contracts that protect investors against the risk of default on particular debt securities. Some commercial banks and other financial institutions buy them in order to protect their own investments in debt securities against default risk. Other banks and financial institutions sell them. The banks that sell credit default swaps receive periodic coupon payments for the term of swap agreement. A typical term of a credit default swap is five years. If there are no defaults on the debt securities, the banks that sold the credit default swaps benefit because they are not required to make any payments. However, when there are defaults on the debt securities, the sellers of credit default swaps must make payments to the buyers to cover the damage. In essence, the sellers of credit default swaps are providing insurance against default.

Terminology

commercial bank	商业银行
bank holding company	银行控股公司
deposit account	存款账户
demand deposit	活期存款
demand deposit account	活期存款账户
savings deposit	储蓄存款
savings account	储蓄账户
time deposit	定期存款
maturity	期限，到期
maturity date	到期日
money market deposit account	货币市场存款账户
yield	收益，收益率
depository institution	存款机构
discount window	贴现窗口
repurchase agreement (repo)	回购协议
off-balance sheet activities	表外业务
loan commitment	贷款承诺
standby letter of credit (SLC)	备用信用证
forward contract on currency	远期外汇合约
interest rate swap contract	利率互换合约
credit default swap contract	信用违约互换合约

Notes on the Text

1. maturity — reaching the date at which a debt instrument is due and payable.
2. creditworthiness — the general eligibility of an individual or firm to borrow money. (信誉)
3. credit risk — the financial and moral risk that an obligation will not be paid and a loss will result. (信用风险)
4. economies of scale — the long run reduction in average (or unit) costs that occurs as the scale of the firm's output is increased (all factor inputs being variable). (规模经济)
5. eurodollar — U.S. dollars that deposited with banks outside the United States, not necessarily in Europe, and lent to borrowers outside the United States. These deposits and loans of dollars are not subject to the same regulations as dealings in domestic currencies, and have grown

rapidly in importance as finance for international trade. (欧洲美元)

6. transaction deposit — a banking deposit that has immediate and full liquidity, with no delays or waiting. Transaction deposits must be held in reserve by the bank at all times; they stand in contrast to time deposits and even deposits into a savings account, which may have monthly limitations on the number of transactions or transfers allowed.

7. negotiable order of withdrawal (NOW) account — an interest-earning bank account with which the customer is permitted to write drafts against money held on deposit.

8. passbook — a book issued by a bank to record deposits, withdrawals, and interest earned in a savings account. The passbook lists the depositor's name and account number as well as all transactions. (存折)

9. certificate of deposit (CD) — a debt instrument issued by a bank that usually pays interest. Institutional CDs are issued in denominations of $100,000 or more, and individual CDs start as low as $100. Maturities range from a few weeks to several years. Interest rates are set by competitive forces in the marketplace.

10. negotiable certificate of deposit (NCD) — a large-dollar-amount, short-term certificate of deposit. Such certificates are issued by large banks and bought mainly by corporations and institutional investors. They are payable either to the bearer or to the order of the depositor, and, being negotiable, they enjoy an active secondary market, where they trade in round lots of $5 million. Although they can be issued in any denomination from $100,000 up, the typical amount is $1 million. They have a minimum original maturity of 14 days; most original maturities are under 6 months.

11. money market deposit account (MMDA) — a market-sensitive bank account that has been offered since December 1982. Under Depository Institutions Deregulatory Committee rules, only three checks may be drawn per month, although unlimited transfers may be carried out at an automated teller machine.

12. federal funds — funds deposited by commercial banks at Federal Reserve banks, including funds in excess of bank reserve requirements. Banks may lend federal funds to each other on an overnight basis at the federal funds rate. Member banks may also transfer funds among themselves or on behalf of customers on a same-day basis by debiting and crediting balances in various reserve banks.

13. discount window — an instrument of monetary policy (usually controlled by central banks) that allows eligible institutions to borrow money from the central bank, usually on a short-term basis, to meet temporary shortages of liquidity caused by internal or external disruptions. The term originated with the practice of sending a bank representative to a reserve bank teller window when a bank needed to borrow money. The interest rate charged on such loans by a central bank is called the discount rate, base rate, or repo rate, and is separate and distinct from the prime rate.

14. standby letter of credit (SLC) — a guarantee of payment issued by a bank on behalf of a client that is used as "payment of last resort" should the client fail to fulfill a contractual commitment with a third party. Standby letters of credit are created as a sign of good faith in

business transactions, and are proof of a buyer's credit quality and repayment abilities. The bank issuing the SLC will perform brief underwriting duties to ensure the credit quality of the party seeking the letter of credit, then send notification to the bank of the party requesting the letter of credit (typically a seller or creditor).

15. credit default swap (CDS) — a swap designed to transfer the credit exposure of fixed income products between parties. A credit default swap is also referred to as a credit derivative contract, where the purchaser of the swap makes payments up until the maturity date of a contract. Payments are made to the seller of the swap. In return, the seller agrees to pay off a third party debt if this party defaults on the loan. A CDS is considered insurance against non-payment. A buyer of a CDS might be speculating on the possibility that the third party will indeed default.

Exercises

I. Reading Comprehension.

Read the text carefully and decide whether the following statements are true (T) or false (F).

___ 1. Commercial banks are the most important type of financial intermediary because they provide all the financial services since they came into being.
___ 2. Commercial banks serve all types of deficit and surplus units.
___ 3. The deposit accounts vary in terms of liquidity and the interest rates offered.
___ 4. Banks usually issue stocks or bonds when they need short-term funds.
___ 5. The off-balance sheet activities do not require an investment of funds, so they are riskless.

II. Vocabulary Building.

A. Match the term in Column A with the definition in Column B.

1. bank holding company
2. commercial bank
3. checking account
4. demand deposit
5. loan commitment
6. off-balance sheet activities
7. repurchase agreement
8. savings account

a. account that allows the holder to write checks against deposited funds
b. business activities that do not involve assets, liabilities on the organization's balance sheet
c. interest-bearing bank deposit that has a specified date of maturity
d. account that pays interest but cannot be used directly as money
e. bank deposit that can be drawn upon on demand, i.e. without prior notice
f. contract in which the seller of securities agrees to buy them back at a specified time and price
g. a company that controls one or more banks, but does not necessarily engage in banking itself
h. financial institution that accepts deposits, makes loans, and offers related services

9. time deposit
10. yield

i. return on an investor's capital investment
j. contractual commitment to loan to a firm a certain maximum amount at given interest rate terms

B. Complete the following sentences with the words given in the box and change the form of the words where necessary.

benefit	critical	excess	flexibility
generate	hedge	intent	maintain
obligation	previously	specify	sufficient

1. Banks use derivatives to _____ against a wide range of risks to operations and earnings.
2. China Guangfa Bank, _____ known as Guangdong Development Bank, is a commercial banking corporation headquartered in Guangzhou.
3. Although there are many institutions involved in the movement of money today, banks remain fundamental to the motion of money that _____ local, national, and global economies.
4. The _____ of the policy is to stimulate the economy by increasing liquidity and promoting bank lending.
5. The $1 billion drawdown will increase both the liquidity and financial _____ of the company, but will not increase its overall net debt position.
6. You have to have _____ funds in your account to cover your purchase.
7. High-tech security measures are increasingly _____ to banking operations between banks and customers, between banks and banks, and between banks and the government.
8. Banks that carry _____ reserves have an extra measure of safety in the event of sudden loan losses or cash withdrawals by customers.
9. Banks can _____ revenue in various ways.
10. A bank failure occurs when a bank is unable to meet its _____ to its depositors or other creditors.

III. Cloze.

There are 10 blanks in the following two passages. For each blank there are four choices marked A, B, C and D. You are supposed to choose the best answer.

Passage 1

In 1995, the Chinese Government introduced the Commercial Bank Law to commercialize the operations of the four (1)_____ banks, Bank of China (BOC), China Construction Bank (CCB), Agricultural Bank of China (ABC), and Industrial and Commercial Bank of China (ICBC). ICBC is the largest bank in China (2)_____ total assets, total employees and total customers. It used to be the major supplier of funds to China's urban areas and manufacturing (3)_____. BOC specializes in foreign-exchange transactions and trade finance. CCB specializes in medium to long-term credit for long-term specialized projects, (4)_____ as infrastructure projects and urban housing development. ABC specializes in (5)_____ financing to China's agricultural sector and offers wholesale and retail banking services to farmers, township and village enterprises (TVEs), and other rural institutions.

(1) A. central   B. private   C. policy   D. state-owned
(2) A. by   B. with   C. at   D. under
(3) A. department   B. circle   C. sector   D. line
(4) A. well   B. such   C. considering   D. regarding
(5) A. providing   B. to provide   C. provided   D. having provided

Passage 2

Commercial banks are the institutions commonly (6)_____ as banks. They do about 60 percent of the deposits and loan (7)_____ in the United States. Commercial banks are so called because, at one time, they (8)_____ their services only to businesses. Today, commercial banks seek the business from any (9)_____ customer and provide a multitude of financial services of many types (10)_____ the traditional practices of holding deposits and lending money.

(6) A. thought   B. thought of   C. thought over   D. thought for
(7) A. trades   B. deals   C. transactions   D. business
(8) A. offered   B. offer   C. will offer   D. have offered
(9) A. worth   B. worthy   C. worthwhile   D. worthless
(10) A. except   B. except for   C. beyond   D. beyond of

IV. Translate the following sentences into English.

1. 历史记录表明，四千多年前寺庙发挥着银行的作用，因为当时寺庙提供了货币兑换和贷款的业务。(indicate)
2. 汇丰银行的信用卡可以通过网点、电话或在线申请。(apply)
3. 这家久负盛名的银行向高端客户提供定制服务以更好地适应他们的需求。(tailor)
4. 参与的商业银行只能使用本银行账户从事债券交易。(conduct)
5. 银行的信息技术成本因其所提供的服务不同而不同。(vary)

V. Translate the following paragraphs into Chinese.

1. Banks are critical to the economy. Although there are many ways that money moves around the economy, banks plays a central role in establishing the financial environment. Transferring money to provide growth and stabilizing the monetary supply are important functions in which banks play a key part. Bank lending makes money available to consumers and businesses to make purchases they might not otherwise be able to make. In addition, banks help determine creditworthiness so that good money is not lost on bad loans.

2. City commercial banks have played an important role in China's economic development, but they face far greater risks than big state-owned banks. Transformed from urban credit cooperatives less than two decades ago, city commercial banks often struggle with high non-performing loan ratios, poor capital adequacy ratios and limited market penetration. After continuous efforts to raise funds, statistics show that city commercial banks are generally performing well.

VI. Self-Testing.

1. Which of the following is NOT one of the main functions of commercial banks?
   A. Accepting deposits.
   B. Providing loans.
   C. Transferring funds.
   D. Managing cash.
2. _____ are funds held in an account from which deposited funds can be withdrawn at any time without prior notice to the depository institution.
   A. Demand deposits
   B. Time deposits
   C. CDs
   D. NCDs
3. Off-balance sheet activities _____.
   A. are the free-of-charge activities off the balance sheet
   B. do not involve risks that add to the overall insolvency exposure on a financial intermediary
   C. include issuing various types of guarantees, making future commitments to lend, and other services
   D. are of little importance, in terms of their value and the income they generate for banks
4. Repurchase agreement _____.
   A. has a collateralized nature
   B. involves the sale of securities by one party to another with a promise to repurchase the securities at a specified date and price in the future
   C. market is highly liquid
   D. all of the above
5. Commercial banks _____.
   A. comprise the largest group of depository institutions in size
   B. only accept deposits and make loans
   C. do not have branches
   D. generally pay higher interest rates on deposits and charge lower interest rates on loans
6. When did the Commercial Bank Law take effect in China?
   A. In 1984. B. In 1994. C. In 1995. D. In 2003.
7. Which of the following is NOT a commercial bank in China?
   A. China CITIC Bank.
   B. China Development Bank.
   C. China Merchants Bank.
   D. China Everbright Bank.
8. Which of the following is a state-owned commercial bank in China?
   A. Bank of China.
   B. The People's Bank of China.
   C. China Development Bank.
   D. The Export-Import Bank of China.
9. _____ is a joint-equity commercial bank operating nationwide in China.
   A. China Development Bank
   B. Shanghai Pudong Development Bank
   C. The People's Bank of China
   D. The Export-Import Bank of China
10. Which of the following is NOT a city commercial bank in China?
    A. Shenzhen Development Bank.
    B. Bank of Beijing.
    C. Bank of Shanghai.
    D. Bank of Ningbo.

VII. Writing.

Please write a letter to Client A in English as follows.
1. 根据规定，我行客户在关闭支票账户前必须退回所有的未使用支票。
2. 请客户 A 退回账号为 8976593 的支票账户下的编号为 2854212 的未使用支票。
3. 我方收到支票后会将支票账户余额汇至客户 A 在花旗银行的账户。
4. 感谢对方的合作。

Supplementary Reading

ICBC Seeks to Boost Sino-Turkish Financial Cooperation

By Li Ping
(*China Daily* October 9, 2018)

Turkey plays an important role in the Belt and Road Initiative due to its geographical and cultural bridge linking the East and West, making it a popular market for Chinese banks going global.

ICBC Turkey, a subsidiary of top Chinese bank — Industrial and Commercial Bank of China — said financial cooperation between China and Turkey still has great potential to grow under the framework of the Belt and Road Initiative and Turkey's Middle Corridor plan.

"Compared to the robust growth in economic and trade exchanges, financial cooperation between the two countries is still in its infancy," said Li Jinhong, deputy general manager of ICBC Turkey, in an interview with media on Sept. 18. She said the company aims to provide more convenient and comprehensive financial services to enhance collaboration in this area via its wide network in Turkey.

ICBC now has 44 branches and 20 securities business offices in 18 major Turkish cities including Istanbul, Ankara and Izmir, according to Li. The company offers a wide variety of financial services for both enterprises and individuals, ranging from deposits, loans and trade financing to investment, acquisition and asset management.

In 2015, ICBC Turkey provided credit support for Kumport Terminal, Turkey's third-largest container terminal, by three Chinese companies: COSCO Pacific, China Merchants Holdings (International) and the China Investment Corporation. It's the biggest acquisition to date from Chinese enterprises in Turkey, in the amount of $940 million.

ICBC entered Turkey in 2015 after buying a 75.5 percent stake of Tekstilbank from GSD Holding, which helped boost the bank's business in countries around the Mediterranean and the Black Sea.

As more Chinese companies are looking for business opportunities overseas, ICBC said it has backed a number of key infrastructure projects in Turkey, including ports, transportation, energy and communications. Globally, the top Chinese commercial bank has established 129 branches in 20 countries and regions involved in the BRI as of the end of 2017, which altogether has supported 358 BRI projects with a loan amount of approximately $94.5 billion.

Unit 8　Commercial Banks

Questions

1. Why does Turkey play an important role in the Belt and Road Initiative?
2. What is ICBC's aim in Turkey?
3. How many branches and offices has ICBC established in Turkey?
4. What services does ICBC provide in Turkey?
5. How did ICBC enter the Turkish market?

Unit 9　Investment Banks

Case

Company ABC is going to sold its stock to interested investors in a cash offer. The offer will be the company's first public equity issue, which is referred to as an initial public offering (IPO). An investment bank will act as the underwriter for Company ABC' IPO. The investment bank will perform services such as formulating the method used to issue the securities, pricing the new securities, and selling the new securities.

Questions

1. What are the services provided by investment banks?
2. Why is an investment bank not a bank in the ordinary sense?

Preview

Skimming

Skim the following text quickly to answer the following questions and discuss your answers with your partners.

1. What are the two basic functions of investment banks?
   _____
   _____.

2. What are the three major investment banking activities?
   _____
   _____.

3. What are the two purposes of transaction activity?
   _____
   _____.

4. What's the main difference between investment banks and commercial banks?
   _____
   _____.

5. According to the text, what is the prospect of investment banking?
   _____
   _____.

Unit 9　Investment Banks

Scanning

Scan the following text quickly to find the specific information.
1. Who undertakes investment banking activities?
   _____
   _____.
2. How many stages has investment banking undergone in its development?
   _____
   _____.
3. What is the traditional view of investment banking?
   _____
   _____.
4. When are new securities by companies brought to market?
   _____
   _____.
5. What does IPO stand for?
   _____
   _____.
6. List three third-generation derivatives.
   _____
   _____.
7. Why did "sell side" research become popular?
   _____
   _____.
8. What is closely connected to the development of investment banking?
   _____
   _____.

Vocabulary in Context

Read the following sentences and try to guess the meaning of the italicized words by using the context. Then replace the italicized words with synonyms (words or phrases that have nearly the same or similar meanings).
1. They are the beginnings of participation by investment banks, on a *modest* scale, in industrial restructuring on capital and other financial markets.
   They are the beginnings of participation by investment banks, on a _____ scale, in industrial restructuring on capital and other financial markets.
2. Investment banking means *first and foremost* the underwriting of securities.
   Investment banking means _____ the underwriting of securities.
3. Other activities are certainly important and have grown substantially, but *prowess* in underwriting and syndication are nevertheless the hallmark of the industry.
   Other activities are certainly important and have grown substantially, but _____ in underwriting and syndication are nevertheless the hallmark of the industry.

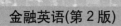

4. Secondary distributions are sales of stock that previously existed in some form or other forms but are too large to be *accommodated* on the stock exchanges.

   Secondary distributions are sales of stock that previously existed in some form or other forms but are too large to be _____ on the stock exchanges.

5. The behavior of investment bankers is *key* to the reception of new issues and directly affects the cost of capital for a company, and a wrong choice could affect its costs over the near term.

   The behavior of investment bankers is _____ to the reception of new issues and directly affects the cost of capital for a company, and a wrong choice could affect its costs over the near term.

6. Many of those that have adopted a full services philosophy which historically means wholesale or institutional banks that actively *courted* consumer deposits, have found that the retail side has helped them when the institutional side has been less profitable than anticipated.

   Many of those that have adopted a full services philosophy which historically means wholesale or institutional banks that actively _____ consumer deposits, have found that the retail side has helped them when the institutional side has been less profitable than anticipated.

7. Investment advisors who do not follow those principles are *liable* for damages to their clients if pursued legally.

   Investment advisors who do not follow those principles are _____ for damages to their clients if pursued legally.

8. As a specialized area within investment banking, financial advising is somewhat *nebulous* and can vary in degrees.

   As a specialized area within investment banking, financial advising is somewhat _____ and can vary in degrees.

9. Acquisitions are either friendly or *hostile*, depending upon the direct reaction of the target company to the proposed bid.

   Acquisitions are either friendly or _____, depending upon the direct reaction of the target company to the proposed bid.

10. A fiduciary is expected to invest clients' money in a *prudent* and reasonable manner in line with the clients' objectives.

    A fiduciary is expected to invest clients' money in a _____ and reasonable manner in line with the clients' objectives.

Text

Investment Banking

Backgrounds

Investment banking is a highly specialized segment of the finance industry. Its basic function is to bring together, directly through the mechanism of financial markets, ultimate savers and savings collecting institutions with those wishing to raise additional funds for investment or consumption. It also facilitates holders of accumulated wealth, held in the form of financial instruments, to reallocate their assets using financial markets in accordance with their changing evaluation of the attraction of the combination of risk/rewards/liquidity attributes of individual financial assets, compared with each other and with real assets[1]. In performing these two basic functions, those involved in investment banking act as market intermediaries.

Investment banking activities are undertaken by specialized and independent investment banking institutions offering all or some of the services described above, or by universal banks alongside their traditional deposit taking and loan business.

History

There are three distinct stages in the evolution of investment banking. The first stage is concerned with classic investment banking business. It is confined almost entirely to the raising of external funds for non-financial companies and various government bodies by issuing securities on capital markets. This covers the well-known function of underwriting.

The second stage covers the expansion of investment banking into closed-end and open-end trusts — acting as agents for the selling and buying of securities on capital markets and dealing in them. They are the beginnings of participation by investment banks, on a modest scale, in industrial restructuring on capital and other financial markets. During this phase, underwriting is still the main area of activity that generates the bulk of profits in the investment banking field.

The third stage, or mature state of the evolution of investment banking is characterized, firstly, by a rapid increase in the relative importance of industrial restructuring by way of acquisitions, mergers, amalgamations[2] and disposals linked to the emergence of an active market for corporate control. This is followed by a rapid growth in the management of funds, especially pension funds and those sponsored by investment banks in the form of open-ended funds[3] and other types of funds held by individual and savings-collecting institutions. The final feature of this stage is direct involvement in risk pricing and transfer markets using a variety of derivatives traded on organized or unorganized markets.

Investment Banking Activities

Investment banking today separates into three distinct kinds of activities: underwriting stocks and bonds, or the new issue of securities; transactions, including trading in the secondary market, proprietary trading for the firm's own account, and retail brokerage; and fee banking, involving activities earning a fee such as advising on mergers and acquisitions, securities and economic research, and other types of financial consulting.

Since investment banking had expanded a lot over the last fifty years, the industry still maintains a traditional view of itself: Investment banking means first and foremost the underwriting of securities. Other activities are certainly important and have grown substantially, but prowess in underwriting and syndication[4] are nevertheless the hallmark of the industry. For this reason, the activity of underwriting will be defined first here.

Underwriting New Issues

New securities by companies are usually brought to market after advice and a commitment to underwrite by an investment banking firm. Underwriting simply means that the investment banker promises to buy the securities. The investment banks help design the securities and buy it from issuer with the intent of selling it to investors as quickly as possible.

New issues of common stock come into two varieties — primary distributions and secondary distributions. Primaries are sales of stock that have never been issued before. There are two types of primary distributions — initial public offerings (IPOs) and additional floats of companies' stock that will dilute each shareholder's existing holding. Of the two, the latter are more common in the new issues market for equities since they involve offerings of shares of larger, more mature companies seeking additional equity capital. Secondary distributions are sales of stock that previously existed in some form or other forms but are too large to be accommodated on the stock exchanges. Procedures for secondaries often follow those for primaries although the offering period is much shorter and may involve a matter of hours rather than days.

The actual marketing for these issues is done by investment bankers directly to the public. On rare occasions, companies have attempted to sell their shares or bonds directly to the public, avoiding investment banking fees. Unless the company is very well known, such attempts are less than successful. The behavior of investment bankers is key to the reception of new issues and directly affects the cost of capital for a company, and a wrong choice could affect its costs over the near term. This is true for bonds as well as for common stocks.

Transactions (Dealing and Broking)

The most obvious place to find transaction activity is in the secondary market for issues. This function serves two purposes. Firstly, it facilitates trading in the instrument, providing a service for both the issuer and investor. Secondly, it allows the bank to act as dealer to make a profit on the spread charged between bid and offer prices[5]. However, not all banks will engage in market making because it requires certain special trading skills that not all banks can develop to the same degree.

In addition to market making in the bond and stock market, another major area of trading is the trading of derivatives: traditional options and financial futures as first-generation derivatives; interest rate swaps[6] and currency swaps as second; instruments which combine the two categories-collars, swaptions, and commodity swaps as third. Development in the market has been so rapid that many investment banks now offer the services to their customers as well as use the products for themselves in hedging exposure risk[7].

When combined with traditional institutional services, retail brokerage provided a complement to the more traditional corporate services. By diversifying into retail, many investment banks realized that brokerage could provide additional revenues when business was good. But their general strategy is quite similar to that of commercial banks. Many of those that have adopted a full services philosophy which historically means wholesale or institutional banks that actively courted consumer deposits, have found that the retail side has helped them when the institutional side has been less profitable than anticipated. Investment bankers have assumed that a retail mix is both good business and a useful hedge against other operations.

Fee Banking

As a specialized area within investment banking, financial advising is somewhat nebulous and can vary in degrees. Advising companies on mergers and acquisitions (M&A), reorganizing capital structures, and advising on market timing are all part of the activity. Most often the clients are corporate, but they can also be governmental, or non-profit organizations.

Mergers and acquisitions simply mean that one company would attempt to take over another by gaining enough of its common stock for control. In the simplest sense, merger means two companies becoming one with the acquirer being in the commanding position.

Mergers come in one of several distinct forms. A horizontal merger brings together two companies in a similar industry — two steel companies for example. It should produce greater scale and efficiency, avoiding duplication of products and production. A vertical merger brings together two companies in related industries. A steel company taking over an energy producer such as a coal mine would be such an example. It is designed to produce a synergy between the two companies that did not exist before. Both forms of merger bring together companies related either directly or indirectly. A conglomerate merger purposely buys another not engaged in the same business at all. Leveraged buyout (LBO) is the purchase of one company by another using mainly borrowed funds.

Generally, most M&A activities involve one company buying another, taking the target company out of the public marketplace. On occasion, the management of a company will itself tender for the outstanding shares of a company, accomplishing the same ends. This type of privatization is referred to as a management buyout, or MBO.

Acquisitions are either friendly or hostile, depending upon the direct reaction of the target company to the proposed bid. If management remains opposed and attempts to dissuade shareholders from accepting the offer of the acquirer, the proposed purchase price is known as a hostile offer, as opposed to a friendly offer where they agree to the terms and conditions. But it should not be assumed that all hostile bids will be successful.

The deals included in the general category of financial advising go far beyond mergers and acquisitions. Investment bankers enter the picture on either side of the deal. They may be asked to represent the acquiring company or the target in the case of an acquisition or may act as advisors. The role of investment banks in financial advising is best seen in M&A activities, but other non-corporate areas of advising also exist, such as non-profit organizations and government.

As the securities business became more and more competitive, many securities firms recognized the need of their investment clients for sound, reliable advice. As a result, "sell side" research became very popular with most firms, and almost all began offering it to clients in one form or another. The establishment of the concept of "prudent man" investing is another driving force. A fiduciary is expected to invest clients' money in a prudent and reasonable manner in line with the clients' objectives. Investment advisors who do not follow those principles are liable for damages to their clients if pursued legally. As more and more investment advisors sought research on securities, the sell side research function became more and more important. It should also be noted that "sell side" research is distinct from "buy side" research, generated by fund managers themselves or by outside contractors whose view may be assumed to be somewhat more distant from that of sell side analysts.

Differences of Investment Banking

Investment banks must be distinguished from commercial banks and other savings collecting institutions who gather and decide themselves on the allocation of savings and who act as financial intermediaries. The use of financial markets is thus at the heart of investment banking. Its development and evolution have been closely linked to the growth and expansion of financial markets (and above all capital markets), the instruments they employ and the mechanisms they use.

There is an important distinction between the activity of the investment banking and the institutions that perform it. Investment banking activity can be, and is also undertaken by banks (who are financial intermediaries), provided that the respective regulatory framework allows it and individual banks (i.e., universal banks) wish to engage in it. Indeed, the history of the development of investment banking is the history of deposit and commercial banks moving into this field, subject to regulatory constraints.

Prospect of Investment Banking

The economic factors are likely to continue to extend their influence in favor of expansion of investment banking. And changes in the financial system regulatory framework will inevitably follow them. Globalization of the world economy can be expected to lead to a rise in the relative importance of investment banking in the financial system. The attention paid to and the need to contain systemic risks are likely to accelerate this trend — placing financial markets and investment banking even more firmly at the center of finance and banking.

Terminology

investment banking	投资银行业务
real asset	实物资产
closed-end/open-end trust	封闭式/开放式信托
acquisition	收购
merger	兼并
amalgamation	合并
proprietary trading	自营交易
retail brokerage	零售经纪
interest rate swap	利率互换
currency swap	货币互换
collar	双限期权
swaption	互换期权
initial public offerings	首次公开募股
bid/offer price	买/卖价
exposure risk	敞口风险
mergers and acquisitions	并购
horizontal merger	同业并购，横向兼并
vertical merger	垂直并购，纵向兼并
synergy	协同效应
conglomerate merger	混合兼并
leveraged buyout	杠杆收购
management buyout	管理层收购
fiduciary	受托人

Notes on the Text

1. real asset — physical or identifiable assets such as gold, land, equipment, patents, etc. They are the opposite of a financial asset.
2. amalgamation — the combination of one or more companies into a new entity. An amalgamation is distinct from a merger because neither of the combining companies survives as a legal entity. Rather, a completely new entity is formed to house the combined assets and liabilities of both companies.
3. open-end fund — a type of mutual fund that does not have restrictions on the amount of shares the fund will issue. If demand is high enough, the fund will continue to issue shares no matter how many investors there are. Open-end funds also buy back shares when investors wish to sell.
4. syndication — a professional financial services group formed temporarily for the purpose of handling a large transaction that would be hard or impossible for the entities involved to handle individually. Syndication allows companies to pool their resources and share risks. There are several different types of syndicates, including underwriting syndicates, banking syndicates and insurance syndicates.
5. bid and offer prices — The bid price is the price a buyer is willing to pay for a security. This is one part of the bid with the other being the bid size, which details the amount of shares the investor is willing to purchase at the bid price. The opposite of the bid price is the offer price, which is the price a seller is looking to get for his or her shares.
6. interest rate swap — a liquid financial derivative instrument in which two parties agree to exchange interest rate cash flows, based on a specified notional amount from a fixed rate to a floating rate (or vice versa) or from one floating rate to another. Interest rate swaps are commonly used for both hedging and speculating.
7. exposure risk — the quantified potential for loss that might occur as a result of some activity. An analysis of the risk exposure for a business often ranks risks according to their probability of occurring multiplied by the potential loss, and it might look at such things as liability issues, property loss or damage, and product demand shifts.

Exercises

I. Reading Comprehension.

Read the text carefully and decide whether the following statements are true (T) or false (F).

___1. Investment banking means the underwriting of securities; other activities are not important.

___2. Procedures for secondaries follow those for primaries, but the offering period is much longer.

___3. Most often the clients of financial advising are corporate, but they can also be governmental, or non-profit organizations.

___4. Conglomerate merger brings together two companies in related industries.

___5. Not all hostile bids will be successful.

II. Vocabulary Building.

A. Match the term in Column A with the definition in Column B.

1. underwriting
2. hedge
3. synergy
4. mergers and acquisitions
5. proprietary trading
6. interest rate swap
7. tender
8. management buyout
9. fiduciary
10. systemic risk

a. an exchange of interest payments on a specific principal amount
b. a transaction where a company's management team purchases the assets and operations of the business they manage
c. trading financial instruments with the firm's own money
d. the process by which investment bankers raise investment capital from investors on behalf of corporations and governments that are issuing either equity or debt securities
e. a person or an organisation that is responsible for managing money or property for another one
f. the consolidation of companies or assets through various types of financial transactions
g. reduce or eliminate (financial risk)
h. risk that can cause serious problem for a whole system
i. make a formal offer to buy shares at a stated price
j. the working together of two things to produce an effect greater than the sum of their individual effects

B. Complete the following sentences with the words given in the box and change the form of the words where necessary.

accelerate	allocate	complement	concern	dilute
employ	link	oppose	serve	sponsor
separate	substantial			

1. After a merger, the acquired firm ceases to exist as a _____ business entity.
2. The company plans to _____ television programmes as part of its marketing strategy.
3. Stockholders will have a strong preference for variance-increasing projects as _____ to variance-decreasing ones, even if that means a lower NPV.
4. The company will further _____ the exportation of high-end and mid-range Chinese cars by exploring 11 overseas markets in South America, the Middle East, and East Europe.
5. Instinct, intuition, and experience should be viewed as _____ to formal analysis, not substitutes.
6. This system creates a separation between Haier's domestic and international activities, meaning that D-shares issued in Germany do not _____ the share ownership of Haier's

existing Chinese investors in China's domestic market.

7. A global commodity trade hub, which _____ as a year-round trade service platform, began its operation.
8. If the issue is oversubscribed, investors will not be able to buy all of the shares they want, and the underwriters will _____ the shares among investors.
9. This book is _____ with the evolution of investment banking.
10. In this case, the costs associated with selling debt are _____ less than the costs of selling equity.

III. Cloze.

There are 10 blanks in the following two passages. For each blank there are four choices marked A, B, C and D. You are supposed to choose the best answer.

Passage 1

Investment banking enables the financial system to (1)_____ some of its basic functions better and more efficiently, and its evolution is one of the important factors (2)_____ the development of the financial system as a whole. The fundamental functions that the financial system must perform are, firstly, to run and manage the payment clearance and settlement system; secondly, to provide liquidity; thirdly, to (3)_____ savings from surplus units to (4)_____ units; fourthly, to monitor and discipline units using (5)_____ raised funds; and finally, to price, transfer and trade risks.

(1) A. perform   B. undertake   C. take   D. hold
(2) A. have propelled B. propel   C. propelling   D. propelled
(3) A. transcend   B. transport   C. transact   D. transfer
(4) A. lost   B. deficit   C. small   D. few
(5) A. internal   B. internally   C. external   D. externally

Passage 2

A firm can offer its securities to the underwriter on (6)_____ a competitive or a negotiated (7)_____. In a competitive offer, the issuing firm sell its securities to the underwriter with the highest (8)_____. In a negotiated offer, the issuing firm works (9)_____ one underwriter. Because the firm generally does not negotiated with many underwriters, negotiated deals may (10)_____ from lack of competition.

(6) A. either   B. neither   C. both   D. all
(7) A. basin   B. base   C. basis   D. baker
(8) A. bid   B. intent   C. attempt   D. ask
(9) A. for   B. with   C. to   D. against
(10) A. come   B. originate C. benefit   D. suffer

IV. Translate the following sentences into English.

1. 投资银行业务不只限于提供承销服务。(be confined to)
2. 公司从事两种一级市场交易——公募和私募。(engage in)
3. 实际结果与分析师的估算相符。(in line with)

4. 账面价值与市场价值的区别很重要，因为账面价值常常与真实的经济价值相去甚远。(be distinguished from)

5. 如果有足够数量的投资人能够方便地得到所有的可得信息，市场就是有效的。(provided that)

V. Translate the following paragraphs into Chinese.

1. Investment banks are at the heart of new security issues. They provide advice and underwrite the securities. An investment banker's success depends on reputation. A good reputation can help investment bankers retain customers and attract new ones. In other words, financial economists argue that each investment bank has a reservoir of "reputation capital".

2. The traditional "merger math" is that one plus one will be greater than two, that merging two companies will create an entity that is greater than the sum of its parts financially. Executives tend to pay the most attention to that principle, focusing on the financial architecture of the deal. However, the "new" merger math has two pieces to it — economic synergy and psychological synergy.

VI. Self-Testing.

1. Which of the following statements concerning investment banks is NOT true?
   A. An investment bank is a financial intermediary that performs a variety of services.
   B. Investment banks specialize in large and complex financial transactions.
   C. Investment banks' clients include corporations, pension funds, other financial institutions, governments and hedge funds.
   D. Investment banks do not provide retail operations that serve small, individual customers.

2. The most common type of primary distributions is _____.
   A. initial public offerings   B. additional floats of companies' stock
   C. secondary distributions   D. seasoned issues

3. A syndicate is _____.
   A. a group of venture capitalists
   B. a group of investors that are the potential buyers of the firm's stocks
   C. a group of underwriters that share the risk of selling a new issue of securities
   D. a group of banks that loan funds to finance the firm

4. Which of the following statements concerning firm commitment underwriting is NOT true?
   A. It is a purchase-resale arrangement.
   B. The underwriter's fee is the spread.
   C. If the underwriter cannot sell all of the issue at the agreed-upon offering price, it cannot lower the price on the unsold shares.
   D. All the risk associated with selling the issue is transferred to the underwriter.

5. Which of the following statements concerning IPO is NOT true?
   A. It is also called the seasoned new issue.
   B. It is the first public equity issue made by a company.
   C. It occurs when a company decide to go public.
   D. It is a cash offer.

6. _____ is the difference between the underwriter's buying price and the offering price.

A. The gross spread   B. The underwriting amount
   C. The commitment fee   D. The retail brokerage
7. _____ brings together two companies in a similar industry.
   A. Conglomerate merger   B. Horizontal merger
   C. Management buyout   D. Vertical merger
8. Which of the following statements concerning mergers and acquisitions is NOT true?
   A. Mergers and acquisitions are transactions in which the ownership of companies, other business organizations, or their operating units are transferred or consolidated with other entities.
   B. Handling mergers and acquisitions is a key element of an investment bank's work.
   C. The main contribution of an investment bank in a merger or acquisition is evaluating the worth of a possible acquisition and helping parties arrive at a fair price.
   D. An investment bank does not assist in structuring and facilitating the acquisition in order to make the deal go as smoothly as possible.
9. _____ is a sell-side investment banking activity.
   A. Underwriting   B. Facilitating transactions
   C. Market-making   D. All of the above
10. _____ is NOT an investment bank.
    A. Morgan Stanley   B. Goldman Sachs
    C. Barclays Investment Bank D. China Merchants Bank

VII. Writing.

Please write a letter to Morgan Stanley Investment Bank in English as follows.
1. 我方与贵方之间有良好的业务关系。
2. 我方决定增发股票，希望贵方给予支持。出于这一良好的意愿，我方随函附上我方去年的年度报告以供参考。
3. 若贵方有兴趣，请写信告知，以便就有关条款进行进一步磋商。
4. 盼佳音。

Supplementary Reading

A Milestone for Haitong in Global Thrust

By Oswald Chan
(*China Daily* October 15, 2018)

   Haitong International Securities Group — a global financial services institution with an established presence in Hong Kong — has hit a milestone in its international business push, becoming the first Chinese-funded market maker on the US Nasdaq Stock Market.

   The development signals that players in the Chinese securities industry have been fast extending their footprints in the global financial arena.

   Haitong International Securities (USA) Inc — the US unit of Haitong International —

launched its market-making business on the Nasdaq market on Oct. 8, filling the void created by the long absence of a Chinese market maker.

"Market makers are a critical component of the financial ecosystem in the US. The company will first focus on China concept stocks as its major market-making target and adjust its coverage gradually based on the market, as well as the needs of clients in an effort to better serve global investors by linking up the Chinese and overseas markets," said Haitong International Deputy Chairman and Chief Executive Officer Lin Yong.

Nasdaq expects Haitong International's market-maker status to elicit a growing number of investors in the Asia-Pacific region to trade on the US bourse.

In contrast with the designated market maker of the New York Stock Exchange, Nasdaq adopts a multiple market-maker framework. Today, it has become the world's second-largest exchange after the NYSE, with nearly 5,400 companies listed with a total market value of $10 trillion, and trading exceeding $1.2 trillion on average monthly. More than 500 of the listed companies are Chinese enterprises.

Since early this year, Haitong International has been extending its operations in the US, having acquired Qualified Intermediary status with the US Internal Revenue Service and becoming a member of Nasdaq.

It completed the first initial public offering of a Chinese company on the NYSE and the first convertible bond issuance in the US by a Chinese company listed on the Nasdaq in June this year.

Haitong International aims to establish a global platform for investment banking, trading and execution and investment services centering on New York, London, Hong Kong and Singapore to serve its 200,000 clients, and continue to foster its business expansion worldwide in electronic trading, market making, institutional client services and investment banking services.

In the first half of this year, Haitong International recorded revenues of HK$3.56 billion — up nearly 21 percent from a year ago. However, its net profit fell 17 percent to HK$859 million in the same period. Haitong International was established in 1996 and was listed in Hong Kong in 2012.

Haitong International's parent company — Haitong Securities Co — was founded in 1988 and is a major securities firm in China, providing services in stocks and futures brokerage, as well as investment banking, corporate finance, mergers and acquisitions, asset management, mutual fund, and private equity.

The parent company was listed on the Shanghai Stock Exchange in 2007 and currently holds a 62.43-percent stake in Haitong International.

As China further opens up its financial market, the nation's securities firms have been venturing abroad to expand their operations. They include China International Capital Corp and CICC Securities, which had set foot in the US market earlier, focusing primarily on sell-side businesses, such as providing underwriting services and advising clients on mergers and acquisitions.

CICC US Securities — CICC's US branch — opened an office in New York in 2009, and CICC became the first Chinese broker — dealer to provide services for securities listed on US exchanges in 2010.

China's securities industry watchdog — the China Securities Regulatory Commission — last month revised relevant regulations regarding securities firms and fund-management companies embarking on overseas business expansion.

It stipulated that Chinese securities companies' net asset size must be not less than 6 billion *yuan* if they want to expand their businesses overseas. For fund managers, the net asset threshold is set at not less than 600 million *yuan*. Both must continue operating their businesses for at least two years.

Questions

1. What is the role of market makers on the US Nasdaq Stock Market?
2. How did Haitong International become a market marker on the US Nasdaq Stock Market?
3. What is Haitong International's aim?
4. What are the services provided by Haitong Securities Co?
5. What is the Chinese Securities Regulatory Commission's requirements for companies that want to expand their businesses overseas?

Unit 10　Financial Services

Case

John is a successful owner of a small business. He wants to plan for his family's financial future. He had his first child, Jerry, at the age of thirty-five. He plans to send Jerry to expensive private schools and he doesn't want to have trouble paying school tuition. He also wants to make sure that he and his wife can live a comfortable life during retirement. John is going to visit various local banks and other financial institutions, looking for services which can meet his needs.

Questions

1. List some services which can meet John's needs.
2. What are the different types of services offered by financial-service providers?

Preview

Skimming

Skim the following text quickly to answer the following questions and discuss your answers with your partners.

1. Name one important financial-service provider.
   _____
   _____.

2. List at least five services offered by banks throughout history.
   _____
   _____.

3. List at least five services offered by banks and other financial institutions more recently.
   _____
   _____.

4. What has been the biggest banking service target in recent years?
   _____
   _____.

5. Why are financial services more convenient for customers today?
   _____
   _____.

Scanning

Scan the following text quickly to find the specific information.

1. Name one of the first services offered by banks.
   _____
   _____.

2. How much did banks in ancient Greece pay to attract savings deposits from wealthy patrons?
   _____
   _____.

3. Which financial service was developed during the Industrial Revolution?
   _____
   _____.

4. Which financial service should be resorted to, if a business customer wants to consult about marketing opportunities?
   _____
   _____.

5. Which financial service should be resorted to, if a business customer wants to acquire a certain piece of equipment immediately but pay for it over time?
   _____
   _____.

6. Which act tore down the legal barriers between banking and insurance in the United States?
   _____
   _____.

7. Which financial service deals in marketing new securities to raise funds for corporations and other institutions?
   _____
   _____.

8. Name one goal of mutual funds.
   _____
   _____.

Vocabulary in Context

Read the following sentences and try to guess the meaning of the italicized words by using the context. Then replace the italicized words with synonyms (words or phrases that have nearly the same or similar meanings).

1. Their success *hinges on* their ability to identify the financial services the public demands, produce those services efficiently, and sell them at a competitive price.
   Their success _____ their ability to identify the financial services the public demands, produce those services efficiently, and sell them at a competitive price.

2. These financial firms would *assay* the market value of their customers' valuables, especially gold and jewelry, and certify whether or not these "valuables" were worth what others had claimed.
   These financial firms would _____ the market value of their customers' valuables, especially gold and jewelry, and certify whether or not these "valuables" were worth what

others had claimed.

3. Frequently banks were chartered under the *proviso* that they would purchase government bonds with a portion of the deposits they received.

   Frequently banks were chartered under the _____ that they would purchase government bonds with a portion of the deposits they received.

4. Providers of this service typically act as trustees for wills, managing a *deceased* customer's estate by paying claims against that estate, keeping valuable assets safe, and seeing to it that legal heirs receive their rightful inheritance.

   Providers of this service typically act as trustees for wills, managing a _____ customer's estate by paying claims against that estate, keeping valuable assets safe, and seeing to it that legal heirs receive their rightful inheritance.

5. Congress acted out of fear that selling insurance would increase bank risk and lead to conflicts of interest in which customers asking for one service would be *compelled* to buy other services as well.

   Congress acted out of fear that selling insurance would increase bank risk and lead to conflicts of interest in which customers asking for one service would be _____ to buy other services as well.

6. Today, these two industries are competing *aggressively* with each other, pursuing cross-industry mergers and acquisition.

   Today, these two industries are competing _____ with each other, pursuing cross-industry mergers and acquisition.

7. Banks, trust departments, mutual funds, and insurance companies are active in managing the retirement plans that most businesses make available to their employees, investing incoming funds and *dispensing* payments to qualified recipients who have reached retirement or become disabled.

   Banks, trust departments, mutual funds, and insurance companies are active in managing the retirement plans that most businesses make available to their employees, investing incoming funds and _____ payments to qualified recipients who have reached retirement or become disabled.

8. Annuities consist of long-term savings plans that promise the payment of a stream of income to the annuity holder beginning on a *designated* future date (e.g., at retirement).

   Annuities consist of long-term savings plans that promise the payment of a stream of income to the annuity holder beginning on a _____ future date (e.g., at retirement).

9. In practice, merchant banking services often *encompass* the identification of possible merger targets for a corporate customer, providing the customer with strategic marketing advice.

   In practice, merchant banking services often _____ the identification of possible merger targets for a corporate customer, providing the customer with strategic marketing advice.

10. This popular financial service has led to *phenomenal* growth in such risk-hedging tools as swaps, options, and future contracts.

    This popular financial service has led to _____ growth in such risk-hedging tools as swaps, options, and future contracts.

Text

Services Offered by Banks and Other Financial-Service Providers

Banks, like their neighboring competitors, are financial-service providers. As such, they play a number of important roles in the economy. Their success hinges on their ability to identify the financial services the public demands, produce those services efficiently, and sell them at a competitive price. What services does the public demand from banks and their financial-service competitors today?

Services Offered Throughout History

Carrying Out Currency Exchanges

History reveals that one of the first services banks offered was currency exchange. A banker stood ready to trade one form of coin or currency for another in return for a service fee. Such exchanges have been important to travelers over the centuries, because the traveler's survival and comfort may depend on gaining access to local funds. In today's financial marketplace, trading in foreign currency is conducted primarily by the largest financial-service firms due to the risks involved and the expense required to carry out the transactions.

Discounting Commercial Notes and Making Business Loans

Early in history, bankers began discounting commercial notes — in effect, making loans to local merchants who sold the debts they held against their customers to a bank to raise cash quickly. It was a short step from discounting commercial notes to making direct loans for purchasing inventories of goods or for constructing new facilities — a service that today is provided by banks, finance companies, insurance firms, and other financial-service competitors.

Offering Savings Deposits

Making loans proved so profitable that banks began searching for ways to raise additional loanable funds. One of the earliest sources of these funds consisted of offering savings deposits — interest-bearing funds left with depository institutions for a period of time. According to some historical records, banks in ancient Greece paid as high as 16 percent in annual interest to attract savings deposits from wealthy patrons and then made loans to ship owners sailing the Mediterranean Sea at loan rates double or triple the rate bankers were paying to their savings deposit customers.

Safekeeping of Valuables and Certification of Value

During the Middle Ages[1], banks and other merchants began the practice of holding gold and other valuables owned by their customers inside secure vaults, thus reassuring customers of their safekeeping[2]. These financial firms would assay the market value of their customers' valuables, especially gold and jewelry, and certify whether or not these "valuables" were worth what others had claimed.

Supporting Government Activities with Credit

During the Middle Ages and the early years of the Industrial Revolution[3], governments in Europe noted bankers' ability to mobilize large amounts of funds. Frequently banks were chartered under the proviso that they would purchase government bonds with a portion of the deposits they received.

Offering Checking Accounts (Demand Deposits)

The Industrial Revolution ushered in new financial services and new service providers. Probably the most important of the new services developed during this period was the demand deposit — a checking account that permitted the depositor to write drafts[4] in payment for goods and services that the bank or other service provider had to honor[5] immediately. Demand deposit services proved to be one of the financial-service industry's most important offerings because it significantly improved the efficiency of the payments process, making transactions easier, faster, and safer. Today the checking account concept has been extended to the Internet, to the use of plastic debit cards[6] that tap your checking account electronically, and to "smart cards" that electronically store spending power. Today, payment-on-demand accounts are offered not only by banks, but also by savings associations, credit unions, securities firms, and other financial-service providers.

Offering Trust Services

For many years, banks and a few of their competitors have managed the financial affairs and property of individuals and business firms in return for a fee. This property management function is known as trust[7] services. Providers of this service typically act as trustees for wills, managing a deceased customer's estate by paying claims against that estate, keeping valuable assets safe, and seeing to it that legal heirs receive their rightful inheritance. In commercial trust departments, trust-service providers manage security portfolios and pension plans for businesses and act as agents for corporations issuing stocks and bonds.

Services Banks and Other Financial-Service Providers Offered More Recently

Granting Consumer Loans

Historically, banks did not actively pursue loan accounts from individuals and families, believing that the relatively small size of most consumer loans and their relatively high default[8] rate would make such lending unprofitable. Early in the 20th century, however, bankers began to rely more heavily on consumers for deposits to help fund their large corporate loans. In addition, heavy competition for business deposits and loans caused bankers increasingly to turn to the consumer as a potentially more loyal customer. Following World War II, consumer loans were among the fastest-growing forms of bank credit.

Financial Advising

Customers have long asked financial institutions for advice, particularly when it comes to the use of credit and the saving or investing of funds. Many service providers today offer a wide range of financial advisory services, from helping to prepare tax returns and financial plans for individuals to consulting about marketing opportunities at home and abroad for business customers.

Managing Cash

Over the years, financial institutions have found that some of the services they provide for themselves are also valuable for their customers. One of the most prominent is cash management services, in which a financial intermediary agrees to handle cash collections[9] and disbursements[10] for a business firm and to invest any temporary cash surpluses in interest-bearing assets until cash is needed to pay bills. Although banks tend to specialize mainly in business cash management services, many financial institutions are offering similar services to customers.

Offering Equipment Leasing

Many banks and finance companies have moved aggressively to offer their business customers the option to purchase equipment through a lease[11] arrangement in which the lending institution buys the equipment and rents it to the customer. These equipment leasing services benefit leasing institutions as well as their customers.

Making Venture Capital Loans

Increasingly, banks, security dealers, and other financial conglomerates[12] have become active in financing the start-up costs[13] of new companies. Because of the added risk involved in such loans, this is generally done through a separate venture capital firm that raises money from investors to support young businesses in the hope of turning a profit when those firms are sold or go public.

Selling Insurance Policies

For many years, bankers have sold credit life insurance to their customers receiving loans, guaranteeing repayment if borrowers die or become disabled. Moreover, during the 19th and early 20th centuries, many bankers sold insurance and provided financial advice to their customers, literally serving as the local community's all-around financial-service store. However, beginning with the Great Depression[14] of the 1930s, U.S. banks were prohibited from acting as insurance agents or underwriting insurance policies. Congress acted out of fear that selling insurance would increase bank risk and lead to conflicts of interest in which customers asking for one service would be compelled to buy other services as well. Many bankers arranged to have insurance companies sell policies to customers by renting space in bank lobbies. This picture of extreme separation between banking and insurance changed dramatically in 1999 when the U.S. Congress passed the Gramm-Leach-Bliley Act[15] and tore down the legal barriers between the two industries, allowing bank holding companies to acquire control of insurance companies and, conversely, permitting insurance companies to acquire banks. Today, these two industries are competing aggressively with each other, pursuing cross-industry mergers[16] and acquisitions[17].

Selling Retirement Plans

Banks, trust departments, mutual funds, and insurance companies are active in managing the retirement plans that most businesses make available to their employees, investing incoming funds and dispensing payments to qualified recipients who have reached retirement or become disabled.

Banks and other depository institutions sell retirement plans to individuals holding these deposits until the funds are needed for income after retirement.

Dealing in Securities: Offering Security Brokerage and Investment Banking Services

One of the biggest of all banking service targets in recent years, particularly in the United States, has been dealing in securities, executing buy and sell orders for security trading customers (referred to as security brokerage services) and marketing new securities to raise funds for corporations and other institutions (referred to as security underwriting or investment banking services).

Offering Mutual Funds and Annuities

Many customers have come to demand investment products from their financial-service providers. Mutual fund investments and annuities that offer the prospect of higher yields than the returns often available on conventional bank deposits are among the most sought-after investment products. However, these product lines also tend to carry more risk than do bank deposits.

Annuities consist of long-term savings plans that promise the payment of a stream of income to the annuity holder beginning on a designated future date (e.g., at retirement). In contrast, mutual funds are professionally managed investment programs that acquire stocks, bonds, and other assets that appear to "fit" the funds' announced goals (such as to maximize current income or to achieve long-term capital appreciation).

Offering Merchant Banking Services

Financial-service providers are offering merchant banking services to larger corporations. These consist of the temporary purchase of corporate stock to aid the launching of a new business venture or to support the expansion of an existing company. Hence, a merchant banker becomes a temporary stockholder and bears the risk that the stock purchased may decline in value. In practice, merchant banking services often encompass the identification of possible merger targets for a corporate customer, providing the customer with strategic marketing advice.

Offering Risk Management and Hedging Services

Many observers see fundamental changes going on in the banking sector with larger banks moving away from a traditionally heavy emphasis on deposit-taking and loan-making toward risk intermediation — providing their customers with financial tools to combat risk exposure in return for substantial fees. The largest banks around the globe now dominate the risk-hedging field, either acting as dealers (i.e., serving as "market makers") in arranging for risk protection for the banks' customers from third parties or directly selling their customers the bank's own risk-protection contracts (i.e., acting as "matched traders") in which banks take on their customers' risk exposure and find creative ways to protect their own institutions from that exposure. This popular financial service has led to phenomenal growth in such risk-hedging tools as swaps, options, and future contracts.

Convenience: The Sum of All Banking and Financial Services

It should be clear from the list of services we have described that not only are banks and their financial-service competitors offering a wide array of comparable services today, but that service menu is growing rapidly. New service delivery methods like the Internet, cell phones, and smart cards with digital cash are expanding and whole new service lines are being launched every year. Viewed as a whole, the impressive array of services offered and the service delivery channels used by modern financial institutions add up to greater convenience for their customers.

Terminology

currency exchange	货币兑换
discount	贴现
commercial note	商业票据
business loan	工商业贷款
safekeeping	保管
debit card	借记卡
smart card	智能卡
trust	信托
trustee	受托人
consumer loan	消费贷款
financial advising	财务咨询
cash management	现金管理
leasing	租赁
lease agreement	租赁协议
security brokerage	证券经纪
security underwriting	证券承销
annuity	年金
merchant banking	商人银行业务
risk management	风险管理

Notes on the Text

1. Middle Ages — a period of European history that lasted from the 5th to the 15th centuries. The Middle Ages is the middle period of the traditional division of Western history into Classical, Medieval, and Modern periods. (中世纪)
2. safekeeping — storage and protection of a customer's financial assets, valuables, or documents, provided as a service by an institution serving as agent and, where control is delegated by the customer, also as custodian.
3. Industrial Revolution — the transition to new manufacturing processes that occurred in the period from about 1760 to some time between 1820 and 1840. This transition included going

from hand production methods to machines, new chemical manufacturing and iron production processes, improved efficiency of water power, increasing use of steam power and development of machine tools. The transition also included the change from wood and other bio-fuels to coal. The Industrial Revolution began in Britain and within a few decades spread to Western Europe and the United States. (工业革命)

4. draft — signed, written order by which one party instructs another party to pay a specified sum to a third party. (汇票)

5. honor — to pay a check, bill of exchange, or promissory note when it becomes due. (承兑)

6. debit card — an electronic card issued by a bank which allows bank clients access to their account to withdraw cash or pay for goods and services. This removes the need for bank clients to go to the bank to remove cash from their account as they can just go to an ATM or pay electronically at merchant locations. This type of card, as a form of payment, also removes the need for checks as the debit card immediately transfers money from the client's account to the business account.

7. trust — fiduciary relationship in which a person, called a trustee, holds title to property for the benefit of another person, called a beneficiary. The agreement that establishes the trust, contains its provisions, and sets forth the powers of the trustee is called the trust indenture. The person creating the trust is the creator, settler, grantor, or donor. The property itself is called the corpus, trust res, trust fund, or trust estate, which is distinguished from any income earned by it. The trustee is usually charged with investing trust property productively and, unless specifically limited, can sell, mortgage, or lease the property as he or she deems warranted.

8. default — failure of a debtor to make timely payments of interest and principal as they come due or to meet some other provision of a bond indenture. (违约)

9. collection — obtaining payment. (收款)

10. disbursement — paying money in the discharge of a debt or an expense, as distinguished from a distribution. (支付)

11. lease — a contract granting use of real estate, equipment, or other fixed assets for a specified time in exchange for payment, usually in the form of rent. The owner of the leased property is called the lessor, the user the lessee.

12. conglomerate — a group of companies resulting from a conglomerate merger. (跨行业公司、集团公司)

13. start-up costs — the capital needed to be spent in starting a business before it begins trading.

14. Great Depression — an economic recession that began on October 29, 1929, following the crash of the U.S. stock market. The Great Depression originated in the United States, but quickly spread to Europe and the rest of the world. The Depression caused massive levels of poverty, hunger, unemployment and political unrest. (大萧条)

15. Gramm-Leach-Bliley Act — law enacted on November 12, 1999, also known as the Financial Services Modernization Act of 1999, which repealed parts of the Glass-Steagall Act of 1933 and the Bank Holding Company Act of 1956, eliminating remaining firewalls

between banks, securities firms, and insurance companies. (《格雷姆-里奇-比利雷法案》)

16. merger — the combining of two or more companies, generally by offering the stockholders of one company securities in the acquiring company in exchange for the surrender of their stock. This decision is usually mutual between both firms. (兼并)

17. acquisition — a corporate action in which a company buys most, if not all, of the target company's ownership stakes in order to assume control of the target firm. Acquisitions are often made as part of a company's growth strategy whereby it is more beneficial to take over an existing firm's operations and niche compared to expanding on its own. Acquisitions are often paid in cash, the acquiring company's stock or a combination of both. Acquisitions can be either friendly or hostile. (收购)

Exercises

I. Reading Comprehension.

Read the text carefully and decide whether the following statements are true (T) or false (F).

___ 1. Banks and other financial-service providers are undergoing changes in function.
___ 2. Safekeeping is not a traditional service offered by banks.
___ 3. Banks always actively pursue loan accounts from individuals and families throughout history.
___ 4. Some financial services offered used to be services financial institutions provided for themselves.
___ 5. One of the principal services offered by banks and other financial-service providers is assisting customers in raising new funds and investing those funds profitably.

II. Vocabulary Building.

A. Match the term in Column A with the definition in Column B.

1. annuity   a. purchase or sell a commercial paper at a reduction equal to the amount of interest that will accumulate before it matures

2. cash management   b. individual or organization that holds and manages assets for the benefit of another

3. debit card   c. card with embedded integrated circuits
4. discount   d. level stream of cash flows occurring for a fixed period of time

5. hedging   e. card issued by a bank to allow customers access to their funds electronically

6. leasing   f. fiduciary relationship in which an individual or organization holds and manages assets for the benefit of another

7. safekeeping   g. strategy used to offset investment risk

8. smart card   h. storage and protection of customers' assets
9. trust   i. activity that grants use of a property for a specified time in exchange for payment
10. trustee   j. efficient mobilization of cash into income-producing applications

B. Complete the following sentences with the words given in the box and change the form of the words where necessary.

aid	certify	charter	dominate
execute	extend	option	practice
prominent	qualified	reveal	valuable

1. Figures from the Bank of England _____ that banks wrote off huge losses on their credit card customers.
2. The first bankers were money changers who _____ travelers by exchanging foreign coins for local money or discounting commercial notes for a fee.
3. The new policy encourages _____ international investors to join the restructuring and reforming of China's banking and financial institutions on a voluntary and commercial basis.
4. Banks invest time and money in training employees to make good decisions about when and to whom to _____ credit and how to make sound financial decisions.
5. Credit unions were first _____ in Germany, providing savings accounts and low-cost credit to industrial workers.
6. One may think of a bank vault or a safe-deposit box when he thinks of safeguarding money, and those on-site measures are certainly ways of protecting _____ assets.
7. Banks devote much time and attention to both the _____ and technology of maintaining and storing accurate records.
8. Career _____ available in the commercial banking sector include bank tellers, loan officers, operations, marketing and branch managers.
9. Banks _____ profits of A-share listed financial firms; 16 banks contributed almost 93 percent of the first-quarter profits of the 50 A-share listed financial service companies.
10. Hedge funds often employ the services of "prime brokerage" divisions at major investment banks to _____ their trades.

III. Cloze.

There are 10 blanks in the following two passages. For each blank there are four choices marked A, B, C and D. You are supposed to choose the best answer.

Passage 1

Every business, no matter how large or small, needs to (1)_____ and collect cash to complete business transactions. Banks are in a good position to provide cash management services to businesses for a number of (2)_____.

• *Experience:* Banks have decades of experience in managing cash.

- *Business Knowledge:* In conducting their own operations, banks (3)_____ the same opportunities and challenges that all businesses face, and they understand the nature and implementation of practices and policies that apply to efficient cash management for all businesses.
- *Technology:* Banks have experience in applying technology to their cash management practices. Banks can afford to invest (4)_____ the applicable technology and develop expertise in its use that most individual firms cannot.
- *Industry* (5)_____: Through their dealing with specific companies over the years, individual banks have developed expert knowledge of the practices of various industries.

(1) A. dispense   B. distribute   C. disburse   D. distinguish
(2) A. causes   B. reasons   C. aspects   D. perspectives
(3) A. will experience   B. will have experienced
     C. have experienced   D. had experienced
(4) A. at   B. on   C. for   D. in
(5) A. Experience   B. Expertness   C. Expert   D. Expertise

Passage 2

A credit card is a payment card that (6)_____ by merchants. Credit cards offer revolving lines of credit to cardholders, (7)_____ means they have the ability to pay balances over time. While debit cards and credit cards are alike in appearance, they differ in one critical aspect: A debit card (8)_____ money from a bank account, while a credit card creates a loan. Think of them as "pay now" (debit) versus "pay later" (credit). Today's debit card users often have the choice of (9)_____ transactions by either PIN or signature. While that choice often makes (10)_____ difference to the consumers, it makes a great deal of difference to the merchants and transaction processors. A PIN transaction uses one payment system; the signature uses another.

(6) A. accept   B. accepted   C. is accepted   D. have accepted
(7) A. that   B. it   C. which   D. what
(8) A. withdraws   B. extracts   C. receives   D. retreats
(9) A. getting   B. dealing   C. paying   D. authorizing
(10) A. no   B. many   C. few   D. a great deal of

IV. Translate the following sentences into English.

1. 这项计划将开辟消费支出的数字时代。(usher in)
2. 据报道，投资银行的巨大亏损将会导致这一行业的重组。(lead to)
3. 1933年，罗斯福总统签署了一项法令以应对美国银行业的危机。(deal)
4. 近期的调查显示，顾客需要更好的信用卡在线服务。(demand)
5. 值得注意的是，这个卫星城将被打造成一个全新的金融服务区。(note)

V. Translate the following paragraphs into Chinese.

1. Off-balance sheet items are contingent assets and liabilities that may affect the future status of a financial institution's balance sheet. Off-balance sheet activities are less obvious and often

invisible to financial statement readers because they usually appear as footnotes to accounts. Although off-balance sheet activities are now an important source of fee income for many financial institutions, they have potential to produce positive as well as negative future cash flows. Efficient management of off-balance sheet items is central to a financial institution's control of overall risk exposure.

2. Banks offering international services help their customers negotiate, finance, transfer, and collect their international accounts. Specialists in international finance and the export-import business help clients make their way through the sea of documents. There are numerous forms of trade financing for international business. Some may take the form of simple domestic loans to an import or other international venture. Some may be direct loans to foreign governments through government-run banks or industries. Using their expertise, banks can help companies assess both their prospects and risks in international commerce and help companies with paperwork associated with international transactions.

VI. Self-Testing.

1. Generally speaking, the relationship between a bank and its client in intermediary services is a _____ one.

   A. principle-agent   B. debtor-creditor   C. bailor-bailee   D. employer-employee

2. In safekeeping services, the relationship between a bank and its client is a _____ one.

   A. principle-agent   B. debtor-creditor   C. bailor-bailee   D. employer-employee

3. _____ is a short-term financing from the nonrecourse sale of accounts receivable to a third party, known as a factor, usually a bank holding company or the bank itself.

   A. Lease   B. Trust service   C. Factoring   D. Forfeiting

4. A _____ is an unconditional promise in writing made by one person (the maker) to another (the payee or the holder), signed by the maker engaging to pay on demand or at a fixed or determinable future time a sum certain in money to, or to the order of a specified person or to bearer.

   A. bank draft   B. bill of exchange

   C. check   D. promissory note

5. Which of the following statement is NOT true?

   A. A bill of exchange is an order, while a promissory note is a promise to pay.

   B. Both a bill of exchange and a promissory note can be accepted.

   C. The maker of a promissory note is always the party primarily liable for payment.

   D. There are only two original parties to the transaction in the case of a promissory note.

6. The advantages of using credit cards to pay for goods and services include _____.

   A. convenience and security   B. increased sales

   C. revenue from the card business   D. all of the above

7. Which of the following statements is NOT true?

   A. Banks set different credit lines for the different groups of credit cardholders.

   B. Debit cards are used in conjunction with a current bank account.

   C. All banks charge an annual fee on both credit cards and debit cards.

D. Intelligent card is another name for smart card.
8. Which of the following is NOT a party involved in the establishment of a trust?
   A. The trustor.   B. The trustee.   C. The beneficiary.   D. The creditor.
9. _____ are deposits made by one person as trustee for the other person.
   A. Time deposits   B. Trust deposits
   C. Demand deposits   D. Transaction deposits
10. Which of the following statements concerning a capital lease is true?
    A. The lessor never transfers ownership of the property to the lessee by the end of the lease term.
    B. The lessee has an option to purchase the leased property at a bargain price.
    C. The lease term is equal to or less than 75 percent of the estimated economic life of the leased property.
    D. The present value of rental and other minimum lease payments is equal to or less than 90 percent of the fair value of the leased property less any investments tax credit retained by the lessor.

VII. Writing.

Please write a letter to HSBC in English as follows.
1. 我行伦敦办事处已向我方发了信用证(No.K4638703)项下的贷记通知书(No.120260-T-15)。我方发现我方账户被贷记金额为33230.00英镑，而不是我方当时电索的33320.00英镑，两者差额为90.00英镑。请对方调查相关情况，把差额迅速付至我方账户，并通知我方。
2. 感谢对方的合作。

Supplementary Reading

Banks to Balance Social Responsibility with Risk Prevention

By Chen Jia
(*China Daily* October 19, 2018)

Chinese financial institutions have vowed to strengthen financial support for poverty-stricken areas while mitigating against debt default risks, as an important element of the country's antipoverty battle.

"Financial institutions need to better balance the relationship between fulfilling social responsibility and preventing financial risks," said Liu Guoqiang, the central bank's vice-governor, at a meeting held in Jinping county in Guizhou province last week.

He called for higher attention to be paid to potential risks in anti-poverty programs, while continuing to earmark financial resources for poverty alleviation-related investment.

Measures will include utilizing the agricultural credit guarantee mechanism to diversify risks; encouraging local governments to effectively integrate fiscal capital and increasing subsidies on interest payments on loans related to poverty alleviation; and establishing risk compensation and guarantee funds.

"(The measures) should remove financial institutions' concerns about loan quality, and promote the proactive issuing of loans," Liu said.

Leaders from 22 financial institutions —Including regulatory bodies, policy and commercial banks, and insurance and asset management companies — gathered at the meeting in Jinping, sharing their achievements in supporting 64 poverty-stricken counties to improve the local people's quality of life, especially in terms of education and healthcare.

The equity market could also play an important role in channeling more capital into the real economy and supporting less-developed regions, said Zhao Zhengping, vice-chairman of the China Securities Regulatory Commission.

In September 2017, the CSRC issued guidelines to encourage the capital market to better support the national anti-poverty program. Since then, 12 companies from poverty-stricken areas have successfully issued A shares on mainland stock markets through a special mechanism called the Green Channel. Together they have raised a total of 6.9 billion *yuan* ($997 million) from the capital market.

Another 66 companies are preparing IPOs, while 98 companies have already listed on the National Equities Exchange and Quotations, known as the New Third Board, according to CSRC data.

During the past five years, financial institutions have invested nearly 33.1 billion *yuan* — in the form of bank loans, funds and risk security funds — into nationwide antipoverty programs, helping more than 720,000 people, the central bank vice-governor said.

China aims to lift all of its citizens out of poverty by 2020. As of the end of 2017, the country had 30 million poor residents, compared with 98.99 million in 2012, according to the National Bureau of Statistics.

Although some of those 30 million people have risen out of extreme poverty, many still struggle to meet their basic daily needs.

In addition to expanding financing channels, many state-owned financial institutions have also transferred managers to local governments, where they have become officials in counties and towns in less-developed regions.

Financial institutions are also introducing new technologies, including e-commerce and fintech, in rural areas to support industrial and business development based on innovative models, according to the speeches delivered at the meeting in Jinping.

Questions

1. What social responsibilities do the Chinese financial institutions take?
2. What are the potential risks involved in the anti-poverty programs?
3. What measures are taken to prevent risks in the anti-poverty programs?
4. What measures are taken to help the poverty-stricken areas?
5. Why is it important for Chinese financial institutions to balance their social responsibilities and risk prevention?

Unit 11　Loans

Case

Tom owns a small company which functions well, and he wants to enlarge his business. But unfortunately, he lacks money to purchase enough facilities and production line. His friends advise him to resort to commercial banks for help. With no idea about loans, Tom goes to several banks and commercial institutions to find out more specific information about loans. He hopes that banks can help him raise enough funds.

Questions

1. Do you know anything about loans?
2. How many kinds of loans do you know, and what kind do you think Tom should choose?

Preview

Skimming

Skim the following text quickly to answer the following questions and discuss your answers with your partners.

1. What is a loan?
   _____
   _____.
2. How many major loan categories are introduced in the text? And what are they?
   _____
   _____.
3. What are the six steps involved to get an individual loan?
   _____
   _____.
4. What is credit review?
   _____
   _____.
5. What are the five loan classifications by risks?
   _____
   _____.

Scanning

Scan the following text quickly to find the specific information.

1. Who borrowed money heavily in feudal European society?
   _____
   _____.

2. In a syndicated loan, who is responsible for the credit risk?
   _____
   _____.

3. What are the two kinds of export credit?
   _____
   _____.

4. What is the usual purpose of consumer loans?
   _____
   _____.

5. What is the fundamental objective of lending?
   _____
   _____.

6. How many components are there in loan disbursement?
   _____
   _____.

7. What does the process of credit review include?
   _____
   _____.

8. What is the purpose of designing the early warning sytem?
   _____
   _____.

Vocabulary in Context

Read the following sentences and try to guess the meaning of the italicized words by using the context. Then replace the italicized words with synonyms (words or phrases that have nearly the same or similar meanings).

1. A loan may be payable on demand (a demand loan), in equal monthly installments (an installment loan), or it may be *good* until further notice or due at maturity (a time loan).

   A loan may be payable on demand (a demand loan), in equal monthly installments (an installment loan), or it may be _____ until further notice or due at maturity (a time loan).

2. The negotiating or "lead" bank wins the "*mandate*" from a number of competitors and underwrites a large portion of the credit and is responsible for organizing the syndication.

   The negotiating or "lead" bank wins the "_____" from a number of competitors and underwrites a large portion of the credit and is responsible for organizing the syndication.

3. Consumer loans' usual purpose is to *finance* the purchase of durable goods.

   Consumer loans' usual purpose is to _____ the purchase of durable goods.

4. Most loans have maturities from one to five years, are repaid in installment, and *carry* a fixed interest rate.

   Most loans have maturities from one to five years, are repaid in installment, and _____ a fixed interest rate.

5. The somewhat competing goals of loan *volume* and loan quality must be balanced with the

bank's liquidity requirements, capital constrains, and rate of return objectives.

The somewhat competing goals of loan _____ and loan quality must be balanced with the bank's liquidity requirements, capital constrains, and rate of return objectives.

6. If any client wants a bank to issue a letter of loan *intent*, then the bank will conduct a preliminary investigation.

   If any client wants a bank to issue a letter of loan _____, then the bank will conduct a preliminary investigation.

7. This agreement formalizes the purpose of the loan, the terms, repayment schedule, collateral required, and any loan *covenants*.

   This agreement formalizes the purpose of the loan, the terms, repayment schedule, collateral required, and any loan _____.

8. Recalling a loan is normally a last *resort* and done only when the borrower does not voluntarily correct the problem.

   Recalling a loan is normally a last _____ and done only when the borrower does not voluntarily correct the problem.

9. After credit review, the bank will find out early warning signals and take remedial measures to *mitigate* risks.

   After credit review, the bank will find out early warning signals and take remedial measures to _____ risks.

10. Early warning signals are *omens* or symptoms that a client may not be able to repay the principal and interest in time or service the loan.

    Early warning signals are _____ or symptoms that a client may not be able to repay the principal and interest in time or service the loan.

Text

Loans

Definition

A loan is a sum of money advanced to a borrower, to be repaid at a later date, usually with interest. Legally, a loan is a contract between a buyer (the borrower) and a seller (the lender), enforceable under relevant law. The terms and conditions for repayment of a loan, including the finance charge or interest rate, are specified in a loan agreement. A loan may be payable on demand (a demand loan[1]), in equal monthly installments[2] (an installment loan), or it may be good until further notice or due at maturity[3] (a time loan). More generally, loan refers to anything given on condition of its return or repayment of its equivalent. A loan may be acknowledged by a bond, a promissory note, or a mere oral promise to repay. Because of biblical injunction against usury, the early Christian church forbade the taking of interest. In feudal European society, loans were little needed by the great mass of relatively self-sufficient and noncommercial peasants and serfs, but kings, nobles, and ecclesiastics were heavy borrowers for personal expenditures. Merchants and other townsmen, especially the Jews, were the moneylenders, and various devices were found for circumventing the prohibition of usury. With the rise of a commercial society, restrictions on the taking of interest were gradually relaxed. Today, banks and finance companies make most loans, usually on collateral, such as stocks, personal effects, and mortgages on land and other property, or on assignments of wages.

A loan is also a type of debt. All material things can be lent but the loan we talked here focuses exclusively on monetary loans. Like all debt instruments, a loan entails the redistribution of financial assets over time, between the lender and the borrower. The borrower initially receives an amount of money from the lender, which may be paid back, usually but not always in regular installments, to the lender. This service is generally provided at a cost, referred to as interest on the debt.

Major Loan Categories

There are several main kinds of loan, which are working capital loans and fixed asset loans, syndicated loan[4], export credit[5], consumer loans, personal residential mortgage loans and overseas fund-raising and on-lending.

Working capital loans are used to fill clients' short-term needs for funds, for projects within the business scope before medium- and long-term loan contracts have been completed. Working capital[6] loan has high liquidity[7], which is applicable to the industrial and commercial customers with medium- and short-term needs. Examples include: preparatory funds, funding for equipment, materials and other costs covered by budget estimates, advances to cover temporary funding shortages before supporting funds are in place, and short-term loans for production and operation. Fixed asset[8] loan refers to loans granted by the bank to meet the demands of enterprises in their investments in fixed asset. Investments by enterprises in fixed assets include capital construction, technical innovation, developing and manufacturing of new products as well as related house purchase, civil engineering, purchase and installation of technical equipment, etc.

A syndicated loan is a very large loan arranged by a lead bank among a single borrower and a group of other banks that are parties to the original credit agreement. These syndicate banks share in credit information and credit risk. It's a large credit, generally more than USD10 million, negotiated between a borrower and a single bank, but actually funded by several banks. The negotiating or "lead" bank wins the "mandate" from a number of competitors and underwrites a large portion of the credit and is responsible for organizing which including inviting other banks to act as manager/co-manager in providing additional underwriting support to the credit before going to market for general syndication to the "participants". The resulting credit is governed by a single loan agreement signed by the borrower and all of the banks involved.

Export credit is government (export credit agencies, e.g., Export-import Bank of the United States) guaranteed lending channeled through a commercial bank to support export trade. There are two kinds of export credit: buyer credit and supplier credit. In buyer credit, exporter's bank provides loans to the importer (importer's bank guarantees) or to importer's bank, which on-lends the loan to the importer. In supplier credit, exporter's bank provides loans to the supplier (exporter) to finance the contract with special payment terms under which importer pays for the contract goods by half-yearly installment. Such terms require the issuance of bill of exchange by the supplier for pre-acceptance by the buyer/borrower. The usual terms and conditions of supplier credit are the same as those of buyer credit.

Consumer loans' usual purpose is to finance the purchase of durable goods, although many individuals borrow to finance education, medical care, and other expenses. The average loan to each borrower is relatively small. Most loans have maturities from one to five years, are repaid in installment, and carry a fixed interest rate. Consumer loans are usually classified as installment, credit card, or non-installment loan. Installment loans require a partial payment of principal plus interest periodically until maturity. Other consumer loans require either a single payment of all interest plus principal or a gradual repayment at the borrower's discretion, as with a credit line[9]. Non-installment loans are for special purpose in which the individual normally expects a large cash receipt to repay the debt, such as a temporary bridge loan for the down payment on a house that is repaid from the sale of the previous house.

Personal residential mortgage loans are long-term loans provided to borrowers (consumers) to purchase house/land. The ownership of the property remains with the mortgagee and the possession of property usually is taken by the mortgagor unless and until the occurrence of default on full repayment.

Overseas fund-raising and on-lending refer to the credit service that a bank, with the mandate from its domestic clients, raises funds overseas first from foreign export credit agencies, commercial banks, investment banks, or other financial institutions, and then on-lends the funds further to its domestic client to facilitate the importing of capital goods, technologies and relevant services.

The Credit Process

Lending business of a bank involves two-level issues. One is the overall business strategy of a bank, mainly referring to the total volume and portfolio[10] structure of loans, which is also called Credit Planning. The other is the decision making of an individual lending business, mainly taking the repayment ability of specific client or project into consideration.

The fundamental objective of lending is to make profitable loans with minimal risk. Management should target specific industries or markets in which lending officers have expertise. The somewhat competing goals of loan volume and loan quality must be balanced with the bank's liquidity requirements, capital constrains, and rate of return objectives. The credit process relies on each bank's systems and control that allow management and credit officers to evaluate risk and return trade-offs[11].

How to Get an Individual Loan

From a bank's perspective, a basic credit process consists of 5 steps, namely, loan application acceptance, investigation and assessment, review and approval, loan disbursement[12] and post-disbursement management.

- Application Acceptance is the first step, mainly consisting of client's application, qualification review, client's submission of material for preliminary review. The associates of a bank to receive applications will decide whether to accept a client's loan application or not, in accordance with relevant laws, rules, regulations and their bank's credit policy.
- Investigation and Assessment is the second step. If any client wants a bank to issue a letter of loan intent, then the bank will conduct a preliminary investigation. If the client is not

qualified according to the investigation result, the application will be handed back. If the client is qualified, the bank will issue a letter of intent first, then, the bank will conduct a comprehensive investigation and assessment. If the client does not need the bank to issue a letter of intent, the bank will directly conduct a comprehensive investigation and assessment which is composed of 3 parts, namely, client assessment, business assessment, and security review.

- Review and Approval is the third step. In Review and Approval (Credit Execution), when materials are submitted, the relevant associates of a bank will conduct a compliance review. Then the associates should judge whether the loan is within their review and approval purview. For a client with or without a credit line, the associates should refer to the credit policy of their own bank.

- Loan Disbursement is the fourth step and consists of 5 components, namely, fulfilling pre-lending conditions, signing contract, fulfilling loan using conditions, loan withdrawal and credit registration.

  Once a loan has been approved, the officer notifies the borrower and prepares a loan agreement. This agreement formalizes the purpose of the loan, the terms, repayment schedule, collateral[13] required, and any loan covenants. It also states what conditions should bring about default by the borrower. These conditions may include late principal and interest payments, the sale of substantial assets, a declaration of bankruptcy, and breaking any restrictive loan covenant. The officer then checks that all loan documentation is present and in order. The borrower signs the agreement along with other guarantors[14], turns over the collateral if necessary, and receives the loan proceeds.

- Post-disbursement Management includes review, collection, extension of lending asset, and non-performing asset management.

The loan review effort is directed at reducing credit risk as well as handling problem loans and liquidating assets of failed borrowers. Effective credit management separates loan review from credit analysis, execution, and administration. The review process has two functions: monitoring the performance of existing loans and handling problem loans. Many banks have a formal loan review committee, independent of calling officers, that reports directly to the chief executive officer and director's loan committee. Loan review personnel audit current loans to verify that the borrower's financial condition is acceptable, loan documentation is in place, and pricing meets the return objective. If the audit uncovers problems, the committee initiates corrective action. Removing the problem may simply involve getting signatures on omitted forms or filing required documents with the state. If the borrower has violated any loan covenants, the loan is in default. The bank can then force the borrower to correct the violation or it can recall the loan. Recalling a loan is normally a last resort and done only when the borrower does not voluntarily correct the problem. It allows the bank to request full payment before repayment prospects worsen.

Post-Disbursement Management

Credit Review

Credit review refers to a bank's on-going monitoring and analysis of its credit clients and the relevant factors that can influence safety of the clients' credit asset. Through credit review a bank can find out early warning signals as early as possible and take remedial measures. The process of credit review includes collecting clients' credit information, reviewing clients' current status, credit business progress, and security status in line with the information. After reviewing, the bank should know whether its clients are still qualified borrowers, whether their financial, operation and credit statuses have been deteriorated, whether there are any events that may incur material and negative impacts on clients' repayment capabilities. After credit review, the bank will find out early warning signals and take remedial measures to mitigate risks. At the same time, relevant reports should be prepared to record the review process.

Early Warning Signals

Early warning system or procedure is designed to warn of a potential or an impending problem. Early warning signals are omens or symptoms that a client may not be able to repay the principal and interest in time or service the loan. When the early warning system sends out signals, situations may be that a client has an undue loan in interest and part of its principal, or that there are no arrears from a client yet, or that a bank has not issued advances to its client yet. But signals show that risks might exist or risks might be extended. Therefore, in the process of credit review, credit associates must identify those early warning signals showing that the asset quality of a client has already or is about to be influenced. Credit associates should report their findings to credit officers as early as possible, take relevant measure and try to eliminate the potential risks of credit loss.

Loan Classification by Risk

There is still no uniform standard for loan classification throughout the world. Nowadays, the five-category loan classification is a popular way for banks to rank loans based on their internal risks. They are pass (normal), special-mention, substandard, doubtful and loss.

"Pass" indicates that borrowers are able to honor the terms of the contracts and there is no reason to doubt their ability to repay the principal and interest of loans in full and in a timely manner.

"Special-mention" means that borrowers are able to serve their loans currently, although repayment may be adversely affected by specific factors.

"Substandard" means that borrowers' abilities to service their loans are in question. Borrowers cannot depend on their normal business revenues to pay back the principal and interest so that losses may ensue, even when guarantees are involved.

"Doubtful" indicates that borrowers cannot pay back the principal and interest in full and significant losses will be incurred, even when guarantees are involved.

"Loss" means that the principal and interest of loans cannot be recovered or only a small portion can be recovered after taking all possible measures and resorting to necessary legal procedures.

Terminology

demand loan	活期借款
installment	分期付款
export credit	出口信贷
syndicated loan	辛迪加贷款
working capital	营运资本
fixed asset	固定资产
credit line	信用额度
portfolio	证券投资组合
trade-off	交易
disbursement	支出
collateral	担保物
guarantor	保证人

Notes on the Text

1. demand loan — Demand loan, also known as the notification loans, is a kind of loan which has an uncertain repayment and the bank can give notice to clients to recover the loans according to the deployment of its own funds at any time.
2. installment — a payment of part of a debt; usually paid at regular intervals.
3. maturity — the date on which a financial obligation must be repaid.
4. syndicated loan — A syndicated loan is one that is provided by a group of lenders and is structured, arranged, and administered by one or several commercial banks or investment banks known as arrangers.
5. export credit — a credit opened by an importer with a bank in an exporter's country to finance an export operation.
6. working capital — It is technically defined as the difference between current assets and current liabilities, and is also known as net working capital. Working capital is the measurement of the availability of liquid assets a company has to build its business.
7. liquidity — In business, economics or investment, market liquidity is an asset's ability to be sold without causing a significant movement in the price and with minimum loss of value. Money, or cash, is the most liquid asset, and can be used immediately to perform economic actions like buying, selling, or paying debt, meeting immediate wants and needs. However, currencies, even major currencies, can suffer loss of market liquidity in large liquidation events. For instance, scenarios considering a major dump of US dollar bonds by China or Saudi Arabia or Japan, each of which holds trillions in such bonds, would certainly affect the market liquidity of the US dollar and US dollar denominated assets. There is no asset whatsoever that can be sold with no effect on the market. An act of exchange of a less liquid asset with a more liquid asset is called liquidation. Liquidity also refers both to a business's ability to meet its payment obligations, in terms of possessing sufficient liquid assets, and to

such assets themselves.
8. fixed asset — It is a long-term, tangible asset held for business use and not expected to be converted into cash in the current or upcoming fiscal year, such as manufacturing equipment, real estate, and furniture or plants.
9. credit line — A person or company's credit line is the amount of credit that they are allowed, for example, by a credit card company or a bank.
10. portfolio — a financial term denoting a collection of investments held by an investment company, hedge fund, financial institution or individual. When determining a proper asset allocation one aims at maximizing the expected return and minimizing the risk. This is an example of a multi-objective optimization problem: more "efficient solutions" are available and the preferred solution must be selected by considering a tradeoff between the risk and return. In particular, a portfolio A is dominated by another portfolio A' if A' has a greater expected gain and a lesser risk than A. If no portfolio dominates A, A is a Pareto-optimal portfolio. The set of Pareto-optimal returns and risks is called the Pareto Efficient Frontier for the Markowitz Portfolio selection problem.
11. trade-off — A trade-off (or tradeoff) is a situation that involves losing one quality or aspect of something in return for gaining another quality or aspect. It often implies a decision to be made with full comprehension of both the upside and downside of a particular choice; the term is also used in an evolutionary context, in which case the selection process acts as the "decision-maker".
12. disbursement — the act of spending or disbursing money.
13. collateral — Properties or assets that are offered to secure a loan or other credit. Collateral becomes subject to seizure on default.
14. guarantor — A surety, surety bond or guaranty, in finance, is a promise by one party to assume responsibility for the debt obligation of a borrower if that borrower defaults. The person or company that provides this promise is also known as a surety or guarantor.

Exercises

I. Reading Comprehension.

Read the text carefully and decide whether the following statements are true (T) or false (F).

____1. Working capital loan has low liquidity, which is applicable to the industrial and commercial customers with long-term needs.

____2. A syndicated loan is a very large loan arranged by a bank among a group of borrowers and a single bank.

____3. In supplier credit, exporter's bank provides loans to the exporter to finance the contract with special payment terms under which importer pays for the contract goods by half-yearly installment.

____4. In personal residential mortgage loans, the ownership of the property remains with the mortgagee and the possession of property usually is taken by the mortgagor unless and until the occurrence of default or full repayment.

_____ 5. Conducting a comprehensive investigation and assessment consists of 2 parts, namely, client assessment and security review.

II. Vocabulary Building.

A. Match the term in Column A with the definition in Column B.

1. demand loan
2. installment
3. credit line
4. disbursement
5. trade-off
6. maturity
7. portfolio
8. collateral
9. guarantor
10. liquidity

a. a monetary part-payment as part of a staged payment plan
b. a situation where you make a compromise between two things, or where you exchange all or part of one thing for another.
c. the date on which a financial obligation must be repaid
d. one who provides a warrant or guarantee to another
e. being in cash or easily convertible to cash; debt paying ability
f. a loan that is repayable on demand
g. money paid out
h. a list of the financial assets held by an individual or a bank or other financial institution
i. the maximum credit that a customer is allowed
j. a security pledged for the repayment of a loan

B. Complete the following sentences with the words given in the box.

maturity	redistribution	discretion	facilitate
covenant	maintenance	monetary	audit
withdrawal	guarantee	mortgage	finance
installment			

1. Both sides undertake to _____ further cultural exchanges.
2. Their house was repossessed when they couldn't keep up their _____ payments.
3. The _____ of the League of Nations bound all signatory states not to go to war.
4. What accounts for this apparent _____ from the practice of price leadership?
5. The most direct approach to income _____ is to levy progressive taxes.
6. Each year they _____ our accounts and certify them as being true and fair.
7. The procedure of buyer credit varies depending on whether the importer's bank provides _____ when the loan is provided to the importer.
8. The government's concern is that concerned proper work of _____ and repair is carried out in order to provide an adequate service.
9. The commercial bank is subjected to the risk-based capital guidelines issued by the central bank or _____ authorities according to the Basle Accord.
10. When an investment such as a savings policy or pension plan reaches _____, it reaches

the stage when you stop paying money and the company pays you back the money you have saved, and the interest your money has earned.

III. Cloze.

There are 10 blanks in the following two passages. For each blank there are four choices marked A, B, C and D. You are supposed to choose the best answer.

Passage 1

The problem is much more serious when the borrower's financial condition (1)_____. These loans are classified as problem loans and require special (2)_____. In many cases, the bank has to (3)_____ the terms of the loan agreement to increase the probability of full repayment. Modifications include deferring interest and principal payments, (4)_____ maturities, and liquidating unnecessary assets. Often the bank requests additional collateral or guarantees and asks the borrower to contribute additional capital. The purpose is to buy time until the borrower's condition (5)_____. Banks often separate loan work-out specialists from traditional loan officers because they are liquidation-oriented and frequently involved in intense negotiations.

(1) A. changes   B. deteriorates   C. improves   D. develops
(2) A. treatment   B. cure   C. remedy   D. improvement
(3) A. develop   B. alter   C. modify   D. recover
(4) A. increasing   B. lengthening   C. expanding   D. contracting
(5) A. worsens   B. exacerbates   C. increases   D. improves

Passage 2

Banks will need to make provision (6)_____ a loan according to the category it is in. A fair level of provision on non-performing loans is an essential (7)_____ in accounting, and in the calculation of bank capital and solvency. Fair provisioning on non-performing loans is of great importance for bank regulators. If there has been (8)_____ discussion on the merits of BASEL 2, the revised capital accord that would much better (9)_____ the actual risks taken by banks, it is quite evident that this accord will not have much relevance if the measurement of bank capital is not satisfactory. A key input in the measurement of bank capital is the amount of loan-loss provisions on non-performing loans. We can see that the loan provisioning of a bank is really essential for regulators and outsiders to (10)_____ its asset quality.

(6) A. for   B. of   C. against   D. with
(7) A. input   B. output   C. job   D. effort
(8) A. different   B. intense   C. fierce   D. tight
(9) A. master   B. gain   C. capture   D. attain
(10) A. sense   B. recognize   C. understand   D. view

IV. Translate the following sentences into English.

1. 次贷危机被认为是股市暴跌的罪魁祸首。(blame for)
2. 中长期贷款主要是为基础设施、基础核心产业和科技升级项目集资。(assemble)

3. 这些公司错误估计了房地产市场低迷时违约的可能性：他们现在持有一堆没人愿意购买的不良贷款。(miscalculate)
4. 许多传统的消费信用贷款有一到五年或更久的每月固定还款计划。(repayment)
5. 信用社在提供相对低利率的私人贷款方面取得了成功，并且事实证明那些提供小额贷款的组织和机构是非常有用的，特别是在发展中国家帮助个人建立小型企业方面。(attain some importance)

V. Translate the following paragraphs into Chinese.

1. Secured loans (in contrast with Unsecured Loans, which are backed only by the borrower's promise to pay) are collateralized by assignment of rights to property and a security interest in personal property or real property taken by the lender. A mortgage borrower gives the lender a mortgage in the property financed. A business loan can be secured by cash, inventory, accounts receivable, marketable securities, or other acceptable collateral. In the event the borrower fails to repay according to the original credit terms, the lender can take legal action to reclaim and sell the collateral.

2. The supplier enters into a contract with the importer for supplying goods and services. The payment terms of the contract requires the importer to pay for the goods in half-yearly installments. The supplier and the importer apply to supplier's bank and importer's bank respectively. Importer's bank issues a letter of guarantee in favor of the supplier after accepting the application. Supplier's bank enters into a loan agreement with the supplier. The loan agreement and the contract come into effect after the export credit agency approves them.

VI. Self-Testing.

1. Which of the following statements concerning syndicated loans is true?
    A. These syndicate banks share in credit information and credit risk.
    B. The syndicated loan is often a small credit.
    C. Its purpose is usually to support export trade.
    D. The syndicate loan is often funded by a single bank.
2. Which one is NOT a loan classification by risk?
    A. Pass.   B. Substandard.
    C. Dangerous.   D. Special-mention.
3. The process of getting an individual loan includes the following EXCEPT_____.
    A. loan application acceptance   B. post-disbursement management
    C. credit-review   D. review and approval
4. A loan may be payable in equal monthly installments is called _____.
    A. a demand loan   B. a time loan
    C. bill of exchange   D. an installment loan
5. What are the functions of the review process in post-disbursement management?
    A. Analyzing its credit clients and monitoring the performance of existing loans.
    B. Monitoring the performance of existing loans and handling problem loans.
    C. Avoiding potential risks and monitoring credit clients.

D. Handling problem loans and analyzing its credit clients.

6. Which of the following statements concerning personal residential loans is true?

    A. Personal residential mortgage loans are short-term loans provided to borrowers (consumers) to purchase house/land.

    B. The ownership of the property remains with the mortgagor unless and until the occurrence of default or full repayment.

    C. The possession of property usually is taken by the mortgagor unless and until the occurrence of default or full repayment.

    D. Personal residential mortgage loans are long-term loans provided to borrowers (consumers) to purchase durable goods.

7. In buyer credit, _____'s bank provides loans to the_____, which on-lends the loan to the _____.

    A. importer…exporter…exporter   B. exporter…importer…exporter

    C. exporter…importer…importer   D. importer…exporter…importer

8. What does "doubtful" mean according to the loan classification by risk?

    A. Borrowers are able to honor the terms of the contracts.

    B. The principal and interest of loans cannot be recovered or only a small portion can be recovered.

    C. Borrowers cannot pay back the principal and interest in full and significant losses will be incurred, even when guarantees are involved.

    D. Borrowers' abilities to service their loans are in question.

9. Which of the following statements is true?

    A. If the borrower has violated any loan covenants, the loan is in default. The bank can request full payment before repayment prospects worsen.

    B. A loan cannot be acknowledged by a bond, a promissory note, or a mere oral promise to repay.

    C. Investigation and assessment is the first step of getting an individual loan.

    D. Consumer loans are usually classified as installment, credit card, or non-installment loan.

10. The somewhat competing goals of loan volume and loan quality must be balanced with the bank's following standards EXCEPT _____.

    A. maturities of loan   B. liquidity requirements

    C. rate of return objectives   D. capital constrains

VII. Writing.

Please write a letter to Standard Chartered Bank in English as follows.

1. 我公司希望能与贵行建立业务关系。
2. 我公司近期因发展需要，有意愿从贵行申请贷款来扩展厂房设备。
3. 我公司将附上公司相关信息供贵行参考，希望贵行能提供可行的贷款额度，还款期限，贷款利率及其他必要信息。我公司愿意与贵行保持长期合作关系。
4. 盼佳音。

Supplementary Reading

AIIB Helps Accelerate Sustainable Infrastructure, Regional Connectivity: Bank Official

By Tao Jun and Bei Long
(*Xinhua net* April 8, 2018)

The Asian Infrastructure Investment Bank (AIIB), a multilateral development bank, has helped many Asian countries have better infrastructure, deeper regional integration and accelerated poverty reduction, an AIIB official told Xinhua recently in an exclusive interview in Hanoi.

"We have three mandates — sustainable infrastructure, regional connectivity and private capital mobilization..." As a Chinese proverb saying, 'Better roads lead to better life,' Supee Teravaninthorn, director general of AIIB's Investment Operations Department, who spoke in English but pronounced the proverb in Chinese.

Regarding regional connectivity, one of the three mandates, or the three strategic priorities of AIIB, the bank prioritizes cross-border infrastructure, ranging from roads and rails, to ports, energy pipelines and telecommunications across Central Asia, the maritime routes in Southeast and South Asia, and the Middle East and beyond, she said.

Concerning sustainable infrastructure, the multilateral development bank promotes green infrastructure, and supports countries to meet their environmental and development goals.

Regarding private capital mobilization, AIIB devises innovative solutions that catalyze private capital, in partnership with other multilateral development banks, governments, private financiers and other partners, she said.

In the first year of operation in 2016, AIIB approved investment of 1.7 billion U.S. dollars for nine infrastructure projects in seven countries, including Pakistan, Bangladesh, Tajikistan, Indonesia, Myanmar, Azerbaijan and Oman, Teravaninthorn noted.

In 2017, another 2.5 billion U.S. dollars worth of investment was approved by AIIB for Egypt, Georgia, India, the Philippines and China.

Regarding Greater Mekong Sub-region (GMS) countries, AIIB has already financed or approved or prepared funds for infrastructure projects there, including an energy efficiency improvement project in Myanmar, and an air quality improvement project in China.

"The third project (in the six-member GMS) we are about to do this year is for Laos. It is the National Road No.13 improvement and we will allocate 40 million U.S. dollars for Laos. The next thing we are discussing to do is in Vietnam, about water resources, energy, and sustainable city development. This project could start in 2018 or 2019," the AIIB official said.

AIIB has yet to finance projects in Cambodia and Thailand, but it is considering technical assistance in the electricity sector in Cambodia, and potential projects in both private and public sectors in Thailand, including one relating to high-speed trains, she added.

AIIB directly invests in infrastructure, which indirectly helps facilitate poverty reduction. "Even though we do not really target poverty reduction, but if we invest successfully in infrastructure, it will have a trickle-down effect the poor benefit from," Teravaninthorn stated, noting that poor people can enjoy cheaper electricity charges with fewer or no blackouts if electricity infrastructure gets improved.

AIIB has helped facilitate infrastructure development and regional integration, bringing about positive direct and indirect impacts, including smoother transport and accelerated poverty reduction, in many Asian countries.

"A lot of people say: You are a Chinese bank, you are a Belt and Road bank, you are a Silk Road bank. No, we are none of those. The uniqueness of AIIB is that we really focus on Asia," Teravaninthorn stated.

This is the first time the major shareholders of a multilateral development bank are developing countries. "You know, the biggest shareholder (of AIIB) is China, 30 percent, India — 10 percent," she said, noting that the major shareholders of the World Bank and the Asian Development Bank are developed countries.

"China doesn't want to borrow from AIIB, so that money can be utilized by other countries. It is very generous. I can say that it is very generous of the Chinese government," Teravaninthorn stated, adding that China has reserved the right to borrow later for only two types of projects.

"One is anything to do with climate change. Because we consider climate change is not a one-country obligation. It's a global obligation. And the second one is regional connectivity," the AIIB said.

As a Beijing-headquartered multilateral development bank operating by international standards, with a mission to improve social and economic outcomes in Asia and beyond, AIIB now counts 84 members — rising from 57 at its commencement in January 2016.

Questions

1. In what particular areas has AIIB helped many Asian countries?
2. Can you explain the innovative solutions which are devised by AIIB?
3. What positive impact can AIIB's investments in infrastructure bring to the assisted regions?
4. What's the role of AIIB in poverty reduction?
5. Who are the major shareholders of AIIB?
6. For what types of projects has China reserved the right to borrow later? Why?

Unit 12 International Settlement

Case

A Chinese businessman wanted to export some tea to America. However, he had no idea of the credit of the customer, so he feared that he might not be able to collect the money when he shipped the goods. What is more, there were problems of currency exchange controls, distance, and different legal systems. After consulting his bank, the businessman finally decided to use the letter of credit to do the business so as to avoid the collecting risk and some other tariffs and got paid successfully.

Questions

1. Do you know why the Chinese businessman chose the letter of credit to do the business?
2. Apart from letter of credit, do you know some other methods of payment in international trade?

Preview

Skimming

Skim the following text quickly to answer the following questions and discuss your answers with your partners.

1. According to the text, what instruments are used in international settlement ?

2. How many documents are used in international trade? And what are they?

3. What are the main methods of international settlement?

4. How many kinds of documentary credits are introduced in the text? And what are the main differences among them?

5. What are the key factors that determine the payment method?

Unit 12 International Settlement

Scanning

Scan the following text quickly to find the specific information.
1. What is international settlement?
   _____
   _____.

2. How has international payment evolved?
   _____
   _____.

3. What are the two typical kinds of bills of exchange?
   _____
   _____.

4. What are the four main functions of a bill of lading?
   _____
   _____.

5. Which method of international settlement benefits the buyers most?
   _____
   _____.

6. What is the major process of the documentary collection?
   _____
   _____.

7. What is the difference between the acceptance credit and the negotiation credit?
   _____
   _____.

8. What is the main procedure of using an irrevocable, confirmed documentary credit?
   _____
   _____.

Vocabulary in Context

Read the following sentences and try to guess the meaning of the italicized words by using the context. Then replace the italicized words with synonyms (words or phrases that have nearly the same or similar meanings).

1. International settlement has evolved from cash settlement to non-cash settlement; from direct payment made between international traders to payment effected through a financial *intermediary*.

   International settlement has evolved from cash settlement to non-cash settlement; from direct payment made between international traders to payment effected through a financial _____.

2. There are two typical kinds of bill, namely, the demand bill and the *usance* bill.

   There are two typical kinds of bill, namely, the demand bill and the _____ bill.

3. As the maker of a promissory note is the person primarily liable on it, there can be no *acceptance.*

   As the maker of a promissory note is the person primarily liable on it, there can be no _____.

4. The traveler's cheque is a draft of a bank or travel agency which is *self-identifying* and may be cashed at banks, hotels and etc., either throughout the world or in particular areas only.

   The traveler's cheque is a draft of a bank or travel agency which is _____ and may be cashed at banks, hotels and etc., either throughout the world or in particular areas only.

5. A bill of lading acts as *a title to goods* being shipped.

   A bill of lading acts as _____ being shipped.

6. Under an open account payment method, title to the goods usually passes from the seller to the buyer prior to payment and subjects the seller to risk of *default* by the buyer.

   Under an open account payment method, title to the goods usually passes from the seller to the buyer prior to payment and subjects the seller to risk of _____ by the buyer.

7. Ultimately, the draft will be debited to either the appropriate *nostro or vostro* account.

   Ultimately, the draft will be debited to either the appropriate _____ account.

8. It may also be defined as the *irrevocable* obligation of a bank to pay a sum of money in the event of non-performance of a contract by the principal.

   It may also be defined as the _____ obligation of a bank to pay a sum of money in the event of non-performance of a contract by the principal.

9. The issuing bank requests a bank to advise the beneficiary, the exporter, of the details. Meanwhile the advising bank is asked to *confirm* the credit.

   The issuing bank requests a bank to advise the beneficiary, the exporter, of the details. Meanwhile the advising bank is asked to _____ the credit.

10. However, in *deferred* payment credits, there is no need for the exporter to draw a bill of exchange.

    However, in _____ payment credits, there is no need for the exporter to draw a bill of exchange.

Text

International Settlement

The sale of goods in other countries is further complicated by additional risks encountered when dealing with foreign customers. In international transactions, contracts usually explicitly include the trade terms specifying how payment under an export invoice shall be made. The terms of payment refer to an agreement between a buyer and a seller, which outlines how goods will be paid for, the length of time between the invoice date, and the due date, and whether a cash discounts apply. It is resulted from the respective perspectives and interests of the buyers and sellers that different methods of payments are adopted. To some extent, the terms of payments reflect which party holds the more advantageous position.

International settlement are financial activities conducted among different countries in which payments are effected or funds are transferred from one country to another in order to settle accounts, debts, claims, etc. emerged in the course of political, economic or cultural contacts among them.

International settlement has evolved from cash settlement to non-cash settlement[1]; from direct payment made between international traders to payment effected through a financial intermediary; from payment under simple price terms to payments under more complex prices terms.

Instruments Used in International Settlement

Bills of Exchange

A bill of exchange[2] (draft) is an unconditional order in writing, addressed by one person (the drawer) to another (the drawee), signed by the person giving it, requiring the person to whom it is addressed to pay on demand, or at a fixed or determined future time, a sum certain in money, to or to the order of a specified person, or to the bearer.

There are two typical kinds of bills of exchange, namely, the demand bill and the usance bill. When a bill is payable on demand or at sight, the drawee is required to pay immediately when the bill is presented to him. This is the demand bill. A usance bill is a bill which may be payable within a fixed period after the date of the bill or after an event which is certain to happen.

Promissory Notes

A promissory note[3] is an unconditional promise in writing made by one person (the maker) to another (the payee or the holder), signed by the maker engaging to pay on demand or at a fixed or determined future time a sum certain in money to, or to the order of a specified person or to the bearer.

A promissory note is a promise, and a bill is an order. There is no need to protest a dishonored note. As the maker of a promissory note is the person primarily liable on it, there can be no acceptance[4].

Cheques

A cheque is an unconditional order in writing, addressed by a person (the drawer) to a bank (the drawee), signed by the person making it, requiring the bank to pay on demand a sum certain in money to or to the order of a specified person or to the bearer (the payee). The traveler's cheque is a draft of a bank or travel agency which is self-identifying and may be cashed at banks, hotels and etc., either throughout the world or in particular areas only.

Documents Used in International Trade

Commercial Invoice

A commercial invoice gives details of the goods, details of the payment and delivery terms, and a detailed breakdown of the monetary amount due. Invoices are usually made by the seller. A formal invoice may include the name and address of the exporter and the importer, reference number, terms of delivery, shipping marks, description of goods, quantity of goods, total amount payable by the importer and the signature of the exporter.

Bills of Lading

There are four main functions of a bill of lading.

- The bill of lading is evidence of the contract for carriage between the shipper and the carrier.
- Bill of lading acts as a receipt of the goods from the shipping company to the shipper.
- A bill of lading is a quasi negotiable document. Any transferee for value who takes possession of an endorsed bill of lading obtain a good title to it, provided the transferor had a good title in the first place.
- A bill of lading acts as a title to goods[5] being shipped.

Insurance Documents

It is a matter for negotiation between the exporter and the importer as to who is responsible for insuring the goods during their journey from the exporter's hands to the importer's hands. Which part to cover the insurance depends on the specific situation. The insurance cover is often based on the standard clauses of the Institute of London, which is called Institute Cargo Clause (ICC). In China, China Insurance Clause (CIC) is used in many cases and accepted by importers abroad.

Main Methods of International Settlement

Open Account

Sales on open accounts are not generally made in foreign trade except to customers of long standing with excellent credit reputations or to a subsidiary or branch of the exporter. Open accounts obviously leave sellers in a position where most of the problems of international commercial finance work to their disadvantage. When sales are made on an open account, the seller should attempt to arrange the insurance. There is no bank involved in such a term of payment, which means no bank credit is available either in most cases. Usually it is an agreement stated in a contract between a seller and a buyer that the payment will be made within a specified period of time.

Under an open account payment method, title to the goods usually passes from the seller to the buyer prior to payment and subjects the seller to risk of default by the buyer. Furthermore, there may be a time delay in payment, depending on how quickly documents are exchanged between the seller and the buyer. There is a possibility that political events will impose regulations which defer or block the movement of funds to him, and his own capital is tied up until the goods are received and inspected by the buyer, or until the services are found to be accepted and payment is made.

Cash in Advance

The buyer places the funds at the disposal of the seller prior to shipment of the goods or provision of services. The parties may agree to fund the operation by partial payments (from 25 to 50 percent) in advance or by progress payments. That is to say, the buyer pays for the goods before they are dispatched or received. Although this means of payment is expensive and includes degrees of risk, it is not uncommon when the manufacturing process or services delivered are specialized and capital intensive. This is used where the buyer is of unknown credit worthiness and is unable to obtain a letter of credit. This is also used as a matter of convenience for small orders. This method of payment is taken into consideration:

(1) When there is an unstable political or economic environment in the buyer's country.
(2) If there is a potential delay in the receipt of funds from the buyer, perhaps due to event beyond his control.

Remittance

Remittance refers to the transfer of funds from one party to another among different countries. That is, a bank (the remitting bank), at the request of its customer (the remitter), transfers a certain sum of money to its overseas branch or correspondent bank (the paying bank) instructing them to pay to a named person or corporation (the payee or beneficiary) domiciled in the country.

There are three types of remittance, namely, M/T, T/T and D/D. First of all, the customer's bank will need to know whether to credit the account of the beneficiary with a named bank. On receipt of the customer's instructions, the book keeping will be applied. The customer's bank will advise the overseas bank of the transaction by airmail, and the payment instruction must be signed by authorized signatures. This is so-called M/T, mail transfer.

If T/T, a telegraphic transfer, is used, the same procedure as for mail is adopted. However, the instructions to the overseas bank are sent by telex or SWIFT[6], and in case of telex, the overseas bank will require a special authenticating code word, which is called "test key", before it will act.

D/D, a demand draft, is in effect a bill of exchange drawn by one bank on another payable on demand. The customer will forward the draft to the beneficiary who will pay it into his bank for credit to his account. Ultimately, the draft will be debited to either the appropriate nostro[7] or vostro[8] account.

Collection

Collection is an arrangement whereby the goods are shipped and the relevant bill of exchange (draft) drawn by the seller on the buyer, and documents are sent to the seller's bank correspondent bank located in the domicile of the buyer. Normally, title to the goods does not pass on to the buyer until the draft is paid or accepted by the buyer.

When collection is to be adopted to settle the cross-border trade, the seller should obtain a credit report on the buyer by consulting credit survey agencies, obtain an economic and political analysis on the destination market. Precaution should also be made by establishing alternative procedures for the resale, reshipment or warehousing of the goods in the event of non-payment by the buyer. There are documentary collection and clean collection, and the difference lies in whether the documents of title to the goods are enclosed.

Documentary collection may be described as collection on financial instruments being accompanied by commercial documents or collection on commercial documents without being accompanied by financial instruments, that is, commercial documents without a bill of exchange.

—The seller ships the goods and obtains the shipping documents, and usually draws a draft, either at sight or with a tenor of XX days on the buyer for the value of the goods.

—The seller submits the drafts to his bank, which acts as his agent.

—The bank acknowledges that all documents as noted by the seller are presented.

—The seller's bank sends the draft and other documents along with a collection letter to a correspondent bank usually located in the same city as the buyer.

—Acting as an agent for the Remitting Bank[9], the Collecting Bank[10] notifies the buyer upon receipt of the draft and documents.

—All the documents, and usually title to the goods, are released to the buyer upon his payment of the amount specified or his acceptance of the draft for payment at a specified later date.

Clean collection is collection on financial instruments without being accompanied by commercial documents, such as invoice, bill of lading, insurance policy.

—An arrangement whereby the seller draws only a draft on the buyer for the value of the goods and presents the draft to his bank.

—The seller's bank sends the draft along with a collection instruction letter to a correspondent bank usually in the same city as the buyer.

The major advantage of a "cash against documents" payment method for the buyer is low cost, versus opening a Letter of Credit. The advantage for the seller is that he can receive full payment prior to releasing control of the documents, although this is offset by the risk that the buyer will, for some reason, reject the documents(or they will not be in order). Since the cargo would already be loaded, the seller has little recourse against the buyer in cases of non-payment. A payment against documents arrangement involves a high level of trust between the seller and the buyer and should be adopted only by parties well known to each other.

Bank Guarantee

A bank guarantee is a written promise issued by a bank at the request of its customer, undertaking to make payment to the beneficiary within the limits. It may also be defined as the irrevocable obligation of a bank to pay a sum of money in the event of non-performance of a contract by the principal.

In international trade, the buyer wants to be certain that the seller is in a position to honor his commitment as offered or contracted. The former therefore makes it a condition that appropriate security is provided. On the other hand, the seller must find a way to be assured of receiving payment if no special security is provided for the payment such as in open account business and documentary collections. Such security may be obtained through banks in the form of guarantee. A bank guarantee is used as an instrument for securing performance or payment especially in international trade.

Documentary Credit

Documentary credit means any arrangement, however named or described, whereby a bank (the issuing bank[11]), acting at the request and the instruction of a customer (the applicant), is to make a payment to or to the order of a third party (the beneficiary), or is to accept and pay bills of exchange (draft) drawn by the beneficiary, against stipulated documents, provided that the terms and conditions of the credit are complied with.

A letter of credit provides the most satisfactory method of setting international transaction. Its primary function is relying on the bank's undertaking to pay, thereby enabling the seller or the exporter to receive payment as soon as possible after the shipment of his goods and also enabling the buyer or the importer to arrange with his bank for the financing of the payment. It is, therefore, of great importance in the sense that it contributes to the smooth conducting of international trade.

Let us assume that an importer and an exporter have agreed that payment terms will be by way of an irrevocable[12], confirmed documentary credit[13]. The procedures are as follows:

— The importer asks their banker (issuing bank) to issue an irrevocable credit and to request confirmation by another bank (confirming bank[14]). And their banker agrees.

— The issuing bank requests a bank (advising bank[15]) to advise the beneficiary, the exporter, of the details. Meanwhile the advising bank is asked to confirm the credit. The advising bank agrees to this.

— The advising bank, now writes to or notifies by other means the beneficiary the details of the credit.

— After consignment, the beneficiary obtains the shipping documents and presents the documents to the confirming bank through their banker (presenting bank). Confirming bank pays the beneficiary provided that the documents are in full compliance with the terms and conditions of the credit.

— The confirming bank sends the documents to the issuing bank and gets reimbursement from the bank.

— The issuing bank settles the payment with the importer, and then the importer is given the documents for taken delivery of the goods.

There are four types of documentary credit:

Payment Credit, the nominated bank will pay the beneficiary on receipt of the specified documents and on fulfillment of all the terms of the credit. The issuing bank can nominates itself as paying bank. On other occasions, usually with confirmed credits, the issuing bank will nominated the advising bank to pay.

Negotiation Credit, the issuing bank will nominate the advising bank to negotiate a credit, or it may even make the credit freely negotiable, in which case any bank may be a nominated bank. If a bank negotiates a credit, it will advance money to the beneficiary on presentation of the required documents and will charge interest on the advance from the date of the advance until such time as it receives reimbursement from the issuing bank. Such negotiation advances are said to be with recourse.

Acceptance Credit, the term "acceptance" can only apply when the credit calls for usance bills, which means that the seller draws a draft on the nominated bank demanding payment at some determined future date. In practice, this means that instead of receiving immediate payment on presentation of the documents, the seller's draft is returned to him accepted on face by the nominated bank.

Deferred Payment Credit, it will include an instruction to the beneficiary to draw bills of exchange, and the issuing bank will guarantee that such bills will be honored, provided all the other terms of the credit are met. However, in deferred payment credits, there is no need for the exporter to draw a bill of exchange.

Key Factors Determining the Payment Method

- The business relationship between the seller and the buyer

- Industry norms
- The nature of the merchandise
- The distance between the seller and the buyer
- Political and economic stability in both the seller and the buyer's country
- The potential for currency fluctuation

Terminology

non-cash settlement	非现金结算
acceptance	承兑
promissory note	本票
bill of exchange	汇票
a title to goods	货物所有权
SWIFT	环球银行金融电信协会
nostro	往账(我方账户)
vostro	来账
remitting bank	汇款行
collecting bank	托收行
bank guarantee	银行保函
irrevocable documentary credit	不可撤销跟单信用证
confirmed documentary credit	保兑跟单信用证
issuing bank	开证行
confirming bank	保兑行
advising bank	通知行

Notes on the Text

1. non-cash settlement — The shipment of gold or silver across national boundaries was both expensive and risky. Freight costs were high, and the speed of transferring funds depended on the speed of transportation facilities. From the thirteenth century A.D., bills of exchange were created, gradually taking the place of coins in the international payments. With the establishment of foreign exchange banks, at the end of the thirteenth century, international payments could be settled by way of transferring funds through the accounts opened in these banks. From then on, the non-cash settlement era began. Nowadays non-cash settlements are universally adopted all over the world.
2. bill of exchange — A bill of exchange or "draft" is a written order by the drawer to the drawee to pay money to the payee. A common type of bill of exchange is the cheque (check in American English), defined as a bill of exchange drawn on a banker and payable on demand. Bills of exchange are used primarily in international trade, and are written orders by one person to his bank to pay the bearer a specific sum on a specific date. Prior to the advent of paper currency, bills of exchange were a common means of exchange. A bill of exchange is essentially an order made by one person to another to pay money to a third person. A bill of

exchange requires in its inception three parties — the drawer, the drawee, and the payee. The person who draws the bill is called the drawer. He gives the order to pay money to the third party. The party upon whom the bill is drawn is called the drawee. He is the person to whom the bill is addressed and who is ordered to pay. He becomes an acceptor when he indicates his willingness to pay the bill. The party in whose favor the bill is drawn or is payable is called the payee. The parties need not all be distinct persons. Thus, the drawer may draw on himself payable to his own order.

3. promissory note — A promissory note is a negotiable instrument, wherein one party(the maker or issuer) makes an unconditional promise in writing to pay a determinate sum of money to the other (the payee), either at a fixed or determinable future time or on demand of the payee, under specific terms.

4. acceptance — That is a promise to pay, the drawee signs on the bill of exchange when the bank presents it to him to promise to pay in the determined future date.

5. a title to goods — a certificate indicating the ownership of the goods.

6. SWIFT — Society for Worldwide International Financial Telecommunication.

7. nostro — From the point of view of a Chinese bank, a nostro account is our bank's account in the book of an overseas bank. When a customer wishes to transfer funds to the bank account of a beneficiary abroad, the bookkeeping is as follows: debit the customer's account with the amount to transfer, and credit the currency to the nostro account for reconciliation. Advise the overseas bank that it can debit the nostro account with the requisite amount and credit the funds to the account of the beneficiary.

8. vostro — A vostro account is an overseas bank's account with our bank. When a customer wishes to transfer funds to the bank account of a beneficiary abroad, the bookkeeping is as follows: debit the customer's account with the amount transfer, and credit the account of the overseas bank under advise to it. This is a vostro account from the customer's bank's point of view. On receipt of the advice, the overseas bank will withdraw the amount from the vostro account, and credit the beneficiary's account.

9. remitting bank — In outward collection (also called payable overseas), a bank acts as the remitting bank, whose functions include: A. receiving the application of the exporter. B. sending the draft with or without shipping documents attached as well as the collection order to the collecting bank in the importer's country.

10. collecting bank — In inward collection, a bank acts as the collecting bank. The collecting bank's inward collection includes: A. receiving the draft with or without shipping documents attached as well as the collection order from a remitting bank abroad. B. endeavoring to collect the payment or obtain the acceptance from the importer.

11. issuing bank — the bank that issues a letter of credit in favor of beneficiary.

12. irrevocable documentary credit — An irrevocable documentary credit constitutes a definite undertaking of the issuing bank, provided that the stipulated documents are presented to the nominated bank or to the issuing bank and that the terms and conditions of the documentary credit are complied with, to pay, accept drafts presented under the documentary credit.

13. confirmed documentary credit — A confirmation of an irrevocable documentary credit by a

bank upon the authorization or request of the issuing bank, constitutes a definite undertaking of the confirming bank, in addition to that of the issuing bank, provided that the stipulated documents are presented to the confirming bank or to any other nominated bank on or before the expiry date and the terms and conditions of the documentary credit are complied with, to pay, to accept draft or to negotiate.

14. confirming bank — a nominated bank who undertakes, at the request or with the consent of the issuing bank, to honor a presentation directly under a letter of credit issued by another, or to honor a presentation to the issuing bank when the bank fails to pay.

15. advising bank — the bank who, at the request of an issuing bank, a confirming bank, or another advising bank, notifies or requests another advising bank to notify the beneficiary that a letter of credit has been issued, confirmed, or amended.

Exercises

I. Reading Comprehension.

Read the text carefully and decide whether the following statements are true (T) or false (F).

___1. International settlement has evolved from payment effected through a financial intermediary to direct payment made between international traders.

___2. A demand bill is a bill which may be payable within a fixed period after the date of the bill or after an event which is certain to happen.

___3. A commercial invoice gives details of the goods, details of the payment and delivery terms, and a detailed breakdown of the monetary amount due.

___4. Documentary collection is collection on financial instruments without being accompanied by commercial documents, such as invoice, bill of lading, insurance policy.

___5. A letter of credit provides the most satisfactory method of settling international transaction.

II. Vocabulary Building.

A. Match the term in Column A with the definition in Column B.

1. nostro
2. SWIFT
3. advising bank
4. vostro
5. a title to goods

a. an overseas bank's account with our bank
b. our bank's account in the book of an overseas bank
c. a credit that must be honored by the issuing bank, provided that the stipulated documents are presented to the nominated bank
d. Society for Worldwide International Financial Telecommunication
e. the bank who, at the request of an issuing bank, notifies another advising bank to notify the beneficiary that a letter of credit has been issued

Unit 12　International Settlement

6. issuing bank　　　　　　　　f. the bank that issues a letter of credit in favor of the beneficiary

7. acceptance　　　　　　　　g. a nominated bank who undertakes, at the request of issuing bank, to honor a presentation under a letter of credit issued by another, when the bank fails to pay

8. irrevocable documentary credit　　h. a promise to pay, the drawee signs on the bill of exchange when the bank presents it to him to promise to pay in the determined future date

9. confirming bank　　　　　　i. a written promise issued by a bank at the request of its customer undertaking to make payment to the beneficiary within the limits

10. bank gurarantee　　　　　　j. a certificate indicating the ownership of the goods

B. Complete the following sentences with the words given in the box and change the form of the words where necessary.

evolve	encounter	undertake	insure	issue
assume	request	tight	unconditional	tenor
carriage	worthiness	stable		

1. The sale of goods in other countries is further complicated by additional risks when _____ dealing with foreign customers.
2. International settlement has _____ from cash settlement to non-cash settlement.
3. A cheque is an _____ order in writing, addressed by a person to a bank, signed by the person making it, requiring the bank to pay on demand a sum certain in money to or to the order of a specified person or to the bearer.
4. The bill of lading is evidence of the contract for _____ between the shipper and the carrier.
5. It is a matter for negotiation between the exporter and the importer as to who is responsible for _____ the goods during their journey from the exporter's hands to the importer's hands.
6. Cash in advance is used where the buyer is of unknown credit _____ and is unable to obtain a letter of credit.
7. The seller ships the goods and obtains the shipping documents, and usually draws a draft, either at sight or with a _____ of XX days on the buyer for the value of the goods.
8. A bank guarantee is a written promise issued by a bank at the _____ of its customer, undertaking to make payment to the beneficiary within the limits.
9. The L/C's primary function is relying on the bank's _____ to pay, thereby enabling the seller or the exporter to receive payment as soon as possible after the shipment of his goods.
10. Let us _____ that an importer and an exporter have agreed that payment terms will be by way of an irrevocable, confirmed documentary credit.

III. Cloze.

There are 10 blanks in the following two passages. For each blank there are four choices marked A, B, C and D. You are supposed to choose the best answer.

Passage 1

Under the advance payment, the buyer agrees a price for goods from an overseas exporter and sends his payment with the firm order i.e., before the goods are shipped. The importer must be confident (1)_____ the reliability of the exporter and the stability of the exporter's country. The risk is borne by the importer. In return the importer may be allowed a discount which is a (2)_____ from the price of goods in consideration of its being paid in advance. This method would be used when an importer is unable or unwilling to open a documentary credit, or when an importer has a good cash position and can negotiate a cash discount, or an individual is buying from a mail order company. Importers can arrange to make advance payment through a bank.

Secondly, open account trading. This is basically payment in arrears, the (3)_____ of advance payment and usually covers a regular flow of shipments. The importer usually agrees (4)_____ the exporter to pay at the end of each month or, say, one month after each shipment. There is usually a long-standing or regular business relationship between the two parties. The exporter must have confidence in the relationship of the importer and the stability of the importer's country. The risk is borne by the exporter. Governments sometimes support their exporters to protect them (5)_____ these risks.

(1) A. of	B. in	C. for	D. on
(2) A. increase	B. deduction	C. raise	D. decrease
(3) A. similar	B. familiar	C. opposite	D. same
(4) A. with	B. to	C. on	D. upon
(5) A. for	B. of	C. against	D. by

Passage 2

Bills of exchange and promissory notes hold an important position in the commercial world. Being (6)_____ the oldest instruments of payment, their origins even date back to the 12th century. The fact that both types of commercial paper have existed to this (7)_____ day is the most conclusive evidence of their substance and relevance. After all, apart from the smooth negotiability the main advantage of the use of a bill of exchange is the legal security it involves.

An additional assert is the protest facility and the ensuring publication in case of non-payment by the drawee: (8)_____, the influence of the statutory publicity on the drawee's creditworthiness constitutes, in practice, an important means of pressure to (9)_____ him to pay promptly.

Whereas a bill of exchange originally functioned as a means of payment, it is now particularly used as a debt-collection or credit (10)_____.

(6) A. with	B. among	C. in	D. as
(7) A. very	B. just	C. only	D. /

(8) A. however   B. nevertheless   C. indeed   D. besides
(9) A. force   B. urge   C. ask   D. tell
(10) A. instrument   B. tool   C. method   D. means

IV. Translate the following sentences into English.

1. 保兑行实际承担了与开证行一样的责任，在所有信用证项下的单据提交且与该证所有的条款和条件都相符的情况下，无追索权(recourse)地向受益人付款、承兑或议付。(assume)
2. 通常情况下，在买方没有付款或承兑远期汇票之前，货权是不会交给买方的。(accept)
3. 如果信用证要进行修改或撤销，实际上必须征得信用证的所有当事人，即开证行、买方、卖方的同意。(agree to)
4. 通过议付受益人提交的汇票，议付行成为该汇票的"善意持票人"，并得到开证行在信用证项下的保证。(protect)
5. 代收行的职责是保证在买方付款或承兑的前提下才向其交付货运单据。(take up the role of)

V. Translate the following paragraphs into Chinese.

1. The importer will have special needs that only his bank will be able to provide such as: assurance that he does not have to pay the seller until he is certain that the seller has fulfilled his side of the contract; the possibility of obtaining loans to finance the cost of the imports until he receives proceeds from the sale of those goods; advice and assistance on trade transaction procedures and advice and assistance with foreign exchange activity.

2. Letters of credit are about documents and not facts; the inability to produce a given document at the right time will make the letter of credit null and void. As a seller/ exporter/ beneficiary you should try and run the compliance issues with the various department or individuals involved within your organization to see if compliance would be a problem. And if so, have the L/C amended before shipping the goods.

VI. Self-Testing.

1. Under the advance payment, the buyer is exposed to the risk that _____.
   A. the exporter might default on the contract
   B. the issuing bank might fail to carry out its promise to pay
   C. the collecting bank might refuse to pay
   D. the bank might refuse to issue a collection instruction
2. _____ is the opposite of advance payment, which is payment in arrears.
   A. Documentary collection   B. Documentary credit
   C. Open account trading   D. None of the above
3. Under the documentary credit, which of the following is false?
   A. The buyer's bank will issue a documentary credit.
   B. The seller has his bank's undertaking to pay.
   C. If the seller presents the correct documents, he will be paid.
   D. A bank acts as an intermediary between the buyer and the seller and is willing to provide

trade finance.

4. Under the documentary collection, the buyer's bank is called the _____ bank.

   A. issuing　　　B. remitting　　　C. collecting　　　D. financing

5. A bill of lading is _____.

   A. a certificate showing the cost of freight has been paid or not

   B. a title to the goods shipped

   C. a receipt for goods shipped issued by the shipper

   D. a certificate issued by the shipping company

6. The advising bank _____.

   A. is authorized by the issuing bank to persuade the beneficiary to accept the amendments

   B. is obliged to persuade the beneficiary to accept partial amendments

   C. is not obliged to persuade the beneficiary to accept or to reject amendments

   D. none of the above

7. If the trader sells the bill of exchange to his bank prior to maturity,_____.

   A. the bank will pay him the amount of the bill of exchange

   B. the trader is using the bill of exchange as a credit instrument

   C. the trader is using the bill as a debt instrument

   D. the trader will receive the payment under the bill of exchange at maturity

8. Exporters and importers who have regular business relationship may choose_____ to settle international trade.

   A. the open account trading　　　B. the payment in advance

   C. the documentary credit　　　　D. the documentary collection

9. The documentary credit is issued by_____and then is transmitted to the beneficiary via_____.

   A. the importer/ the issuing bank　　　B. the importer / the advising bank

   C. the issuing bank / the advising bank　D. the advising bank / the importer

10. Under _____, the nominated bank will pay the beneficiary on receipt of the specified documents and on fulfillment of all the terms of the credit.

    A. payment credit　　　　B. negotiation credit

    C. acceptance credit　　　D. deferred credit

VII. Writing.

Please write a letter to the importer Bill American in English as follows.

1. 希望向贵公司出口我公司的优质茶叶，并保持长期合作关系。
2. 我公司生产并对外出口各种优质茶叶，希望对方公司做我方在美国的代理。我方希望对方公司提供当地银行开具的信用证作为结算工具。
3. 出于这一良好意愿，我方随函附上我们各类茶叶的报价。
4. 盼佳音。

Unit 12　International Settlement

Supplementary Reading

What Is the Bank for International Settlements?

By Filed Under

Headquartered in Basel, Switzerland, the Bank for International Settlements (BIS) is a bank for central banks. Founded in 1930, the Bank for International Settlements is the oldest global financial institution and operates under the auspices of international law. But from its inception to the present day, the role of the BIS has been ever-changing, as it adapts to the dynamic global financial community and its needs. Read on as we explain this bank and its role in global banking.

Financial Chameleon

The BIS was created out of the Hague Agreements of 1930 and took over the job of the Agent General for Repatriation in Berlin. When established, the BIS was responsible for the collection, administration and distribution of reparations from Germany — as agreed upon in the Treaty of Versailles — following World War I. The BIS was also the trustee for Dawes and Young Loans, which were internationally issued loans used to finance these repatriations.

After World War II, the BIS turned its focus to the defense and implementation of the World Bank's Bretton Woods System. Between the 1970s and 1980s, the BIS monitored cross-border capital flows in the wake of the oil and debt crises, which in turn led to the development of regulatory supervision of internationally active banks.

The BIS has also emerged as an emergency "funder" to nations in trouble, coming to the aid of countries such as Mexico and Brazil during their debt crises in 1982 and 1998, respectively. In cases like these, where the International Monetary Fund is already in the country, emergency funding is provided through the IMF structured program.

The BIS has also functioned as trustee and agent. For example, from 1979 to 1994, the BIS was the agent for the European Monetary System, which is the administration that paved the way for a single European currency.

Notwithstanding all the roles mentioned above, the BIS has always been a promoter of central bank cooperation in an effort to ensure global monetary and financial stability.

Lean On Me

Given the continuously changing global economic structure, the BIS has had to adapt to many different financial challenges. However, by focusing on providing traditional banking services to member central banks, the BIS essentially gives the "lender of last resort" a shoulder to lean on. In its aim to support global financial and monetary stability, the BIS is an integral part of the international economy.

To promote such stability, the BIS offers a forum of cooperation among member central banks (including monetary agencies). It does so by offering support and banking services for central banks:

The BIS offers its support by:

- ***Contributing to international cooperation*** — As a crucial resource for central banks and other financial institutions, the BIS produces research and statistics, and organizes seminars and workshops focused on international financial issues. For example, the Financial Stability Institute (FSI) organizes seminars and lectures on themes of global financial stability. The governors of member central banks meet at the BIS twice a month to share their experiences, and these meetings function as the core of central bank cooperation. Other regular meetings of central bank executives and specialists, as well as economists and supervisory specialists, contribute to the goal of international cooperation, while also ensuring that each central bank serves its country effectively. The ultimate goal of all these high-level meetings is global financial stability.
- ***Offering services to committees established and working at the BIS*** — By offering its services to various secretariats of financial committees and organizations created under its patronage, the BIS also functions as an international "think tank" for financial issues. Committees such as the Markets Committee debate and improve upon fundamental issues regarding the workings and regulations of the international financial infrastructure. As the bankers' bank, the BIS serves the financial needs of member central banks. It provides gold and foreign exchange transactions for them and holds central bank reserves. The BIS is also a banker and fund manager for other international financial institutions.

How the Bank Operates

The BIS does compete directly with other private financial institutions for global banking activities; however, it does not hold current accounts for individuals or governments. At one time, private shareholders as well as central banks held shares in the BIS. But in 2001 it was decided that the private shareholders should be compensated and that ownership of the BIS should be restricted to the central banks (or equivalent monetary authorities). There are currently 55 member central banks.

The BIS's unit of account is the IMF's special drawing rights, which are a basket of convertible currencies. The reserves that are held account for approximately 7% of the world's total currency.

Like any other bank, the BIS strives to offer premium services in order to attract central banks as clients. In order to provide security, it maintains abundant equity capital and reserves that are diversely invested following risk analysis. The BIS ensures liquidity for central banks by offering to buy back tradable instruments from central banks; many of these instruments have been specifically designed for the central bank's needs. In order to compete with private financial institutions, the BIS offers a top return on funds invested by central banks.

The statutes of the BIS are presided over by three bodies: the general meeting of member central banks, the board of directors and the management of the BIS. Decisions on the functions of the BIS are made at each level and are based on a weighted voting arrangement.

Conclusion

The BIS is a global center for financial and economic interests. As such, it has been a principal architect in the development of the global financial market. Given the dynamic nature of social, political and economic situations around the world, the BIS can be seen as a stabilizing force, encouraging financial stability and international prosperity in the face of global change.

Questions

1. Why was the BIS created?
2. What does the author mean by "financial chameleon"?
3. What was the role of the BIS after World War II?
4. How does the BIS support its members' central banks?
5. Who are presiding over the BIS?

Unit 13 Banking Supervision

Case

A crowd of angry investors packed in the local branch of H Bank as they had heard that the first of four phases of repayment in a RMB 119 million *yuan* wealth management plan had not been made and demanded the bank to return their investments. They said the bank's employees had recommended the product and all the contracts had been signed at the bank with the help of the bank staff. However, the bank refused to commit to any compensation and said that this wealth product had not been sold by the bank but by a now former employee, who had been dismissed one week before the plan was due.

Questions

1. If you were one of the investors, whom would you turn to for help?
2. Why is it necessary to supervise and regulate financial institutions?

Preview

Skimming

Skim the following text quickly to answer the following questions and discuss your answers with your partners.

1. What kind of roles do banks play in a market economy?
   _____
   _____.

2. What kind of risks are banks faced with?
   _____
   _____.

3. What are the core principles of banking supervision?
   _____
   _____.

4. What are the preconditions for effective banking supervision?
   _____
   _____.

5. What are the methods of ongoing banking supervision?
   _____
   _____.

Unit 13 Banking Supervision

Scanning

Scan the following text quickly to find the specific information.
1. What is " delegated monitoring"?
   _____
   _____.

2. Why is it important to regulate banks?
   _____
   _____.

3. What is the primary activity of most banks?
   _____
   _____.

4. How do banks act as "market makers" in the foreign exchange market?
   _____
   _____.

5. When are banks vulnerable to legal risks?
   _____
   _____.

6. Who put forward the Core Principles for Effective Banking Supervision?
   _____
   _____.

7. What should licensing process be composed of ?
   _____
   _____.

8. What is CAMELS rating system?
   _____
   _____.

Vocabulary in Context

Read the following sentences and try to guess the meaning of the italicized words by using the context. Then replace the italicized words with synonyms (words or phrases that have nearly the same or similar meanings).
1. …on behalf of their depositors, banks *tackle* asymmetric information problems in financial transactions.
   …on behalf of their depositors, banks _____ asymmetric information problems in financial transactions.
2. When this happens, depositors lose their savings, which can have *devastating* implications for public trust in the whole banking system.
   When this happens, depositors lose their savings, which can have _____ implications for public trust in the whole banking system.
3. Given that banks play a *pivotal* role for the real economy in providing ways of clearing and settling payments, transforming claims in terms of…

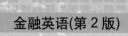

Given that banks play a _____ role for the real economy in providing ways of clearing and settling payments, transforming claims in terms of…

4. …basis risk, which arises from imperfect *correlation* in the adjustment of the rates earned and paid on different instruments with otherwise similar repricing characteristics.

   …basis risk, which arises from imperfect _____ in the adjustment of the rates earned and paid on different instruments with otherwise similar repricing characteristics.

5. Special attention should be paid to this risk in countries where interest rates are being *deregulated*.

   Special attention should be paid to this risk in countries where interest rates are being _____.

6. Liquidity risk arises from the inability of a bank to *accommodate* decreases in liabilities or to fund increases in assets.

   Liquidity risk arises from the inability of a bank to _____ decreases in liabilities or to fund increases in assets.

7. Banks are particularly *susceptible* to legal risks when entering new types of transactions and when the legal right of a counterparty to enter into a transaction is not established.

   Banks are particularly _____ to legal risks when entering new types of transactions and when the legal right of a counterparty to enter into a transaction is not established.

8. The Core Principles *address* the following main areas:

   The Core Principles _____ the following main areas:

9. These requirements should not *supplant* management decisions but rather impose minimum prudential standards to ensure that banks conduct their activities in an appropriate manner.

   These requirements should not _____ management decisions but rather impose minimum prudential standards to ensure that banks conduct their activities in an appropriate manner.

10. Their purpose is to limit *imprudent* risk-taking by banks.

    Their purpose is to limit _____ risk-taking by banks.

Text

Banking Supervision

The Role of Banks in a Market Economy

In a market economy, banks provide means of clearing and settling payments to facilitate trade; they collect and hold savings/deposits of households, firms and government; and they use this funding to grant credits for investment purposes.

As such, banks are financial intermediaries that can be seen as engaging in volume transformation[1], maturity transformation[2], liquidity transformation[3], risk transformation[4] and regional transformation[5]. In carrying out these transformation activities, banks benefit from economies of scale in gathering information from a large number of depositors, borrowers and market participants that is not available to each single depositor of the bank and would be too costly to acquire. In economic theory, this is often referred to as the role of "delegated monitoring": on behalf of their depositors, banks tackle asymmetric information problems in financial transactions.

More generally, one can also say that banks manage the "blood" that helps keep the real economy of goods and services alive. They manage the capital flows from savers, and take on risks in connection with this intermediation process. When market elements work properly, banks optimize capital flows under risk/return perspectives and thereby support the economy by providing loans for profitable investments. As intermediaries, banks also play an important role in the monetary policy transmission process.

Importance of Banking Supervision

Banks play a crucial role in the efficient allocation of savings and investments in a market economy and are important for the stability of the whole financial system. Because banks take risks in fulfilling this function, they can fail and potentially go bankrupt. When this happens, depositors lose their savings, which can have devastating implications for public trust in the whole banking system[6]. Given that banks play a pivotal role for the real economy in providing ways of clearing and settling payments, transforming claims in terms of volume, maturity, liquidity, risk and region, and acting as delegated monitors, a primary reason for regulating banks is to maintain confidence and trust in the banking system by setting minimum standards for the safety and soundness of the operation of banks.

Banking Risks

Banking, by its nature, entails taking a wide array of risks. Banking supervisors need to understand these risks and make sure that banks are adequately measuring and managing them.

There are mainly six risk categories faced by banks: credit risk, market risk, liquidity risk and operational risk, legal risk and reputation risk.

Credit Risk

The extension of loans is the primary activity of most banks. Lending activities require banks to make judgments related to the creditworthiness of borrowers. These judgments do not always prove to be accurate and the creditworthiness of a borrower may decline over time due to various factors. Consequently, a major risk that banks face is credit risk or the failure of a counterpart to perform according to a contractual arrangement. This risk applies not only to loans but also to other on-and-off-balance-sheet exposures such as guarantees, acceptances and securities investments. Serious banking problems have arisen from the failure of banks to recognize impaired assets, to create reserves for writing off these assets, and to suspend recognition of interest income when appropriate.

Market Risk

Banks may also face a risk of losses in on-and-off-balance-sheet positions arising from movements in market prices. Established accounting principles cause these risks to be typically most visible in a bank's trading activities, whether they involve debt or equity instruments, or foreign exchange or commodity positions.

One specific element of market risk is foreign exchange risk. Banks act as "market-makers" in foreign exchange by quoting rates to their customers and by taking open positions[7] in currencies. The risks inherent in foreign exchange business, particularly in running open foreign exchange positions, are increased during periods of instability in exchange rates.

Interest rate risk is another main element of market risk. This risk impacts both the earnings of a bank and the economic value of its assets, liabilities and off-balance-sheet instruments. The primary forms of interest rate risk to which banks are typically exposed are: (1) repricing risk, which arises from timing differences in the maturity (for fixed rate) and repricing (for floating rate) of bank assets, liabilities and off-balance-sheet positions; (2) yield curve[8] risk, which arises from changes in the slope and shape of the yield curve; (3) basis risk[9], which arises from imperfect correlation in the adjustment of the rates earned and paid on different instruments with otherwise similar repricing characteristics; and (4) optionality, which arises from the express or implied options embedded in many bank assets, liabilities and off-balance sheet portfolios.

Although such risk is a normal part of banking, excessive interest rate risk can pose a significant threat to a bank's earnings and capital base. Managing this risk is of growing importance in sophisticated financial markets where customers actively manage their interest rate exposure. Special attention should be paid to this risk in countries where interest rates are being deregulated.

Liquidity Risk

Liquidity risk arises from the inability of a bank to accommodate decreases in liabilities or to fund increases in assets. When a bank has inadequate liquidity, it cannot obtain sufficient funds, either by increasing liabilities or by converting assets promptly, at a reasonable cost, thereby affecting profitability. In extreme cases, insufficient liquidity can lead to the insolvency of a bank.

Operational Risk

The most important types of operational risk involve breakdowns in internal controls and corporate governance. Such breakdowns can lead to financial losses through error, fraud, or failure to perform in a timely manner or cause the interests of the bank to be compromised in some other way, for example, by its dealers, lending officers or other staff exceeding their authority or conducting business in an unethical or risky manner. Other aspects of operational risk include major failure of information technology systems or events such as major fires or other disasters.

Legal Risk

Banks are subject to various forms of legal risk. This can include the risk that assets will turn out to be worthless or liabilities will turn out to be greater than expected because of inadequate or incorrect legal advice or documentation. In addition, existing laws may fail to resolve legal issues involving a bank; a court case involving a particular bank may have wider implications for banking business and involve costs to it and many or all other banks; and, laws affecting banks or other commercial enterprises may change. Banks are particularly susceptible to legal risks when entering new types of transactions and when the legal right of a counterpart to enter into a transaction is not established.

Reputation Risk

Reputational risk arises from operational failures, failure to comply with relevant laws and regulations, or other sources. Reputational risk is particularly damaging for banks since the nature of their business requires maintaining the confidence of depositors, creditors and the general market place.

Internationally Recognised Principles for Banking Supervision

Instability or a poor banking system in one country can negatively influence financial stability not only in that country but also internationally. The Core Principles for Effective Banking Supervision ("the Core Principles") is a document prepared by the Basel Committee on Banking Supervision ("the Basel Committee[10]") in close cooperation with the Group of Ten (G10)[11] central banks and additional supervisory authorities. They supplement the so-called Basel Concordat[12], which deals with international supervisory cooperation. Whereas the Core Principles were originally developed for internationally active banks, they have become the benchmark for assessing the effectiveness of supervision by international financial institutions.

The Core Principles

The Basel Committee issued the Core Principles in September 1997. They comprise 25 basic principles that form the foundation for the establishment and effective functioning of banking supervision. The Core Principles address the following main areas:
— Preconditions for effective banking supervision (Principle 1)
— Licensing and structure (Principles 2 to 5)
— Prudential regulations and requirements (Principles 6 to 15)
— Methods of ongoing banking supervision (Principles 16 to 20)
— Information requirements (Principle 21)
— Formal powers of supervision (Principle 22)
— Cross-border banking (Principles 23 to 25)

The principles are understood as minimum requirements to be implemented in national legislation. They can significantly support the efforts of public authorities and international institutions to strengthen the stability and soundness of the banking systems worldwide. The Basel Committee believes that the implementation of the Core Principles can help to improve financial stability nationally as well as internationally.

Preconditions for Effective Banking Supervision

The basic precondition for effective banking supervision is a clear definition of the responsibilities, authorities and objectives of each supervision agency, which should also be independent and legally protected. Banking supervision can only be effective if it works within a suitable macroeconomic frame with a sound and sustainable macroeconomic policy, a well-developed infrastructure, effective market discipline, procedures for the efficient resolution of problems, and a mechanism for providing an appropriate level of systemic protection.

Licensing Process and the Approval of Changes of the Structure

In order to promote a sound financial system, it is necessary to define the group of institutions to be regulated and supervised. The licensing process plays a key role in setting up this process by regulating market access. Licensing should as a minimum consist of an assessment of the bank's ownership structure, its directors and senior management, its operating and business plans, its projected financial condition, and its internal control system. The assessment of an acquirer of shares in a bank is also an important precondition for a healthy financial system. A bank's major investments or acquisitions should also be taken into account, so that the supervisor has a good sense of the bank's group structure.

Prudential Regulations and Requirements

The risks inherent in banking must be recognized, monitored and controlled. Supervisors play a critical role in ensuring that bank management does this. An important part of the supervisory process is the authority of supervisors to develop and utilize prudential regulations and requirements to control these risks, including those covering capital adequacy, loan loss reserves, asset concentrations, liquidity, risk management and internal controls. These may be qualitative and/or quantitative requirements. These requirements should not supplant management decisions but rather impose minimum prudential standards to ensure that banks conduct their activities in an appropriate manner. The dynamic nature of banking requires that supervisors periodically assess their prudential requirements and evaluate the continued relevance of existing requirements as well as the need for new requirements.

Methods of Ongoing Banking Supervision

Supervision requires the collection and analysis of information. This can be achieved by on-site and off-site supervision. On-site and off-site supervision are two sides of one coin: they supplement each other, and would not be complete without each other.

On-site Supervision

On-site inspection is the cornerstone of the supervisory process with two primary objectives: (1) to allow the supervisor to understand better the business and risks of an individual bank, its risk profile[13] and how qualified its management and staff are; and (2) to obtain the assurance that the regulatory framework is being implemented correctly and that banks are managed and organized in a proper and sound way, including the risk management framework.

On-site examination includes: interviews with management, inspecting the written policies and procedures of the bank and the degree to which those written policies and procedures are followed; evaluating whether the bank's financial statements accurately show the bank's capital, which requires a determination of the value of the bank's assets; checking the accuracy of accounting records; checking the adequacy of internal controls and the audit function; checking for compliance with laws and regulations; writing a "Report of Examination" that summarizes findings and assigns a rating to the bank.

The Report of Examination and the Ratings are often organized according to the CAMELS rating system.

CAMELS:
— Capital adequacy
— Asset quality (is the bank making good loans or bad loans)
— Management (including internal controls, corporate governance, audit)
— Earnings (profitability)
— Liquidity (does the bank have enough cash or assets easily converted to cash to meet a temporary, unexpected excess of deposits over withdrawals)
— Sensitivity to market risk (is the bank's capital or profitability overly sensitive to changes in interest rates, foreign exchange rates, or share prices, and does the bank adequately measure and monitor that risk).

The Report of Examination assigns a rating for each CAMELS component (rating is 1 through 5 — where 1 is the best, and 5 is the worst). In addition, a "composite" rating is assigned, again 1 through and the composite rating is not necessarily the average of individual component ratings.

Example: C = 2, A = 3, M = 3, E = 4, L = 1, S = 2

Average is between 2 and 3.

Generally, more weight is placed on management than other components.

The CAMELS rating is the single, comprehensive, informed supervisory opinion about the condition and performance of the bank.

Off-site Supervision

Off-site supervision covers the period in the supervisory cycle between on-site examination. It has three main objectives: (1) to monitor the development and levels of risk at individual banks and in a benchmarking exercise, comparing the bank with a peer group of comparable institutions; (2) to monitor a bank's compliance with prudential limits; and (3) to provide input for the prioritization of supervisory resources and for planning of inspections.

Off-site monitoring includes the following activities:

Looking back at the results of the last on-site examination and checks for the correction of financial problems revealed at the last examination.

Looking ahead to the next examination and identifies areas of emerging risk for the examiners to focus on.

Describing in a written analysis the current condition and performance of the bank.

Comparing the bank's condition and performance to similar banks.

Recommending changes to the CAMELS rating, a targeted examination, or a full-scope examination earlier than scheduled, if necessary.

Supervisors must have adequate means to collect proper and sufficient information on banks, on an individual and on a consolidated basis. Issues generally covered in supervisory reporting by banks include capital adequacy, liquidity, asset quality, liability, earnings, risk concentration, management, and internal control system.

Banking supervision departments require banks to submit financial data on a daily, weekly, monthly, quarterly, semi-annual, and annual basis. The data are usually required to be submitted according to International Financial Reporting Standards (IFRS), but sometimes the bank supervisors require different standards ("regulatory accounting practices"). In addition to the balance sheet and profit and loss statement, banks are usually required to submit data on non-performing loans, financial assets and liabilities categorized by remaining time to maturity and by currency, and other details. The data are used in both on-site examinations and off-site monitoring.

Terminology

banking supervision	银行监管
depositor	存款人
creditor	债权人
volume	交易量
maturity	期限；(票据)到期
liquidity	流通性，变现能力
economies of scale	规模经济
delegated monitoring	受托监控
credit risk	信贷风险
market risk	市场风险
liquidity risk	流通风险
operational risk	经营风险
legal risk	法律风险
reputation risk	声誉风险
on-and-off-balance-sheet	(资产负债表)表内、表外项目
guarantee	担保
acceptance	承兑
position	投资持有量
market maker	做市者
open position	持仓
repricing risk	重新定价风险
yield curve risk	收益曲线风险
basis risk	基差风险
optionality	期权风险
capital base	资本金基础
corporate governance	公司治理
liabilities	债务
capital adequacy	资本充足
loan loss reserves	贷款损失储备金
asset concentration	资产集中
risk management	风险管理
on-site supervision	现场监管

| off-site supervision | 非现场监管 |
| risk profile | 风险状况 |

Notes on the Text

1. volume transformation — transformation of small individual deposits into large-sum loans.
2. maturity transformation — transformation of short-term deposits into long-term lending.
3. liquidity transformation — transformation of liquid deposits into illiquid loans.
4. risk transformation — transformation of a depositor's demand for repayment security into the risk for the bank that the lender will not repay the loan.
5. regional transformation — transformation of high levels of saving in one region/country into high lending activity in a different region country.
6. banking system — the structural network of institutions that offer financial services within a country. The member of the banking system and function they typically perform include: (1) commercial banks that take deposits and make loans, (2) investment banks which specialize in capital market issues and trading, and (3) national central banks that issue currency and set monetary policy.
7. open position — It refers to any trade in investing that has been established or entered and that has yet to be closed with an opposing trade. An open position can exist following a buy (long) position, or a sell (short) position. In either case, the position will remain open until an opposing trade has taken place. For example, an open long position is the state in which an investor owns a security and has not sold it.
8. yield curve — It refers to a line that plots the interest rates, at a set point in time, of bonds having equal credit quality, but differing maturity dates. It is used as a benchmark for other debt in the market, such as mortgage rates or bank lending rates. The curve is also used to predict changes in economic output and growth.
9. basis risk — The risk is associated with imperfect hedging using futures, which could arise due to the difference between the asset whose price is to be hedged and the asset underlying the derivative, or due to a mismatch between the expiration date of the futures and the actual selling date of the asset. (Basis = spot price of hedged asset−futures price of the contract.)
10. The Basel Committee — It refers to a committee of banking supervisory authorities established by the central bank governors of the G10 countries in 1974. It now consists of senior representatives of banking supervisory authorities and central banks from Argentina, Australia, Belgium, Brazil, Canada, China, France, Germany, Hong Kong SAR, India Indonesia, Italy, Japan, Korea, Luxembourg, Mexico, the Netherlands, Russia, Saudi Arabia, Singapore, South Africa, Spain, Sweden, Switzerland, Turkey, the UK and the US. The committee's Secretariat is located at the Bank for International Settlements (BIS) in Basel, Switzerland.
11. The Group of Ten (G10) — It originally refers to the group of countries that agrees to participate in the *General Arrangements to Borrow* (*GAB*) established in 1962, including

Belgium, Canada, France, Germany, Italy, Japan, the Netherlands, Sweden, the United Kingdom and the U.S. Now, G10 actually is made of eleven industrial countries (Switzerland joined the group in 1964), which consult and cooperate on economic, monetary and financial matters. The Ministers of Finance and central bank Governors of the Group of Ten meet as needed in connection with the meetings of the International Monetary Fund and the World Bank.

12. Basel Concordat — It is a 1983 agreement by the Basel Committee stating banks opening subsidiaries in foreign countries must submit those subsidiaries to the full regulatory authority of the relevant countries. It also requires the parent banks to allow their own regulators to review the foreign subsidiaries. It accomplishes both of these by encouraging the regulatory authorities to share information with each other.

13. risk profile — It is an evaluation of an individual or organization's willingness to take risks as well as threats to which an organization is exposed. A risk profile identifies: (1) the acceptable level of risk an individual or corporation is prepared to accept; and (2) the risks and threats faced by an organization. The risk profile may include the probability of resulting negative effects, and an outline of the potential costs and level of disruption of each risk.

Exercises

I. Reading Comprehension.

Read the text carefully and decide whether the following statements are true (T) or false (F).

_____ 1. The key objective to supervise and regulate banks is to maintain stability and public confidence in the financial system.

_____ 2. Banking supervision only involves monitoring and examining banks' compliance with laws and regulations.

_____ 3. The collapse of a bank's computer network is a typical operational risk event.

_____ 4. In the course of the licensing process, one of the aspects that supervisors shall pay due attention to is the fit and proper nature of the management.

_____ 5. Banking supervisors are also responsible for banks' identification, measurement, management and control of risks.

II. Vocabulary Building.

A. Match the term in Column A with the definition in Column B.

1. open position   a. eliminate an investment from one's portfolio, by either selling a long position or covering a short position

2. close position   b. a person or company that places money in a bank account

3. liquidity risk   c. exposure to the loss of principal or financial reward due to a counterparty's failure to perform according to a contractual arrangement

4. credit risk   d. any stock or equity which is owned

5. market risk   e. the risk that a given security or asset cannot be traded quickly enough in the market to prevent a loss or make the required profit

6. creditor   f. the date on which payment of a financial obligation is due

7. depositor   g. exposure to uncertain market prices

8. maturity   h. the number of shares or contracts traded in a security or in an entire market during a given period of time

9. guarantee   i. a person or company to whom one owes money

10. volume   j. a promise made by a third party to provide payment on a bond, loan, or other liability in the event of default

B. Complete the following sentences with the words given in the box and change the form of the words where necessary.

subject	deregulate	optimize	pose	grant
sound	impair	susceptible	comprise	compose
benchmark	impose			

1. The health of the economy and the effectiveness of monetary policy depend on a _____ financial system.

2. Bank charter is usually _____ by the central bank or a separate supervisory body of a country.

3. A weak bank is one whose liquidity or solvency is or will be _____ unless there is a major improvement in its financial resources.

4. These standards are applied as a set of _____ and a code for improving the effectiveness of regulation.

5. Institutions that are _____ to regulation must have access to timely and accurate data to underpin rational decision making and management in accordance with the requirements of regulatory departments.

6. Some believe that the _____ of the sector contributed to the U.S. financial crisis 2007−2009 and the global financial crisis of 2008−2009.

7. Service sectors like finance, trading and tourism are more _____ to financial risk when compared to other traditional sectors.

8. The CBRC have made it clear that they will _____ the regulatory organization system, enhance the efficiency of off-site regulation and on-site inspections on an ongoing basis.

9. The regulatory framework that _____ Basel III was developed in response to perceived flaws in financial regulation that were revealed during the global financial crisis of 2008.

10. The growing use of complex financial instruments known as derivatives does not _____ a threat to the country's financial system.

III. Cloze.

There are 10 blanks in the following two passages. For each blank there are four choices marked A, B, C and D. You are supposed to choose the best answer.

Passage 1

Banking supervisors play an indirect role in protecting depositors against losses arising from the failure of an individual bank. Direct responsibility lies (1) _____ the bank's management, who have to ensure, under monitoring by the supervisors, that they are responsible and are able to meet depositors' demands for repayment. (2)_____ the role of the supervisor can substantially influence the quality and soundness of the banking system, and the supervisor can for instance play a role in educating bank managers on how they may (3)_____their responsibilities towards stakeholders. One contribution that the supervisor can make is to express clearly to managers (4)_____ principles and processes the bank should have in (5)_____in order to identify, measure, monitor and control banking risks. The supervisor must tread a delicate balance between helping bank managers understand and develop such principles and processes, and at the same time avoid being too prescriptive and thereby performing a management function for the bank.

(1) A. in   B. behind   C. with   D. on
(2) A. Nevertheless B. Thus   C. Therefore   D. Consequently
(3) A. complete   B. fulfill   C. achieve   D. bear
(4) A. which   B. that   C. what   D. these
(5) A. order   B. common   C. array   D. place

Passage 2

While anyone may lend out money, only registered banks are allowed to take deposits from the general public. Should a bank run into financial difficulties and (6)_____ unable to repay its depositors, the public will lose their money. As a result, in order to (7) _____ that the deposits taken from the public are not used irresponsibly and to protect the public (8)_____, banks have to be supervised. The Bank Supervision Department (BSD) plays a pivotal role in this regard.

As one of the Bank's core departments, the BSD is fully (9)_____to achieving its mission of promoting the soundness of the domestic banking system and contributing to financial stability. In its interminable endeavour to continuously improve on its supervisory programme and practices, the BSD steadfastly models its regulatory and supervisory framework (10)_____ the following highly-regarded and internationally recognized key supervisory methodologies, namely, the *25 Core Principles for Effective Banking Supervision*; and the *Basel II, Basel 2.5 and Basel III frameworks*.

(6) A. is   B. would be   C. be   D. will be
(7) A. assure   B. ensure   C. insure   D. reassure
(8) A. at large   B. in the large C. by and large D. at the large
(9) A. committed   B. admitted   C. remitted   D. submitted
(10) A. after   B. for   C. in   D. on

IV. Translate the following sentences into English.

1. 网上商业银行会遭遇的风险和其他类型的银行是一样的。(entail)
2. 银行监管涉及对银行的经营状况及其对法律法规的遵守情况进行监督检查。(compliance)

3. 人们认为银行经营效率低主要是源于不良贷款，而大多数时候不良贷款是因管理不善引起的。(arise from)
4. 银行监管机构在评估一家银行的资本金是否足以应对其贷款、投资和其他资产的损失时会考虑这些资产的风险水平。(take into account)
5. 在市场经济体中，银行的主要作用就是分配金融资源，并根据对将要借款人偿还能力的积极评估，充当有多余资金的存款人和将要借款人之间的中介人。(play a role)

V. Translate the following paragraphs into Chinese.

1. A global financial meltdown will affect the livelihoods of almost everyone in an increasingly inter-connected world. The primary goals of supervision and regulations include protecting depositors' funds, maintaining a stable monetary system, promoting an efficient and competitive banking system and protecting consumer rights related to banking relationships and transactions.

2. According to Principle 3, the licensing process, at a minimum, should consist of assessment of the ownership structure and governance of the bank and its wider group, including the fitness and propriety of Board members and senior management, its strategic and operating plan, internal control and risk management, and its projected financial condition, including its capital base. Where the proposed owner or parent organization is a foreign bank, the prior consent of its home country supervisor should be obtained.

VI. Self-Testing.

1. Which of the following combinations correctly represents the goals of banking supervision?
    A. Maintaining confidence in the banking sector, protecting both depositors and banks and avoiding systemic risk.
    B. Maintaining confidence in the banking sector, protecting both depositors and creditors and avoiding systemic risk.
    C. Protecting depositors and financial institutions, promoting sound practices for banking operations and avoiding systemic risks.
    D. Regulating banks, controlling banks' activities, protecting depositors and supporting banks financially as the lender of the last resort.
2. The following are the three pillars in the Basel II framework EXCEPT _____.
    A. minimum capital requirements   B. on-site supervision of banks
    C. the supervisory review process   D. market discipline
3. Which of the following assets does not carry credit risk?
    A. Loan.
    B. Guarantee.
    C. A government bond.
    D. The head office building owned by the bank.
4. Which of the following statements regarding market risk is correct?
    A. Markets are fundamentally stable and banks do not need to have timely information in order to manage market risks. Information about the purchase price of a given asset

is sufficient.

B. A bank must monitor the development of the market price on a government bond although there is no risk that the government will default on the payment obligation.

C. Banks should not enter into transactions carrying market risks without understanding the risk involved in a specific instrument.

D. Banking supervisors are not responsible for banks' identification, measurement, management and control of market risk. The responsibility rests with the bank's management.

5. Which of the following instruments carries liquidity risk?
   A. Loan.   B. Share.   C. Equity reserves.   D. Subordinated debt.

6. Who issued the Core Principles for Effective Banking Supervision?
   A. The International Organization of Banking Supervisors.
   B. The Financial Stability Forum.
   C. The Basel Committee on Banking Supervision.
   D. The Bank for International Settlements Regulatory Committee.

7. Which of the following principles is not part of the Core Principles for Effective Banking?
   A. Principles for licensing and structure.
   B. Principles for information requirements.
   C. Principles for prudential regulations.
   D. Principles for capital adequacy.

8. Which of the following statements relating to off-site and on-site supervision is correct?
   A. One of the objectives of off-site supervision is to monitor a bank's compliance with prudential limits.
   B. Off-site supervision is about the collection of quantitative information, its storage and evaluation. On-site supervision uses the information collected for peer group analysis, prioritization of resources and takes action where necessary.
   C. Off-site and on-site supervision are complementary with off-site supervision being best suited to address quantitative elements of supervisory analysis and on-site supervision best suited for qualitative elements.
   D. Urgent on-site inspections are most efficient for the banking supervisor, because they are not announced to the bank which cannot therefore correct misdoings before the supervisor arrives to look for breaches of rules and regulations.

9. What do the off-site supervisory tools aim to assess?
   A. The ongoing performance of banks.
   B. The current compliance of a bank with quantitative standards.
   C. A bank's past performance.
   D. A bank's current performance.

10. Which of the following statements correctly reflects the supervisory aspects assessed in a "CAMELS" model?
    A. Capital, Adequacy, Management, Earnings, Liability, Sensitivity to market risk.
    B. Capital adequacy, Asset quality, Management, Earnings, Liability, Sensitivity to market risk.

C. Capital, Asset quality, Management, Earnings, Liquidity, Sensitivity to market risk.
D. Capital, Adequacy, Management, Earnings, Liquidity, Sensitivity to market risk.

VII. Writing.

Please write an invitation letter in English as follows.
1. 国际清算银行金融稳定学院与中国银行业监督管理委员会将于 20××年 5 月 29 — 31 日在北京联合举办"金融稳定和宏观审慎监管"高层政策论坛(Regional Policy Forum on Financial Stability and Macroprudential Supervision)。
2. 诚邀您出席。
3. 此次会议与会者主要是东亚和太平洋地区中央银行行长会与组织(Executive Meeting of East Asia Pacific，EMEAP)成员国中央银行和监管机构的高级官员，因此，这是各国监管机构高级官员增进相互交流与合作的大好机会。
4. 欢迎在大会上演讲，演讲摘要须在 3 月 15 日之前提交。欲了解情况更多详情，请与王启明先生联系，电子邮箱是：wangqiming@cbrc.gov.cn。

Supplementary Reading

Regulatory and Supervisory Issues from FinTech

Remarks by Svein Andresen, Secretary General, Financial Stability Board
June 29, 2017
(Abridged)

Good morning, everyone. I would like to start by thanking our hosts here at the Cambridge Center for Alternative Finance for organizing today's conference and for inviting me.

In the last few years, we have seen rapid growth and an increasing maturity in FinTech, including peer-to-peer (P2P) platforms, blockchain, algo trading, InsurTech, RegTech, SupTech and others. FinTech, which the FSB defines as technology-enabled innovation in financial services, is transforming — many say "disrupting" — financial services at a rapid pace. This applied to activities performed by both start-ups and incumbent financial institutions. Our focus is on FinTech activities, rather than the entities.

FinTech encompasses a broad range of tech-fuelled innovations, which are not all of a similar nature. Distributed ledger technology, robo-advice, smart contracts, big data applications and P2P lending may all be TinTech innovations, but as we all know, they mean and do very different things. In fact, FinTech innovations are such different animals from one another that it's difficult to classify them as one species, and many instead refer to "a whole ecosystem".

Today, I will discuss the work of FSB, focusing on:
- the framework the FSB has used for drawing out the potential financial stability benefits and risks of FinTech,
- how FinTech fits within existing regulatory frameworks.

FinTech: new technologies, same functions

The financial system performs a number of important economic functions, and in this light, FinTech is not fundamentally different. For instance:

- Loans can be granted by banks, which engage in deposit taking, money creation and delegated monitoring, or by FinTech credit platforms, which pool funds and streamline the sharing of information outside traditional financial intermediaries. Or as we see more and more, loans be granted by FinTech platforms in cooperation with traditional banks.
- Payments can be executed in physical currency, bank currency or in mobile and web-based payment platforms, and need obviously not be operated by banks.
- Investment advice can be given by a human advisor or by robo-advisors that use artificial intelligence and machine learning.
- Securities and currency transactions can be cleared and settled through traditional financial infrastructures, or in new ways with distributed ledgers.

And, of course, digital interfaces can unbundle and rebundle access to all of these services. Classifying FinTech by their economic functions is one means of cutting through the fog and understanding what many of these innovations entail.

Looking at FinTech in this way also helps to understand the drivers of its growth, and its financial stability implications. And in principle, financial services through FinTech can be subject to the same microfinancial and macrofinancial risks as traditional finance.

On the microfinancial side, authorities and providers are focused on financial and operational risks. Where there is maturity mismatch, this entails run risk, and where there is liquidity transformation, there is the possibility for fire sales. In this light, it is encouraging that most FinTech credit platforms and digital wallets do not engage in such maturity transformation. Leverage is not typically associated with FinTech activities, either, though there are exceptions. Algorithmic trading can involve substantial leverage. And in some cases, FinTech business and consumer lending or equity crowdfunding platforms may borrow funds in order to finance temporary holdings (or "warehousing") of bond or equity issuance. FinTech platforms that lend on their balance sheet may also build up leverage. Of operational risks, third-party dependencies and cyber risks are relevant. More on this later. There are also public policy concerns and risks around data privacy.

On the macrofinancial side, we distinguish between contagion, procyclicality, volatility and systemic implications. For FinTech, there may be reputational contagion, particularly where activities interact directly with households and businesses. Potential breaches of confidential consumer data could undermine confidence in the sector more broadly. Procyclicality may arise if FinTech credit platforms grow large and investors suddenly lose confidence, for example due to rising non-performing loans. And in terms of systemic implications, it is possible that new highly connected single point of failure entities emerge in the future.

For these reasons, financial authorities need to take FinTech into account in their existing risk assessments and regulatory frameworks in light of its rapid evolution. Indeed, many authorities have already done so, and quite a few have already made regulatory changes where existing framework were considered inadequate.

Regulatory approaches: learning by doing

A second part of the work looks at approaches of FSB member jurisdictions, and some non-FSB members, to regulating and supervising FinTech. Of the 26 jurisdictions taking part, 20 have taken or plan to take policy measures on FinTech. Other jurisdictions are considering changes, and only one has decided after review that its existing framework sufficiently addresses current national FinTech developments.

Importantly, the scope and scale of these changes or planned changes vary substantially. This depends, among other things, on the size and structure of domestic FinTech activities — and the flexibility of the existing regulatory framework. Some authorities have recently issued publications or proposals on aspects of FinTech. And several jurisdictions as you know have introduced so-called innovation facilitators — such as regulatory sandboxes, innovation hubs or accelerators — in order to promote innovation and improve interactions with new FinTech firms.

Where authorities have regulatory changes:
- The policy objectives have been to strengthen consumer and investor protection, to include FinTech in market integrity regulation, to promote financial inclusion and to foster innovation or competition.
- Financial stability considerations have not so far motivated recent or planned regulatory reforms around FinTech. In part, this reflects the small size of activities. However, several authorities see this as an issue going forward.

Looking at the FinTech activities that have been the subject of regulatory change, the focus has been on crowdfunding or FinTech credit, payments, virtual currencies, cybersecurity, and in some cases specific technologies, such as big data or cloud computing. Cross-border issues are not frequently discussed, but will gain relevance as innovations are increasingly used across borders. There are substantial contacts between regulators who are learning from one another's experience.

Conclusion

Let me sum up.

First, FinTech may be a new area, but the economic functions it delivers are not fundamentally different from existing financial services. Healthy innovations can expand on their economic benefits. But FinTech activities are also subject to similar microfinancial and macrofiancial risks. As such, authorities will continue to regulate for the same reasons they regulate traditional financial activities.

Second, authorities are adapting their regulatory approaches in a number of ways, sometimes with innovation facilitators, and sometimes with means of fitting FinTech activities into existing frameworks. For now, regulatory lenses other than financial stability policy considerations are at the fore, but that will likely change as the sector become larger.

Notes

Financial Stability Board (FSB) — It is an international body that monitors and makes recommendations about the global financial system. It was established after the G20 London summit in April 2009 as a successor to the Financial Stability Forum. The Board includes all G20 major economies, and the European Commission. Hosted and funded by the Bank for International Settlements, the Board is based in Basel, Switzerland.

Questions

1. What is FinTech? What does it include?
2. Why do some people use the term "a whole ecosystem" to refer to FinTech?
3. In what ways is FinTech similar to traditional finance?
4. Why should governments regulate and supervise FinTech?
5. How are the authorities of FSB members going to regulate and supervise FinTech?

Unit 14　Basics of Insurance

Case

Ben, 40 years old, is the sales director of a company. He has a very happy family with 2 kids, one being 6 and the other 8. His wife does not work, so he is the bread winner of the family.

As the head of the sales department, he is constantly under great pressure and has to work overtime almost every day. Since his company is 20 miles away from his home, he has to drive to work and in addition, he has to fly frequently for business purpose. Sometimes he is worried that if something unexpected and disastrous should happen to him, how his wife and kids would get the money they need to buy food and make mortgage payments. They have just bought a big apartment with 20 years mortgage to pay.

Questions

1. If you were Ben, what would you do to get rid of the worries?
2. What kind of insurance is appropriate for Ben?

Preview

Skimming

Skim the following text quickly to answer the following questions and discuss your answers with your partners.

1. What are the three main functions of insurance?
   _____.

2. What are the factors to be considered when the premium level is determined?
   _____.

3. What is the insurance market made up of?
   _____.

4. What are the basic principles of insurance?
   _____.

5. What are the two types of reinsurance treaties?
   _____.

Scanning

Scan the following text quickly to find the specific information.

1. How can people transfer some of the risks in their life on to others?
   _____
   _____.

2. Who fixes the level of premium?
   _____
   _____.

3. What is the difference between an insurance broker and an insurance agent?
   _____
   _____.

4. Why do insurance companies seek reinsurance?
   _____
   _____.

5. How are the risks considered under a facultative treaty?
   _____
   _____.

6. How are risks shared under a quota share treaty?
   _____
   _____.

7. How are risks shared under a surplus line treaty?
   _____
   _____.

8. How much is the reinsurer obligated to pay under an excess-loss treaty?
   _____
   _____.

Vocabulary in Context

Read the following sentences and try to guess the meaning of the italicized words by using the context. Then replace the italicized words with synonyms (words or phrases that have nearly the same or similar meanings).

1. The insured's premium, which is fixed at the *inception* of the contract, is received by the insurer into a fund or pool for the type of risk.

   The insured's premium, which is fixed at the _____ of the contract, is received by the insurer into a fund or pool for the type of risk.

2. For example, a timber-built house presents a different *hazard* from that of one of standard brick construction.

   For example, a timber-built house presents a different _____ from that of one of standard brick construction.

3. ….someone *grossly* overweight has a higher chance of early death than a person of average weight.

   …someone _____ overweight has a higher chance of early death than a person of average weight.

4. ... and *in aggregate,* the contributions to the fund must be sufficient to meet the total cost of claims brought about by these factors.

... and _____, the contributions to the fund must be sufficient to meet the total cost of claims brought about by these factors.

5. ... there will be the costs of administering the fund, of creating reserves to ensure that *abnormally* heavy claims in future years can still be met, and an allowance for a margin of profit to the insurers in their operations.

... there will be the costs of administering the fund, of creating reserves to ensure that _____ heavy claims in future years can still be met, and an allowance for a margin of profit to the insurers in their operations.

6. The concept requires that the insured have a "*stake*" in the loss or damage to the life or property insured.

The concept requires that the insured have a "_____" in the loss or damage to the life or property insured.

7. *Proximate* cause. The cause of loss (the peril) must be covered under the insuring agreement of the policy, and the dominant cause must not be excluded.

_____ cause. The cause of loss (the peril) must be covered under the insuring agreement of the policy, and the dominant cause must not be excluded.

8. For example, the insurer may sue those *liable* for the insured's loss.

For example, the insurer may sue those _____ for the insured's loss.

9. ....while the company *assuming* part of the risk is known simply as the reinsurer.

....while the company _____ part of the risk is known simply as the reinsurer.

10. Normally, the amount the reinsurer *is obligated to* accept is referred to as a number of "lines" and is expressed as some multiple of the retention.

Normally, the amount the reinsurer _____ accept is referred to as a number of "lines" and is expressed as some multiple of the retention.

Text

Introduction to Insurance

The Function of Insurance

The primary function of insurance is to provide a risk transfer mechanism by means of a common pool[1] into which each policy-holder[2] pays a fair and equitable premium[3], according to the risk of loss he or she brings to the pool.

Risk transfer Insurance is a risk transfer mechanism, whereby the individual or the business enterprise can shift some of the uncertainty of life on to the shoulders of others. In return for a known premium, usually a very small amount compared with the potential loss, the cost of that loss can be transferred to an insurer. Without insurance, there would be a great deal of uncertainty experienced by an individual or an enterprise, not only as to whether a loss would occur, but also as to what size it would be if it did occur.

The common pool The insured's premium, which is fixed at the inception of the contract, is received by the insurer into a fund or pool for the type of risk, and the claims[4] of those suffering losses are paid out of this pool. An insurance company will pay its motor claims out of the monies[5] it has received from those insuring motor cars, and so on. Because of the large number of clients in any particular fund or pool the insurance company can predict, with reasonable accuracy, the amount of claims likely to be incurred in the coming year. There will be some variation in claims costs from year to year and the premiums include a small margin to build up a reserve[6] upon which the company can draw in bad years. Therefore, subject to the limitations of the type of cover bought, the insured will not be required to make further contributions[7] to the common pool after the loss.

Equitable contributions or premiums Assuming that a risk mechanism has been set up through a common fund or pool, the third primary function is that the contributions paid into the fund should be fair to all the parties participating.

Each party wishing to insure will bring to the fund differing degrees of risk of loss to the fund. For example, a timber-built house presents a different hazard from that of one of standard brick construction; an 18-year old driver is more hazardous than one aged 35; someone grossly overweight has a higher chance of early death than a person of average weight; the man with a house worth $500,000 has a potentially larger claim on the fund than one with a house worth $250,000.

These examples could be summarized under two main headings, hazard and value, and in aggregate the contributions to the fund must be sufficient to meet the total cost of claims brought about by these factors. In addition, there will be the costs of administering the fund, of creating reserves to ensure that abnormally heavy claims in future years can still be met, and an allowance for a margin of profit to the insurers in their operations.

Factors such as these must be taken into account by the underwriter[8]. In fixing the level of premium of each case he must try to ensure that the level of contribution made to the fund by a particular policy-maker[9] is equitable compared with the contributions of others, bearing in mind the likely frequency and severity of claims which may be made by that policy-holder. Finally the level of premium fixed must be relatively competitive otherwise the insurer will go out of business due to lack of new orders.

Insurance Market

Like any other market, the insurance market comprises sellers — the insurance companies and Lloyd's underwriting members[10]; buyers — the general public, industry and commerce; and middlemen — the insurance brokers and agents.

The Insured

The buyer of insurance, whether a private individual or a large corporation, is called the insured. It is the buyer's financial risk which is being assured by the insurer in return for a premium.

The Insurer

The seller or supplier of insurance is called the insurer, and insurers can be divided into two broad classes.

Companies These may transact one form of insurance only, e.g., life business, or they may transact many forms of cover, e.g., motor, fire, liability and perhaps life business.

Lloyd's　This is an association of individual underwriting members who form themselves into groups or syndicates but each retain their individuality.

The Intermediary

A buyer of insurance (the insured) may approach a company direct, but the majority of business is placed through intermediaries. Indeed a buyer can place business at Lloyd's only through an intermediary called a Lloyd's broker. Intermediaries can be classified as follows.

Broker　An individual or firm whose full time occupation is the placing of business with insurance companies on behalf of clients.

Lloyd's broker　Similar to a broker but in addition business can be placed at Lloyd's as the firm has been approved by the committee of Lloyd's.

Agent　Someone who places insurance with companies but whose main occupation is in some field which brings him into contact with members of the public who require insurance. Examples of this class are solicitors[11], accountants, garage proprietors[12] and the like.

Basic Doctrines

When a company insures an individual entity, there are basic legal requirements. Several commonly cited legal principles of insurance include:

Insurable interest　The insured typically must directly suffer from the loss. Insurable interest must exist whether property insurance[13] or insurance on a person[14] is involved. The concept requires that the insured have a "stake" in the loss or damage to the life or property insured. What that "stake" is will be determined by the kind of insurance involved and the nature of the property ownership or relationship between the persons.

Indemnity　The insurance company indemnifies, or compensates, the insured in the case of certain losses only up to the insured's interest.

Utmost good faith　The insured and the insurer are bound by a good faith bond of honesty and fairness. Material facts must be disclosed.

Proximate cause　The cause of loss (the peril) must be covered under the insuring agreement of the policy, and the dominant cause must not be excluded.

Subrogation　The insurance company acquires legal rights to pursue recoveries on behalf of the insured. For example, the insurer may sue those liable for the insured's loss.

Contribution　Insurers who have similar obligations to the insured contribute in the indemnification, according to some methods.

Reinsurance

Nature of Reinsurance

Reinsurance is a device whereby an insurance company may avoid catastrophic hazard in the operation of the insurance mechanism. As the term indicates, reinsurance is insurance for insurers. It is based on the same principles of sharing and transferring as insurance itself. To protect themselves against the catastrophe of a comparatively large single loss or a large number of small losses caused by a single occurrence, insurance companies devised the concept of reinsurance. In a reinsurance transaction the insurer seeking reinsurance is known as the direct writer or the ceding company, while the company assuming part of the risk is known simply as the reinsurer. That portion of a risk that the direct writer retains is called the net line or the net retention. The act of transferring a part of the risk to the reinsurance company is called ceding, and that portion of the risk passed on to the reinsurer is called the cession.

Type of Reinsurance Treaties

Two types of reinsurance treaties are available: facultative and automatic. Under a facultative treaty, the risks are considered individually by both parties. Each risk is submitted by the direct writer to the reinsurer for acceptance or rejection, and the direct writer is not even bound to submit the risks in the first place. However, the terms under which reinsurance will take place are spelled out, and once the risk has been submitted and accepted, the advance arrangements apply; until then, the direct writer carries the entire risk.

Under an automatic treaty, the reinsurer agrees — in advance — to accept a portion of the gross line[15] of the direct writing company or a portion of certain risks that meet the reinsurance underwriting rules of the reinsurer. The direct writer is obliged to cede a portion of the risk to which the automatic treaty applies.

Reinsurance in Property and Liability Insurance[16]

There are two essential ways in which risk is shared under reinsurance agreements in the field of property and liability insurance. The reinsurance agreement may require the reinsurer to share in every loss that occurs to a reinsured risk, or it may require the reinsurer to pay only after a loss reaches a certain size. The first arrangement is called proportional reinsurance[17] and includes quota share treaties and surplus line treaties. The second approach is called excess loss reinsurance[18].

Quota Share Treaty Under a quota share treaty, the direct-writing company and the reinsurance company agree to share the amount of each risk on some percentage basis. Thus, the ABC Mutual Insurance Company (the direct writer) may have a 50 percent quota share treaty with the DEF Reinsurance Company (reinsurer). Under such an agreement, the DEF Reinsurance Company will pay 50 percent of any losses arising from those risks subject to the reinsurance treaty. In return, the ABC Mutual Insurance Company will pay the DEF Reinsurance Company 50 percent of the premiums it receives from the insured with a reasonable allowance made to ABC for the agent's commission and other expenses connected with putting the business on the books[19].

Surplus Treaty Under a surplus line treaty, the reinsurer agrees to accept some amount of insurance on each risk in excess of a specified net retention. Normally, the amount the reinsurer is obligated to accept is referred to as a number of "lines" and is expressed as some multiple of the retention. A given treaty might specify a net retention of $10,000, with five lines. Under such a treaty, if the direct writer writes a $10,000 policy, no reinsurance is involved, but the reinsurer will accept the excess of policies over $10,000 up to $50,000. These treaties may be first-surplus treaties, second-surplus, and so on. A second-surplus treaty fits over a first-surplus treaty, assuming any excess of the first treaty, and so on for a third and fourth treaty. To illustrate, let us assume that the ABC Mutual Insurance Company (the direct writer), has a first-surplus treaty with a $10,000 net retention and five lines with the DEF Reinsurance Company and a second-surplus treaty with the GHI

Reinsurance Company, also with five lines. If ABC sells a $100,000 policy, it must, under the terms of both agreements, retain $10,000. The DEF Reinsurance Company will then assume $50,000 and GHI will assume $40,000.

Any loss under this policy would be shared on the basis of the amount of total insurance each company carries. Thus, ABC would pay 10 percent of any loss, DEF would pay 50 percent and GHI would pay 40 percent. The premium would be divided in the same proportion, again with a reasonable allowance from the reinsurers to the direct writer for the expense of putting the policy on the books.

Excess-Loss Treaty Under an excess-loss treaty, the reinsurer is bound to pay only when a loss exceeds a certain amount. In essence, an excess-loss treaty is simply an insurance policy that has a large deductible taken out by the direct writer. The excess-loss treaty may be written to cover a specific risk or to cover many risks suffering loss from a single occurrence. Such a treaty might, for example, require the reinsurer to pay after the direct-writing company had sustained a loss of $10,000 on a specific piece of property, or it might require payment by the reinsurer if the direct writer suffered loss in excess of $50,000 from any one occurrence. There is, of course, a designated maximum limit of liability for the reinsurer.

Reinsurance in Life Insurance

In the field of life insurance, reinsurance may take one of two forms: the term insurance approach and the coinsurance approach. Under the term insurance approach, the direct writer purchase yearly renewable term insurance[20] equal to the difference between the face value of the policy and the reserve, which is the amount at risk for the company. The coinsurance approach to reinsurance in life insurance is quite similar to the quota share approach in property and liability. Under this approach, the ceding company transfers some portion of the face amount[21] of the policy to the reinsurer, and the reinsurer becomes liable for its proportional share of the death claim. In addition, the reinsurer becomes responsible for the maintenance of the policy reserve[22] on its share of the policy.

Terminology

pool	共保集团；分享基金
insurance	保险
risk transfer	风险转移
risk sharing	风险分散
policyholder	保单持有人
premium	保险费
insurer	保险人
the insured	被保险人
claim	索赔
insurance company	保险公司
profit margin	盈余，利润
reserve	准备金
type of cover	投保险别

equitable contribution	公平分摊
hazard	危险因素
underwriter	核保人
Lloyd's	劳合社
insurance broker	保险经纪人
insurance agent	保险代理人
intermediary	保险中介人
Lloyd's broker	劳合社经纪人
solicitors	招保人，保险业务员
garage proprietor	汽车维修和经销商
insurable interest	可保利益(原则)
property insurance	财产保险
indemnity	补偿(原则)
utmost good faith	最大诚信原则
proximate cause	近因原则
peril	风险
policy	保单
subrogation	代位求偿原则
contribution	分摊原则
recoveries	追偿款
reinsurance	再保险，分保
direct writer	直接承保人
ceding company	分保公司
reinsurer	分保人
net line	净线数
net retention	净自留额
ceding	再保，分保
cession	再保金额，分保金额
reinsurance treaty	分保(再保)合同
facultative reinsurance	临时再保，临时分保
automatic reinsurance	自动生效分保
gross line	分保总额
underwriting	承保
liability insurance	责任保险
proportional reinsurance	比例再保险
quota share treaty	成数再保险合同，定额分保合同
surplus line treaty	溢额线数再保险合同
excess loss reinsurance	超额损失再保险
direct-writing company	直接承保公司
commission	佣金
books	账目

first-surplus treaty	第一次溢额分保合同
second-surplus treaty	第二次溢额分保合同
deductible	免赔额
life insurance	人身保险；人寿保险
term insurance	定期(人寿)保险
yearly renewable term	每年更新式保单
coinsurance	共同保险
face amount	面额
policy reserve	保单责任准备金

Notes on the Text

1. pool — fund: a risk-sharing mechanism in which the members of a group agree to be collectively responsible for losses. (共保集团)

2. policy-holder — a person who has an insurance policy and who receives the specific types of coverage stated in the policy, subject to the payment of premiums, usually on a monthly basis. (保单持有人)

3. premium — the payment, or one of the periodical payments a policyholder agrees to make for an insurance policy. (保险费)

4. claim — notification to an insurance company that payment of an amount is due under the terms of a policy. (索赔)

5. monies — amounts of money. (款项)

6. reserve — liability set up for particular purposes. (准备金)

7. contribution — a participation, as two insurance policies in the same loss. (分摊)

8. underwriter — an individual who decides whether the insurance company will issue coverage, and in some cases, the rate at which it will be issued. (核保人)

9. policy-maker — a person who buys the insurance. (投保人)

10. Lloyd's underwriting members — Lloyd's refers to a British insurance market, which serves as a meeting place where multiple financial backers or "members", whether individual (traditionally known as "names") or corporations, come together to pool and spread risks. It is a home to 45 managing agents and 66 syndicates, which offers an unrivalled concentration of specialist underwriting expertise and talent. It is a group of individual underwriters and syndicates that underwrite insurance risks severally, using facilities maintained by the Lloyd's of London Corporation. (劳合社)

11. solicitor — a person who solicits insurance business on behalf of an insurance enterprise, an insurance broker company, or an insurance agent company. (招保人；保险业务员)

12. garage proprietor — a person who owns a commercial establishment in which motor vehicles are repaired, serviced, bought and sold. (汽车维修和经销商)

13. property insurance — It is insurance that provides protection against risks to property, such as fire, theft or weather damage. This includes specialized forms of insurance such as fire insurance, flood insurance, earthquake insurance, home insurance or boiler insurance. (财产保险)

14. insurance on a person — insurance that includes life insurance, health insurance, personal injury insurance, and annuities. (人身保险)

15. gross line — the amount of liability an insurer has written on a risk, including the amount it has reinsured. Net line plus reinsurance equals gross line. (分保总额)

16. liability insurance — a contract of insurance in respect of liability incurred by the insured for loss or damage to a third party. (责任险；第三方损失或伤害险)

17. proportional reinsurance — system whereby the reinsurer shares losses in the same proportion as it shares premium and policy amounts. (比例再保险)

18. excess loss reinsurance — also called non-proportional reinsurance. (超额再保险)

19. books — a set of records or accounts. (账目)

20. term insurance — a type of life insurance policy that provides coverage for a certain period of time, or specified "term" of years. (定期人寿保险)

21. face amount — the amount stated on the face of a life insurance policy that will be paid in case of death or at the maturity of the contract; it does not include dividend additions, or additional amounts payable under accidental death or other special provisions. (面额)

22. policy reserve — It is the amount that a life insurance company allocates specifically for the fulfillment of its policy obligations; reserves are so calculated that, together with future premium and interest earnings, they will enable the company to pay all future claims. (保单责任准备金)

Exercises

I. Reading Comprehension.

Read the text carefully and decide whether the following statements are true (T) or false (F).

____ 1. The main function of insurance is to provide individuals or businesses with protection against financial aspects of risk.

____ 2. People can buy insurance direct in Lloyd's.

____ 3. The premiums include claims costs and profit margin.

____ 4. Under a facultative treaty, the direct writing company needs to submit each case to the reinsurer for scrutiny.

____ 5. Under a surplus line treaty, one line is equal to the ceding company's net retention.

II. Vocabulary Building.

A. Match the term in Column A with the definition in Column B.

1. liability insurance   a. the right for an insurer to pursue a third party that caused an insurance loss to the insured

2. term insurance   b. a person who tries to obtain insurance orders

3. solicitors   c. a contract of insurance in respect of liability incurred by the insured for loss or damage to a third party

4. indemnity   d. compensation for damage or loss sustained

Unit 14　Basics of Insurance

5. subrogation
6. direct writer
7. ceding company
8. net retention
9. facultative reinsurance
10. excess loss reinsurance

e. a type of life insurance policy that provides coverage for a certain period of time, or specified "term" of years
f. the amount of insurance that a ceding company keeps for its own account and does not reinsure
g. reinsurance effected item by item and accepted or declined by the reinsuring company after scrutiny
h. the company that originally writes the insurance business
i. reinsurance by a company agreeing to bear any loss in excess of a stipulated amount often with some maximum limit
j. a company that has placed reinsurance

B. Complete the following sentences with the words given in the box and change the form of the words where necessary.

claim	subject	hazard	chance	assure
catastrophe	inception	indemnification	exceed	assume
submit	include			

1. In insurance, the insured makes payments called "premiums" to an insurer, and in return is able to _____ a payment from the insurer if the insured suffers a defined type of loss.
2. In most countries, life and non-life insurers are _____ to different regulations, tax and accounting rules.
3. In general, insurance carriers (or insurers) are large companies that provide insurance and _____ the risks covered by the policy.
4. Property insurance protects against losses or damage to property resulting from _____ such as fire, theft, and natural disasters.
5. An increasing number of insurers have expanded their websites to enable customers to access online account and billing information and allow claims to be _____ online.
6. An insurer is liable to _____ for damage caused by unforeseeable events or force majeure.
7. The insurer may be aware of certain potential claim payments may _____ his financial resources, so he will wish to pass on part of the liability for these claims to another insurer by purchasing reinsurance.
8. Insurance companies spend a lot of time trying to work out the _____ of their customers having to make a claim and the potential cost of that claim.
9. An endorsement is a written document attached to an insurance policy that modifies the policy by changing the coverage afforded under the policy and can be added at the _____ of the policy or later during the term of the policy.
10. The main uses of reinsurance are to allow the ceding company to assume individual risks greater than its size would otherwise allow, and to protect the direct insurer

against _____ losses.

III. Cloze.

There are 10 blanks in the following two passages. For each blank, there are four choices marked A, B, C and D. You are supposed to choose the best answer.

Passage 1

Insurance is based on two principles: risk transference and the law of large numbers.

Risk transference, sometimes called "pooling", (1)_____ the transfer of risk from the individual to a pool of the insurance company's policyholders. The insurance company charges a fee, the premium, for accepting the risk and (2) "_____" the premium from a group of policyholders into a general fund to fund the death benefits (3)_____ contract.

For example, if 10,000 policy owners in the pool pay $1,000 each in annual premiums, the pool would amass $10,000,000 each year to (4)_____ claims resulting from losses. Should 500 members of the pool have losses during the year of $10,000 each, the pool (5)_____ be able to reimburse the members for their losses.

(1) A. addresses   B. indicates   C. involves   D. deals with
(2) A. pooling   B. pool   C. pools   D. pooled
(3) A. under   B. from   C. in   D. on
(4) A. make   B. meet   C. file   D. cover
(5) A. will   B. would   C. should   D. is

Passage 2

The law of large numbers basically relies on the principle that the larger the pool, the more predictable the amount of losses will be in a given period. (6)_____ not all members of the pool are the same age or in the same health condition, we can assume not all of them will be making a claim at the same time.

In fact, by recording and studying the number of (7)_____ over a very large population, the number of 62-year-old men, for example, who will die in a particular year, can be fairly predicted. This is not to say the year a (8)_____ person will die can be predicted. It only says that in a given year there is a high (9)_____ that X number of men who are 62 will die at that age.

Accordingly, with enough data, a statistician can comfortably predict the number of persons of a given age who will (10)_____ a serious illness in a given year. With enough data, the statisticians can assemble all of this information into tables.

(6) A. When   B. If   C. Since   D. While
(7) A. cases   B. claims   C. losses   D. men
(8) A. particular   B. specific   C. given   D. special
(9) A. chances   B. occurrence   C. probability   D. opportunity
(10) A. afflict with B. suffer   C. conceive   D. inflict on

IV. Translate the following sentences into English.

1. 根据保险合同规定的义务,所承保的危险事故一旦发生,保险人应负有赔偿责任。(liable)
2. 中国保监会(China Insurance Regulatory Commission)开始向偿付能力监管转变,这将使各

保险公司越来越重视资本金和责任准备金的充足问题。(shift)
3. 保险人有义务对在开展保险业务时所获得的有关投保人、被保险人和受益人的经济状况和个人隐私等信息进行保密。(obligate)
4. 保险公司在对保险基金进行投资时，总的目标是使公司能到期履行契约责任，同时能在不承担太大风险的情况下获得尽可能高的收益。(incur)
5. 如果合同约定保费分期支付，那么投保人应在合同订立时支付首期保费，并应按时支付续期保费。(at the inception of)

V. **Translate the following paragraphs into Chinese.**

1. Underwriting is the process of evaluating the risk to be insured. This is done by the insurer when determining how likely it is that the loss will occur, how much the loss could be and then using this information to determine how much you should pay to insure against the risk. The underwriting process will enable the insurer to determine what applicants meet their approval standards. For example, an insurance company might only accept applicants that they estimate will have actual loss experiences that are comparable to the expected loss experience factored into the company's premium fees.

2. Coinsurance and reinsurance differ fundamentally. With coinsurance, there is a contractual relationship between the policyholder and the coinsurer, so that in the event of a loss each is directly and separately responsible to the policyholder for paying its share of the loss. A reinsurance contract, on the other hand, is between the ceding company and the reinsurer — the original policyholder is not a party to that contract. By the principle of privity of contract, the original policyholder thus neither enjoys any benefit nor incurs any liability under a contract of reinsurance.

VI. **Self-Testing.**

1. All of the following are characteristics of insurance EXCEPT _____.
   A. risk avoidance
   B. pooling of losses
   C. payment of fortuitous losses
   D. indemnification
2. Indeterminacy and loss are the two common elements of _____.
   A. risk
   B. peril
   C. hazard
   D. insurance
3. The value of a policyholder's loss is generally determined _____.
   A. when the contract is entered into
   B. at the time of the loss
   C. after the policyholder makes a claim
   D. when the adjuster investigates the loss
4. _____ is the process by which the insurer decides whether or not to accept a proposal of insurance, on what condition, in what proportion and at what price.
   A. Premium rating
   B. Underwriting
   C. Ceding
   D. Investigating
5. Peter is a claims adjustor for ABC Insurance Company. After the insurer is notified that there has been a loss, Peter meets with the insured. The first step in the claims process that Peter should follow is to _____.

A. determine the amount of the loss

B. attempt to deny the claim regardless of whether he believes the claim is covered

C. verify that a covered loss has occurred

D. delay paying the claim if the claim is covered

6. What happens to the premiums for yearly renewable term insurance as an insured gets older?

   A. They increase at an increasing rate.   B. They increase at a decreasing rate.

   C. They decrease at a constant rate.   D. They remain level.

7. In _____, the face amount is paid if the insured dies during the policy period or at the end of the policy period if the insured is still alive.

   A. whole life insurance   B. endowment life insurance

   C. temporary life insurance   D. ordinary life insurance

8. If a direct insurer had a five-line surplus treaty, they could accept business from the public up to _____ times their retention.

   A. four   B. five   C. six   D. seven

9. ABC Insurance Company is a property insurer that is interested in protecting itself against cumulative losses that exceed $200 million during the year. This protection can best be obtained using_____.

   A. a quota-share reinsurance treaty   B. a surplus-share reinsurance treaty

   C. an excess-of-loss reinsurance treaty   D. a reinsurance pool

10. A reinsurance contract that is entered into on a case-by-case basis after an application for insurance is received by a primary insurer is called _____.

    A. a reinsurance pool   B. automatic treaty reinsurance

    C. retrocession   D. facultative reinsurance

VII. Writing.

Please write a letter to ABC Insurance Company in English in the following content to ask about the insurance rate.

1. 你们将船运 120 箱价值 5,050 英镑的皮鞋去英国伦敦。
2. 这批货从上海出发，由"东风号"船承运。
3. 请保险公司报出优惠的包括战争险的海运险费率。
4. 因"东风号"要在 8 月 4 日左右启航，请保险公司尽快回复。

Supplementary Reading

Insurtech — the Threat That Inspires

By Tanguy Catlin, Johannes-Tobias Lorenz
(www.mckinsey.com, March 2017)
(Abridged)

Incumbents need to keep their eyes out for new entrants that use technology to create a strategic advantage. The size of their share in the next generation of the insurance industry is at stake.

The rise of insurtechs

"Insurtechs" are technology-led companies that enter the insurance sector, taking advantage of new technologies to provide coverage to a more digitally savvy customer base. Over the past few years, insurtechs have emerged in the insurance space. Investments have grown by leaps and bounds — whereas $140 million was invested annually in 2011, investment climbed to $270 million in 2013, and $2.7 billion in 2015. Over this same period, the most successful insurtech ventures moved beyond the seed and venture-capital rounds of financing to advanced funding rounds. The average investment per insurtech has risen fivefold, from $5 million in 2011 to $22 million in 2015. After the US, the UK and then Germany are the homes of most insurtech companies. Asia-Pacific region accounts for only 14 percent of the insurtechs but is expected to be the fastest growing region in the coming years. Insurtechs are active in all major insurance products and business lines, with concentrations in the P&C business and in the marketing and distribution areas of the value chain.

Where insurtechs are now

Not unlike fintechs in banking, the initial focus of the insurtechs has been on the retail segment: 75 percent of insurtech business is in serving retail clientele, with the remainder in the commercial segment. Online and mobile channels and digital technologies offer many quick wins in retail, as millennials and more youthful age segments take over from the baby boomers. Young, digitally savvy segments are less company-loyal and tend to treat financial products and services, including insurance policies, as interchangeable as long as they fulfill personal needs. They value convenience and like to execute transactions remotely — if possible, without direct interaction with the institution. For the plugged-in cohorts, the use of 24/7 digital channels to receive an insurance quote or submit a claim is infinitely preferable to a branch or office visit.

Although much of the focus of insurtechs is on personal lines, they are also starting to move into the commercial segment. As in personal lines, insurtechs in commercial lines are bringing innovation to products, for instance, peer-to-peer and digital brokerage, often targeting the small- and medium-sized business segment. However, commercial lines insurtechs are also focusing on loss prevention and efficiency (e.g., drone inspection for underwriting and claims). In terms of lines of business, 46 percent of insurtechs in McKinsey Panorama Insurtech database are focused on property and casualty, 33 percent on health, and the remaining on life. Insurtechs target primarily pure risk insurance, where they have developed access points to the value chain based on innovation. Technologies such as telematics and the Internet of Things have enabled new product development in motor, home, and health that drive customer engagement and retention. Insurtechs have attracted consumers with selective discounting based on the intersection of smart devices and risk-minimizing behaviors, offering, for example, meters for car mileage or calories burned, or in-home flood and fire detectors that autonomously signal emergency services. Along the insurance value chain, insurtechs are active in distribution (37 percent) and pricing (23 percent). Within distribution, 75 percent of insurtechs focus on enabling distribution, by making products available to customers at their convenience, facilitating product comparison, and simplifying the purchasing process. These activities build on the successes of aggregators such as comparethemarket.com or confused.com —

e-commerce pioneers that moved into financial services in the 21st century and are now the leaders in digital insurance.

The insurtech edge is in its early adoption (and adaptation) of new technology. Almost all insurtechs rely on a digital customer interface for sales and service but many insurtechs are also adopting newer technologies and concepts that incumbents are only just beginning to experiment with. Eight important new technologies that have not been widely adopted by incumbents are already being used by insurtechs to solve real business problems. Certain of the new technologies specifically support insurance product innovations, including microinsurance, usage-based insurance, and peer-to-peer insurance; others have applications in many industries and include machine learning, robo-advisory, and the Internet of Things. Blockchain is an example of a new technology that is being used by insurtechs.

How insurtechs differ from incumbents

Insurtechs are able to go to market in fundamentally different ways than incumbents can. One advantage insurtechs exploit is their freedom from legacy products, processes, and IT systems. They are able to design digital processes, products, and systems from the ground up, relying on the latest technology. Like the fintechs, insurtechs target particular value pools in the sector, rather than seek to provide end-to-end solutions. Simpler IT and simpler operations translate into less investment and quicker returns. Insurtechs use their digital expertise to maximize value in a number of ways characteristic of truly digital enterprises:

- Increased connectivity. Insurtechs such as digital brokers Knip in Germany and Clark in Switzerland are using artificial intelligence and bots to provide robo-advice through a digital customer interface with digital distribution.

- Targeted product concepts. Insurtechs are able to offer personalized smallticket products based on usage or value-added services. Cuvva allows customers to buy hourly car insurance on demand using their mobile phone. Kasko and Simplensurance offer insurance coverage as an add-on purchase within e-commerce websites.

- Full automation. By an automatedonly approach, insurtechs cut costs and accelerate processes to meet customer expectations. SnapSheet, for example, offers end-to-end automated claims management, while the Claim Di mobile app "shake and go" allows claimants to interact with their carriers on the accident site just by shaking their phone.

- Data-driven decision making and insights. With access to diverse sources of data, including telematics from installed boxes and smartphone apps, insurtechs are applying machine-learning techniques to offer innovative, personalized products and services. Metromile, for example, offers pay-per-mile auto insurance to low-mileage drivers in some US states. FitSense allows life and health insurers to use data from wearable technology in underwriting, pricing and claims handling.

Insurtechs build their business models by addressing the pain points customers experience in their relationships with incumbent insurers. They especially seek to heighten customer interest and foster interaction. They do this in a number of ways:

- Social engagement. Peer-to-peer insurers, such as Friendsurance, Lemonade, Guevara, and Inspeer, use policyholder pooling to lower rates, but also create a social contract with the policy holder that many traditional insurers would envy. ERSTE Digital, a digital broker offering add-on coverage, sells through social media channels, including YouTube, Instagram, and Facebook.
- More frequent interactions. On-demand insurers like Trōv are able to offer consumers a mobile-enabled on-off switch for coverage. These innovations promote customer relationships and raise awareness of insurance by making it more relevant.
- Digitizing "moments of truth". Customer pain points, whether arising in advice or claims, can make or break customer relationships. Advisory solutions to these "moments of truth", such as PolicyGenius and HeyBrolly, tackle customer concerns about being over- or underinsured. Likewise in claims, Bauxy allows its customers instantly to initiate straight-through claims processing by taking a photo of an invoice and submitting it electronically.

The risks insurtechs present to traditional business models are real, as digital innovation relentlessly redefines the next-generation insurance ecosystem. Incumbents must adapt or lose market share, this much is known. In particular, they will have to address the much higher level of customer engagement that the insurtechs are attaining. Adaptation will bring benefits in many operational areas, leading to cost improvements, better capital allocation, and greater revenue generation. Insurers need to analyze the innovation landscape, compare their in-house technological capabilities with insurtech solutions, and consider their options for moving forward — from digitizing operations to acquiring or partnering with insurtechs.

Questions

1. What are insurtechs?
2. Which market segment do insurtechs target at? Why?
3. What are the focuses of insurtechs in the commercial segment?
4. What is the competitive edge of insurtechs?
5. How do insurtechs differ from traditional insurance companies?
6. What are traditional insurance companies supposed to do to meet the challenges imposed by insurtechs?

Unit 15　Basics of Accounting

Case

Daisy lived with her parents near a university campus. In order to help support the family, she decided to embark on a small business venture at home by offering printing and photocopying services to students. She began her business venture with $5,000 cash. She also invested her desktop computer and laser printer into the business. In addition, she leased a second-hand photocopier for $600 per month and purchased $1,000 of paper. Daisy provided $2,000 in printing and photocopying services during the first week. She had about $600 worth of paper left at the end of the first week. She was very happy, so she took $200 from the business to celebrate with her parents.

Questions

1. How much net profit did Daisy get in the first week of operations?
2. Why do businesses need an accounting system?

Preview

Skimming

Skim the following text quickly to answer the following questions and discuss your answers with your partners.

1. What is accounting?
   _____
   _____.

2. Why is accounting called the language of business?
   _____
   _____.

3. What are the two groups of users of accounting?
   _____
   _____.

4. What does GAAP stand for?
   _____
   _____.

5. What is the accounting equation?
   _____
   _____.

Unit 15   Basics of Accounting

Scanning

Scan the following text quickly to find the specific information.

1. What is the important aim of accounting?
   _____
   _____.

2. What does the term "general-purpose" refer to?
   _____
   _____.

3. Which group of users are similar to directors in information needs?
   _____
   _____.

4. List five internal information users.
   _____
   _____.

5. How long is the primary accounting period for most organizations?
   _____
   _____.

6. According to the revenue recognition principle, when is revenue recognized?
   _____
   _____.

7. What are the three basic forms of business organizations?
   _____
   _____.

8. What are the nonowners' claims on an organization's assets?
   _____
   _____.

Vocabulary in Context

Read the following sentences and try to guess the meaning of the italicized words by using the context. Then replace the italicized words with synonyms (words or phrases that have nearly the same or similar meanings).

1. Recordkeeping, or bookkeeping, is the recording of transactions and events, either *manually* or electronically.
   Recordkeeping, or bookkeeping, is the recording of transactions and events, either _____ or electronically.

2. Shareholders (investors) are the owners of a corporation. They use accounting reports in deciding whether to buy, *hold*, or sell stock.
   Shareholders (investors) are the owners of a corporation. They use accounting reports in deciding whether to buy, _____ or sell stock.

3. External (independent) auditors examine financial statements to *verify* that they are prepared according to generally accepted accounting principles.
   External (independent) auditors examine financial statements to _____ that they are

227

prepared according to generally accepted accounting principles.

4. Suppliers use accounting information to judge the *soundness* of a customer before making sales on credit, and consumers use financial reports to assess the staying power of potential suppliers.

   Suppliers use accounting information to judge the _____ of a customer before making sales on credit, and consumers use financial reports to assess the staying power of potential suppliers.

5. Research and development managers need information about *projected* costs and revenues of proposed changes in products and services.

   Research and development managers need information about _____ costs and revenues of proposed changes in products and services.

6. Comparable information is helpful in *contrasting* organizations.

   Comparable information is helpful in _____ organizations.

7. General principles *stem from* long-used accounting practices. Specific principles arise more often from the rulings of authoritative groups.

   General principles _____ long-used accounting practices. Specific principles arise more often from the rulings of authoritative groups.

8. The objectivity principle means that accounting information is supported by independent, *unbiased* evidence.

   The objectivity principle means that accounting information is supported by independent, _____ evidence.

9. The time period principle assumes that an organization's activities can be divided into specific time periods such as a month, a three-month quarter, a six-month *interval*, or a year.

   The time period principle assumes that an organization's activities can be divided into specific time periods such as a month, a three-month quarter, a six-month _____, or a year.

10. The revenue recognition principle provides guidance on when a business must *recognize* revenue. To recognize means to record it.

    The revenue recognition principle provides guidance on when a business must _____ revenue. To recognize means to record it.

Text

Accounting in Business

Today's world is one of information — its preparation, communication, analysis, and use. Accounting is at the heart of this information age. Knowledge of accounting gives us career opportunities and the insight to take advantage of them.

Importance of Accounting

We live in an information age — a time of communication and immediate access to data, news, facts, and commentary. Information affects how we live, whom we associate with, and the opportunities we have. To fully benefit from the available information, we need knowledge of the information system. An information system involves the collecting, processing, and reporting of information to decision makers.

Providing information about what businesses own, what they owe, and how they perform is an important aim of accounting. Accounting is an information and measurement system that identifies, records, and communicates relevant, reliable, and comparable information about an organization's business activities. Identifying business activities requires selecting transactions and events relevant to an organization. Recording business activities requires keeping a chronological log of transactions and events measured in monetary units and classified and summarized in a useful format. Communicating business activities requires preparing accounting reports such as financial statements[1]. It also requires analyzing and interpreting such reports.

We must guard against a narrow view of accounting. The most common contact with accounting is through credit approvals, checking accounts, and payroll. These experiences are limited and tend to focus on the recordkeeping parts of accounting. Recordkeeping, or bookkeeping, is the recording of transactions and events, either manually or electronically. This is just one part of accounting. Accounting also identifies and communicates information on transactions and events, and it includes the crucial processes of analysis and interpretation.

Technology is a key part of modern business and plays a major role in accounting. Technology reduces the time, effort, and cost of recordkeeping while improving clerical accuracy. Some organizations continue to perform various accounting tasks manually, but even they are impacted by information technology. As technology has changed the way we store, process, and summarize masses of data, accounting has been freed to expand. Consulting, planning, and other financial services are now closely linked to accounting. These services require sorting through data, interpreting their meaning, identifying key factors, and analyzing their implications.

Users of Accounting Information

Accounting is often called the language of business because all organizations set up an accounting information system to communicate data to help people make better decisions. The accounting information serves many kinds of users who can be divided into two groups: external users and internal users.

External Information Users

External users of accounting information are not directly involved in running the organization. They include shareholders (investors), lenders, directors, customers, suppliers, regulators, lawyers, brokers, and the press. External users have limited access to an organization's information. Yet many of their important decisions depend on information that is reliable, relevant, and comparable.

Financial accounting[2] is the area of accounting aimed at serving external users by providing them with financial statements. These statements are known as general-purpose financial statements. The term general-purpose refers to the broad range of purposes for which external users rely on these statements.

Each external user has special information needs depending on the types of decisions to be made. Lenders (creditors[3]) loan money or other resources to an organization. Banks, savings and loans, co-ops[4], and mortgage and finance companies are often the lenders. Lenders look for information to help them assess whether an organization is likely to repay its loans with interest. Shareholders (investors) are the owners of a corporation. They use accounting reports in deciding whether to buy, hold, or sell stock. Shareholders typically elect a board of directors[5] to oversee their interests in an organization. Since directors are responsible to shareholders, their information needs are similar. External (independent) auditors[6] examine financial statements to verify that they are prepared according to generally accepted accounting principles[7]. Employees use financial statements to judge the fairness of wages, assess future job prospects, and bargain for better wages. Regulators often have legal authority over certain activities of organizations.

Accounting serves the needs of many other external users. Contributors to nonprofit organizations use accounting information to evaluate the use and impact of their donations. Suppliers use accounting information to judge the soundness of a customer before making sales on credit, and consumers use financial reports to assess the staying power of potential suppliers.

Internal Information Users

Internal users of accounting information are those directly involved in managing and operating an organization. They use the information to help improve the efficiency and effectiveness of an organization. Managerial accounting[8] is the area of accounting that serves the decision-making needs of internal users. Internal reports are not subject to the same rules as external reports and are designed with special needs of internal users in mind.

There are several types of internal users, and many are managers of key operating activities. Research and development managers need information about projected costs and revenues of proposed changes in products and services. Purchasing managers need to know what, when, and how much to purchase. Human resource managers need information about employees' payroll, benefits, performance, and compensation. Production managers depend on information to monitor costs and ensure quality. Distribution managers need reports for timely, accurate, and efficient delivery of products and services. Marketing managers use reports about sales and costs to target consumers, set prices, and monitor consumers needs, tastes, and price concerns. Service managers require information on both the costs and benefits of looking after products and services.

Both internal and external users rely on internal controls[9] to monitor and control an organization's activities. Internal controls are procedures set up to protect property and equipment, ensure reliable accounting reports, promote efficiency, and encourage adherence to policies.

Generally Accepted Accounting Principles

Financial accounting practice is governed by concepts and rules known as generally accepted accounting principles (GAAP). To use and interpret financial statements effectively, we need to understand these principles. A main purpose of GAAP is to make information in financial statements relevant, reliable, and comparable. Relevant information affects the decisions of its users. Reliable information is trusted by users. Comparable information is helpful in contrasting organizations.

Accounting principles are of two types. General principles are the basic assumptions, concepts, and guidelines for preparing financial statements. Specific principles are detailed rules used in reporting business transactions and events. General principles stem from long-used accounting practices. Specific principles arise more often from the rulings of authoritative groups.

Some of the general principles are as follows:

The objectivity principle means that accounting information is supported by independent, unbiased evidence. It demands more than a personal opinion. Information is not reliable if it is based only on what a preparer thinks might be true. A preparer can be too optimistic or pessimistic. The objectivity principle is intended to make financial statements useful by ensuring they report reliable and verifiable information.

The going-concern principle means that accounting information reflects an assumption that the business will continue operating instead of being closed or sold. This implies, for example, that property is reported at cost instead of, say, liquidation values that assume closure.

The monetary unit principle means that we can express transactions and events in monetary, or money, units. Money is the common denominator in business. The monetary unit a business uses in its accounting reports usually depends on the country where it operates, but many companies today are expressing reports in more than one monetary unit.

The time period principle assumes that an organization's activities can be divided into specific time periods such as a month, a three-month quarter, a six-month interval, or a year. Most organizations use a year as their primary accounting period[10]. Reports covering a one-year period are known as annual financial statements. Many organizations also prepare interim financial statements[11] covering one, three, or six months of activity.

The consistency principle prescribes that an organization use the same accounting methods period after period so that financial statements are comparable across periods – the only exception is when a change from one method to another will improve its financial reporting. The consistency principle does not require an organization to use one method exclusively.

Revenue is the amount received from selling products and services. The revenue recognition principle provides guidance on when a business must recognize revenue. To recognize means to record it. The following three concepts are important to revenue recognition. (1) Revenue is recognized when earned. The earnings process is normally complete when services are rendered or a seller transfers ownership of products to the buyer. (2) Proceeds[12] from selling products and services need not be in cash. A common noncash proceed received by a seller is a customer's promise to pay at a future date, called credit sales. (3) Revenue is measured by the cash received plus the cash value of any other item received.

Expenses are outflows or using up of assets as part of operations of a business to generate sales. The matching principle aims to record expenses in the same accounting period as the revenues that are earned as a result of these expenses.

The business entity[13] principle means that a business is accounted for separately from other business entities, including its owner. The reason for this principle is that separate information about each business is necessary for good decisions. A business entity can take one of three legal forms: sole proprietorship[14], partnership[15], or corporation[16].

Accounting Equation

The accounting system[17] reflects the basic aspects of an organization: what it owns and what it owes. Assets are resources with future benefits that are owned or controlled by an organization. The claims on an organization's assets — what it owes — are separated into owner and nonowner claims. Liabilities are what an organization owes its nonowners (creditors). Equity (also called owner's equity) refers to the claims of its owner(s). Together, liabilities and equity are the source of funds to acquire assets. The relation of assets, liabilities, and equity is reflected in the following accounting equation:

$$\text{Assets} = \text{Liabilities} + \text{Equity}$$

The accounting equation applies to all transactions and events, to all forms of organization, and to all points in time.

Assets are resources owned or controlled by an organization. These resources are expected to yield future benefits. Examples are Web servers for an online services company, and musical instruments for a rock band. The term receivable is used to refer to an asset that promises a future inflow or resources.

Liabilities are creditors' claims on assets. These claims reflect obligations to provide assets, products or services to others. The term payable refers to a liability that promises a future outflow of resources.

Equity is the owner's claim on assets. Equity is equal to assets minus liabilities. This is the reason why equity is called net assets[18] or residual equity. A corporation's equity — often called stockholders' or shareholders' equity — has two parts: contributed capital and retained earnings. Contributed capital refers to the amount that stockholders invest in the company. Retained earnings refer to income (revenues less expenses) that is not distributed to its stockholders. The distribution of assets to stockholders is called dividends, which reduce retained earnings. Revenues increase retained earnings and are the assets earned from a company's earnings activities. Examples are consulting services provided, sales of products, facilities rented to others, and commissions from services. Expenses decrease retained earnings and are the cost of assets or services used to earn revenues. Examples are costs of employee time, use of supplies, and the advertising, utilities, and insurance services from others.

Net income occurs when revenues exceed expenses. Net income increases equity. Net loss occurs when expenses exceed revenues, which deceases equity. The accounting equation can be used to track changes in an organization's assets, liabilities, and equity.

Terminology

accounting	会计，会计学
financial statement	财务报表
recordkeeping	簿记
bookkeeping	簿记
financial accounting	财务会计
creditor	债权人

Unit 15　Basics of Accounting

shareholder	股东
managerial accounting	管理会计
internal control	内部控制
generally accepted accounting principles (GAAP)	公认会计原则
objectivity principle	客观性原则
going-concern principle	持续经营原则
monetary unit principle	货币计量原则
time period principle	会计分期原则
consistency principle	一致性原则
revenues	收入
revenue recognition principle	收入确认原则
expenses	费用
matching principle	配比原则
accounting period	会计期间
business entity principle	会计主体原则
sole proprietorship	个人独资企业
partnership	合伙制企业
corporation	公司
accounting equation	会计等式
assets	资产
liabilities	负债
equity	权益，所有者权益
owner's equity	所有者权益
net assets	净资产
contributed capital	投入资本
retained earnings	留存收益
dividends	股利

Notes on the Text

1. financial statement — a report containing financial information about an organization.
2. financial accounting — the field of accounting concerned with the summary, analysis and reporting of financial transactions pertaining to a business. It involves the recording and summarization of business transactions and events. Financial accounting relates to the preparation of financial statements for users such as creditors, investors, and suppliers.
3. creditor — a business or individual that has extended credit and is owed money.
4. co-op — a business organization owned and run by a society of persons or of groups of persons whose aim is not to make a profit but to give benefits to the members. It is also called cooperative. (合作社)
5. board of directors — a group of individuals elected, usually at an annual meeting, by the shareholders of a corporation and empowered to carry out certain tasks as spelt out in the

corporation's charter. (董事会)

6. external auditor — an independent public accountant who examines a business entity's books. The external auditor is not an employee of the business. (外部审计员)

7. generally accepted accounting principles (GAAP) — standards, conventions, and rules accountants follow in recording and summarizing transactions, and in the preparation of financial statements.

8. managerial accounting — process of identification, measurement, accumulation, analysis, preparation, interpretation, and communication of financial information that is used by management to plan, evaluate, and control within an organization.

9. internal control — all the methods and measures used by a business to monitor assets, prevent fraud, minimize errors, verify the correctness and reliability of accounting data, promote operational efficiency, and ensure that established managerial policies are followed.

10. accounting period — the length of time covered by financial statements, which is usually annual, semi-annual, quarterly, or monthly.

11. interim financial statement — a financial statement issued for an accounting period of less than one year. (中期财务报表)

12. proceeds — funds received from the sale of assets or issuance of securities such as capital stock or bonds.

13. entity — a separate economic unit subject to financial measurement for accounting purposes. (主体/会计主体)

14. sole proprietorship — an unincorporated business owned by a single person. The individual proprietor has the right to all the profits from the business and also has responsibility for all the liabilities of the business. (个人独资企业)

15. partnership — an unincorporated business owned by two or more persons. The partners agree to pool their funds and talent and share in the profits and losses of the business. (合伙制企业)

16. corporation — a legal entity, separate and distinct from the person who owns it. It is regarded by the courts as an artificial person; it may own property, incur debts, sue, or be sued. (公司)

17. accounting system — methods, procedures, and standards followed in accumulating, classifying, recording, and reporting business events and transactions.

18. net assets — total assets less total liabilities.

Exercises

I. Reading Comprehension.

Read the text carefully and decide whether the following statements are true (T) or false (F).

___ 1. Bookkeeping is a subset of accounting.

___ 2. Technology increases accuracy, efficiency and convenience in accounting.

___ 3. Managerial accounting is governed by GAAP.

___ 4. The consistency method means that an organization uses the same accounting methods period after period. That is to say, the consistency principle requires an organization to use one method exclusively.

___ 5. The accounting equation is always in balance.

II. Vocabulary Building.

A. Match the term in Column A with the definition in Column B.

1. accounting equation
2. assets
3. bookkeeping
4. expenses
5. financial accounting
6. going-concern principle
7. liabilities
8. managerial accounting
9. owner's equity
10. revenues

a. detailed and accurate recording of all transactions
b. accounting assumption that a business will continue in existence for the foreseeable future
c. accounting that supports the decision-making process through planning and controlling operations
d. obligations that legally bind an individual or organization to settle a debt
e. items of economic value owned or controlled by an individual or organization
f. any cost of doing business resulting from revenue-generating activities
g. income that an organization receives from its normal business activities
h. the process of recording, summarizing and reporting the myriad of transactions from a business, so as to provide an accurate picture of its financial position and performance
i. interest of the owners in the assets of the business represented by capital contributions and retained earnings
j. equation displays that all assets are either financed by borrowing funds or the owners' funds

B. Complete the following sentences with the words given in the box and change the form of the words where necessary.

| assume | assess | authority | concern | crucial | ensure |
| evaluate | focus | impact | insight | involve | sort |

1. Thorough and proper accounting procedures are _____ to the financial sustainability of an organization.
2. Historical cost refers to the sum of money was or is _____ to have been spent on a purchase or an operation of a firm.
3. Identity theft is a growing _____ in the economy, and bank officials work closely with technology experts and law enforcement agencies to prevent various forms of identity fraud.
4. Source documents are checked, _____, batched ready for entry into journals.

5. It is easier to _____ a firm using financial statements when the firm uses the same accounting procedures as other firms in the industry.

6. Investors _____ the impact of several large one-time charges and asset sales on the company.

7. Trial balance _____ listing the name of the accounts with their respective balances, then adding up the debits and credits to check if the two totals are equal.

8. Auditors use the accounting information to _____ that internal controls are working effectively.

9. Tax _____ have established special units to monitor the "offshoring" of revenues by companies.

10. Managerial accounting _____ on providing economic and financial information so that managers can make informed decisions.

III. Cloze.

There are 10 blanks in the following two passages. For each blank, there are four choices marked A, B, C and D. You are supposed to choose the best answer.

Passage 1

A bank reconciliation is the process that explains the difference between the bank (1)_____ shown in an organization's bank statement, as supplied by the bank, and the corresponding amount shown in the organization's own accounting records at a particular point in time. Such differences may occur, for example, because a (2)_____ issued by the organization has not been presented to the bank, a banking transaction, such as a credit received, or a charge made by the bank, has not yet been recorded in the organization's books, or either the bank or the organization itself has (3)_____ a mistake. It may be easy to reconcile the difference by looking at very recent transactions in either the bank statement or the organization's own accounting records. Otherwise it may be necessary to (4)_____ through and match every single transaction in both sets of records since the last reconciliation, and see which transactions remain (5)_____.

(1) A. amount   B. balance   C. number   D. result
(2) A. check   B. paper   C. contract   D. account receivable
(3) A. done   B. made   C. found   D. resulted
(4) A. put   B. add   C. go   D. see
(5) A. uneven   B. unequal   C. under   D. unmatched

Passage 2

Financial statements are the statements (6)_____ by an entity to communicate information about its financial performance, financial position and cash flows. There are typically three basic financial statements: the statement of financial position, the statement of financial performance, and the statement of cash flows. The statement of financial position (also referred (7)_____ as the balance sheet) sets out the financial position of an entity at a specific point in time and is often used to indicate the (8)_____ wealth of the entity at the end of a particular period of time. The statement of financial performance (also called the (9)_____ statement) shows how much profit was generated by an entity over a particular period of time. The statement of cash flows (10)_____ the cash movements that took place in the entity over a particular period of time.

(6) A. prepared   B. organized   C. set   D. established
(7) A. for   B. in   C. to   D. with
(8) A. accumulating   B. accumulated
    C. being accumulating   D. having accumulated
(9) A. profit   B. performance   C. result   D. income
(10) A. indicates   B. is indicated   C. will indicate   D. will be indicated

IV. Translate the following sentences into English.
1. 公允价值会计能够更好地反映经济环境，增加会计信息的相关性。(reflect)
2. 证券交易委员会有权规定上市公司应遵循的会计原则。(prescribe)
3. 一致性原则是指会计处理方法前后各期应当一致，不得随意变更。(imply)
4. 提供税务咨询服务的人员应当具备全面的税法知识。(render)
5. 根据复式记账规则，每一项经济业务都会影响至少两个账户。(affect)

V. Translate the following paragraphs into Chinese.
1. Accrual basis accounting recognizes revenues when earned and expenses when incurred. Adjustment entries have to be made at the end of the accounting period to account for any accruals and prepayments so as to determine the net income for the period. Cash basis accounting recognizes revenues when cash is received and records expenses when cash is paid. This means that cash basis net income for a period is the difference between cash receipts and cash payments. Cash basis accounting is not consistent with generally accepted accounting principles. It is commonly held that accrual basis accounting better reflects business performance than cash basis accounting.

2. An account is a record of increases and decreases in a specific asset, liability, equity, revenue, or expense item. The left side of an account is called the debit side, often abbreviated Dr. The right side is called the credit side, abbreviated Cr. Whether a debit or a credit is an increase or decrease depends on the account. The difference between total debits and total credits for an account, including any beginning balance, is the account balance. Double-entry accounting requires that each transaction affect, and be recorded in, at least two accounts. It also means the total amount debited must equal the total amount credited for each transaction.

VI. Self-Testing.
1. _____ is a system that measures business activities, processes the information into reports, and communicates the findings to decision makers.
    A. Financial accounting   B. Bank accounting
    C. Managerial accounting   D. Auditing
2. Which of the following statements concerning the accounting entity is NOT true?
    A. An accounting entity is an organization or a section of an organization that stands apart

from other organizations and individuals as a separate economic unit.

B. According to the accounting entity principle, business transactions should not be confused with personal transactions.

C. An accounting entity is a legal entity.

D. All of the above.

3. The key factor in determining whether an asset is liquid is _____.

   A. whether it can be sold in the money market without a significant loss being incurred

   B. whether it can be converted into cash as required without a significant loss being incurred

   C. whether it can be sold to the customers without a significant loss being incurred

   D. whether it can be converted into current assets as required without a significant loss being incurred

4. Given total assets are 760,000 *yuan* and total liabilities are 250,000 *yuan*, owner's equity is _____.

   A. 1,100,000 *yuan*   B. 510,000 *yuan*

   C. 160,000 *yuan*   D. 500,000 *yuan*

5. A bank's operating activities include cash inflows from _____.

   A. disposal of fixed assets   B. fees for services

   C. salaries and wages   D. financial investments

6. The accounting break-even occurs when _____.

   A. NPV is zero

   B. operating cash flow is zero

   C. net income is zero

   D. none of the above

7. According to _____, revenues are recognized when they are earned and expenses are recognized when they are incurred.

   A. accrual basis accounting   B. cash basis accounting

   C. modified cash basis accounting   D. basic basis accounting

8. A bank's budget should include _____.

   A. assets and liabilities   B. income and expenses

   C. profit and loss   D. all of the above

9. _____ is the value today of a future payment or series of payments discounted at the appropriate discount rate.

   A. Future value   B. Net future value

   C. Present value   D. Net present value

10. _____ is the catchall term that describes the wide scope of advice CPAs provide to help managers run a business.

    A. Budgeting   B. Cost accounting

    C. Auditing   D. Management consulting

VII. Writing.

Please write a letter to CitiBank in English as follows.

1. 对方行到20××年10月31日截止的对账单没有10月2日借方金额10,350美元和10月17日借方金额5,680美元的详情。我行无法在我方记录中查到。
2. 希望对方告知上述会计事项的性质和编号，以便我方采取必要措施。

Supplementary Reading

Traditional Accounting Company Embraces AI Tech

By Lu Hui
(*Xinhuanet* October 4, 2018)

SHANGHAI, Oct. 4 (Xinhua) — Accounting services including audits and tax preparation, which have long relied on human workers, are embracing artificial intelligence (AI).

Ernst & Young (EY), one of the Big Four accounting companies, said "yes" to the advancements brought by the cutting-edge technology, according to EY Global Chief Innovation Officer Jeff Wong.

A technology enthusiast himself, Wong shared his views on AI development and its impact on business with Xinhua during his business trip to Shanghai recently.

For him, AI is not a single technology but a set of methods and tools that can be applied to countless situations in enterprise systems.

Wong expects that in the next three to five years, AI will have a huge impact on a variety of areas such as healthcare, the financial sector and professional services involving traditional accounting companies like EY.

"AI could be a game changer for business generally, and professional services in particular. But actually, we are not disrupted by the new technology. However, we are moving forward and constantly evolving," Wong said.

"AI can alleviate mundane tasks performed by the human workforce so that we can focus more on complex work that ultimately provides a greater level of professional fulfillment, which is absolutely positive," he said.

EY is also making large investments into AI, according to Wong, without giving details.

During his business trip to Shanghai, Wong was impressed by China's AI development, calling it an explosion in creativity and innovation fueled by education improvements, intensified R&D, government policy and the availability of capital.

"In China, everybody seems to be moving in the same direction for the development of AI, on university levels, research levels, the corporate levels and investment levels, which is incredible," Wong added.

Benson Ng, partner of advisory services with EY, also mentioned in the interview with Xinhua that the Chinese Ministry of Industry and Information Technology published a document on how to foster AI development from 2018 to 2020 on a national level.

"China is a data-rich country, which is a very good starting point. Meanwhile, there are a lot of very encouraging progressions in different provincial governments," Ng said, adding that the municipal government of Shanghai unveiled plans to open up more space for the autonomous driving pilot program.

According to a newly released report from UBS in September, Chinese innovation is helping cast off the doubts over investment and credit toward new growth engineers. Based on government targets and the rate of change on a number of the innovation metrics, China is highly likely to emerge as a major innovating and high value-added economy in the coming decade.

Questions

1. What is AI?
2. What are the big accounting firms' attitudes towards AI?
3. How does AI impact the accounting services?
4. Will AI replace the human workforce in accounting business? Why?
5. How does AI develop in China?

Reference Key for the Exercises in the Texts

Unit 1

I. Reading Comprehension.

1. T   2. T   3. F   4. T   5. F

II. Vocabulary Building.

A. Match the term in column A with the definition in column B.

1. b   2. a   3. f   4. g   5. i
6. e   7. d   8. c   9. h   10. j

B. Complete the following sentences with the words given in the box.

1. tighten   2. liquidity   3. dominated   4. issuance   5. adjustment
6. monitoring   7. enforcement   8. implement   9. stability   10. accessed

III. Cloze.

Passage 1
(1) C   (2) A   (3) D   (4) B   (5) A

Passage 2
(6) C   (7) B   (8) A   (9) B   (10) A

IV. Translate the following sentences into English.

1. After the commercial banks raise the interest rates charged on mortgages, those who buy their houses on mortgage will have to pay more each month.

2. The People's Bank of China is the central bank of the People's Republic of China. Its chief mandate is to formulate and implement monetary policy and supervise and regulate the financial industry.

3. Before the Great Depression of the 1930s, many economists tended to see the economy as inherently stable with strong self-correcting tendencies.

4. The non-bank financial institutions mainly consists of trust and investment companies, asset management companies, securities firms, finance companies and insurance firms as well as many urban and rural credit cooperatives.

5. It is widely accepted that the first national paper notes in the world date from around 960 AD when the Chinese Song Dynasty began to issue paper currency after a shortage of copper limited its coin production.

V. Translate the following paragraphs into Chinese.

1. 美国联邦储备系统，通常简称为"美联储"，是一家独立的美国联邦政府机构。其主要负责监管美国的银行系统。自1931年起，美联储一直是美国的中央银行。美联储的主要职能是通过买卖政府债券来影响货币和信贷的成本和供给，进而实现相关的货币政策。假如美联储的货币供给量太少，利率往往会上升，借贷成本就会增加，经济发展速度会缓下来；反之，假如货币供应量太多，利率就会下降，借贷数量的增加会导致对货币的过度需求，从而推高商品价格，加剧通货膨胀。

2. 中国人民银行上周降息，这是自2008年12月起的首次降息。降息后一年期的借贷利率为6.13%，依然有进一步的降息空间，有利于经济增长速度的放缓。截至4月份，当年的工业生产增长率为9.3%，这是自2009年以来最缓的增长，但是5月份工业生产的增长率又上升到了9.6%。中国目前的通货膨胀率也为实施更为宽松的货币政策留出了空间。截至5月份，消费者价格指数只上升了3%，比4月份的3.4%有所下降，这也是自2010年6月以来上升幅度最缓的，远低于历来让政府担心的4%的临界点。

VI. Self-Testing.

1. D   2. D   3. D   4. D   5. B   6. B   7. A   8. B   9. C   10. B

VII. Writing.

Dear Sir/Madam,

Establishing Correspondent Relationship

We are writing you this letter in the hope of establishing the correspondent relationship with your esteemed bank.

As you may also have noticed, there has been a rapid growth of trade volume between our two countries in the past years. We believe the establishment of the correspondent relationship between us can help handle quickly the ever increasing banking transactions between us.

With this good wish, we enclose here a copy of our annual report for the fiscal year of 2018 for your reference.

We are looking forward to receiving a favorable reply from you.

Yours sincerely,

×××

Unit 2

I. Reading Comprehension.

1. T   2. F   3. T   4. T   5. T

II. Vocabulary Building.

A. Match the term in column A with the definition in column B.

1. c   2. e   3. a   4. f   5. g
6. b   7. h   8. j   9. i   10. d

Reference Key for the Exercises in the Texts

B. Complete the following sentences with the words given in the box.

1. discouraging   2. pursue   3. volatility   4. regime   5. curb
6. band   7. adverse   8. relevant   9. incentive   10. diversifying

III. Cloze.

Passage 1
(1) B   (2) C   (3) D   (4) A   (5) D

Passage 2
(6) B   (7) D   (8) B   (9) A   (10) C

IV. Translate the following sentences into English.

1. What factors do we need to take account of when forecasting the foreign exchange rate movements?

2. In order to eliminate the exchange risk, he hedged by selling the U.S. Dollars three months forward.

3. The exchange regulations of some countries do not allow the conversion of bank notes into foreign exchange.

4. People's Bank of China has ordered banks conducting yuan/dollar trading on the domestic foreign exchange market to abide by the restrictions limiting the currency's daily trading range of no more than 1 percent on either side of the midpoint it sets each morning.

5. We should accelerate the development of a multilevel capital market, take steady steps to make interest rates and the RMB exchange rate more market-based, and promote the RMB's convertibility under capital accounts in due course.

V. Translate the following paragraphs into Chinese.

1. 几乎每个国家都有其自己的货币或货币单位(美元、比索、卢比等)，用于在本国进行支付结算。但外汇通常是用于与他国的支付结算。因此，在任何国家，假如其居民要在国外做生意或是与外国人要有金融业务往来，一定会有途径能使他们获得外汇，这样，他们就能用外国人可以接受的货币来进行支付。换言之，存在这样一种"外汇"交易的需要，即将一种货币转换成另一种货币。

2. 决定外汇汇率远期升水或贴水幅度的因素包括两国间相对的利率。两国间利率的差异使外汇远期汇率较即期汇率升水或贴水。此外，如果预计宏观经济活动会出现变化，如国内生产总值会增长，或是预期的通货膨胀率也会对外汇的远期汇率产生影响。

VI. Self-Testing.

1. C   2. C   3. A   4. B   5. D   6. A   7. A   8. D   9. A.   10. D

VII. Writing.

Dear Mr. ×××,

Acceptance of Correspondent Relationship Proposal

Thank you for your letter regarding the establishment of the correspondent relationship between our two banks.

We are pleased to inform you that we have decided to accept your proposal. With the increasing banking transactions, we also find it necessary to establish the correspondent relationship, which we believe will be beneficial to both parties.

In response to your request, we are enclosing here our annual report for the fiscal year of 2018. We assure you of our best service to you.

Yours sincerely,

×××

Unit 3

I. Reading Comprehension.

1. T   2. F   3. F   4. F   5. T

II. Vocabulary Building.

A. Match the term in column A with the definition in column B.

1. b   2. g   3. a   4. h   5. c
6. f   7. i   8. e   9. j   10. d

B. Complete the following sentences with the words given in the box.

1. well-being   2. explore   3. distribution   4. facilitated   5. consume
6. accumulate   7. deposit   8. entity   9. adjust   10. entitle

III. Cloze.

Passage 1

(1) B   (2) A   (3) C   (4) A   (5) D

Passage 2

(6) A   (7) D   (8) B   (9) A   (10) A

IV. Translate the following sentences into English.

1. Since they are private banks, why do we have to pay for their mistakes?

2. In terms of financial reforms, experts say there is widespread support for some proposals to control risks.

3. Authorities will push for greater access for private and foreign capital while keeping proper capital account regulations.

4. It has become increasingly apparent that the market doesn't know what to expect and that many financial institutions are sitting on the sidelines, waiting to see what regulators will do next.

5. China has also accomplished huge progress in changing the financing structure of its financial market, with the proportion of its bank credit to the country's whole financing volumes declining from 90 percent a decade ago to the current 60 percent.

V. Translate the following paragraphs into Chinese.

1. 金融市场的首要作用是帮助撮合借方和储户(出借者)，促进资金从有盈余资金的个人、

Reference Key for the Exercises in the Texts

企业向需要的资金超过他们的收入的个人、企业、政府流动。在发达经济体中，金融市场有效帮助储户将剩余资金调配给需要资金用于投资或消费的个人和组织。无论是在制造业还是金融业，资金流转越高效，经济的有效性也越高。

2. 短期金融工具市场被称为货币市场，长期金融工具市场被称为资本市场。更具体地说，货币市场是包括到期日距发行日的期限等于一年或更少的金融工具的市场，资本市场包括到期日距发行日的期限大于一年的金融工具的市场。根据定义，货币市场只包括债务工具，因为权益工具(即股票)没有特定的期限，而资本市场则包括权益工具和长期债务工具如抵押贷款、企业债券和政府债券等。

VI. Self-Testing.

1. A 2. C 3. C 4. A 5. A 6. C 7. C 8. D 9. D 10. D

VII. Writing.

Dear Sirs,

We have examined the test key arrangements that we have with banks abroad, with the purpose of rationalizing them and consequently cutting into the relevant costs.

We have realized that in many circumstances, test keys are seldom, if ever, used, and this means that keeping and administering these documents would entail superfluous costs which could otherwise be avoided.

For this reason, if you agree, we would propose a cancellation of the test key arrangements with your ×× branches.

If, by January 1, 2013, nothing is heard from you to the contrary, we would suspend the arrangements with your ×× branches and would instruct our branches to discontinue using them. Please destroy those test key tables of ours now in the possession of your said branches and confirm that fact by returning the enclosed copy of this letter duly signed.

Thank you for your cooperation in this matter.

Yours sincerely,

×××

Unit 4

I. Reading Comprehension.

1. F   2. T   3. T   4. T   5. F

II. Vocabulary Building.

A. Match the term in column a with the definition in column B.

1. a   2. d   3. g   4. b   5. i
6. c   7. e   8. f   9. j   10. h

B. Complete the following sentences with the words given in the box.

1. repay   2. channel   3. exceed   4. incur   5. upsurge
6. collapsed   7. default   8. redeem   9. dump   10. confirm

III. Cloze.

Passage 1

(1) B　　(2) D　　(3) A　　(4) C　　(5) C

Passage 2

(6) A　　(7) B　　(8) C　　(9) D　　(10) A

IV. Translate the following sentences into English.

1. Desirable forms of financial regulation differ across countries depending on their preferences and levels of development.

2. The great increase of money supply has also increased the market liquidity which would result in a rise of price, followed by the pressure of inflation.

3. In effect, dealers bidding the highest prices faced a real "winner's curse", they attempted to resell the securities won in the auction to their customers.

4. Thus, the dealers had a strong incentive to share information with each other on the size of the orders they planned to place with the government and on the prices they hoped to bid.

5. Money market transactions are wholesale, meaning that they are for large dimensions and take place between financial institutions and companies rather than individuals.

V. Translate the following paragraphs into Chinese.

1. 全球货币市场有一些共同特征。他们在借贷双方都处于低风险的水平上为社会、个人和机构协调现金失衡。货币市场传导政府的经济政策，协助政府赤字融资(财政政策)和管理货币和信贷的增长(货币政策)。

2. 在发展中国家，由于他们的证券市场通常不发达，货币市场通常由大型银行把持。就如同在20世纪90年代亚洲经历的经济危机所显示的一样，银行主导的货币市场有一个潜在的弱点。他们可以很容易由于政府压力而导致坏账，这可能会延缓可以促进经济稳定长期的资本市场发展。

VI. Self-Testing.

1. D　　2. B　　3. B　　4. D　　5. C

6. A　　7. A　　8. B　　9. D　　10. C

VII. Writing.

Dear Sirs,

Private and Confidential

This is to reply to your letter of April 3, 2018 concerning the information on the Bank of China.

Bank of China is the most internationalized domestic Chinese bank. It is the only Chinese bank to open branches and representative offices in Asia, Europe, Australia, Africa, South and North America. It has a strong foreign exchange funding capacity. Its business now encompasses commercial banking, investment banking and insurance, making it a real universal bank.

In the process of assisting the government to introduce foreign capital into the country and handling foreign exchange business for many years, Bank of China accumulated a talent pool in dealing with domestic business and foreign exchange business and established a highly competitive customer service model.

Any above information must be treated as strictly private and confidential. We shall hold no responsibility for any irregularity therein.

Yours sincerely,
×××

Unit 5

I. Reading Comprehension.

1. T   2. T   3. F   4. T   5. T

II. Vocabulary Building.

A. Match the term in column a with the definition in column B.

1. b   2. i   3. a   4. f   5. c
6. e   7. d   8. g   9. h   10. j

B. Complete the following sentences with the words given in the box.

1. recall   2. reliable   3. transmit   4. purchase   5. tangible
6. disclosure 7. commission   8. principal   9. feasibility 10. estimate

III. Cloze.

Passage 1
(1) A   (2) C   (3) B   (4) D   (5) C

Passage 2
(6) C   (7) A   (8) B   (9) D   (10) A

IV. Translate the following sentences into English

1. Since taking office in late October last year, the minister has announced a series of high-profile policies to promote the healthy development of the stock market.

2. The Xinhua News Agency commented that the current effort to clear up the stock market is far from adequate.

3. The pension funds, corporate annuities and other forms of social insurance funds will need professional services from securities companies to preserve and increase their assets.

4. Analysts yesterday urged authorities to impose stricter regulations on the stock market after officials talked about the possibility of investing the country's huge pension funds in the market.

5. The Ministry of Human Resources and Social Security stipulates that social insurance funds can only be stored in designated banks or used to purchase national debt before the government hands out rules on any other forms of investment.

V. Translate the following paragraphs into Chinese.

1. 资本市场的一个主要切分是初级市场和二级市场。在初级市场，一般通过一种被称为承销的机制，新发行的股票或债券被出售给投资者。在初级资本市场，寻求筹集长期资金的主要实体是政府(可能是市政府、当地政府或国家)和企业(公司)。政府只倾向于发行债券，而公司经常发行股票或债券。购买债券或股票的主要实体包括养老基金、对冲基金、主权财富基金和较少的代表自己利益交易的富人和投资银行。在二级市场，已发行的证券在投资者和交易员之间通常通过证券交易所、场外交易或其他方式进行出售和购买。

2. 如果想要筹集长期资金，政府往往会在资本市场出售债券。对于发展中国家而言，一个多边发展银行有时会提供一个附加层的承销，这样可以使得风险由投资银行、多边发展银行和最终投资者三者共同分担。然而，自1997年以来，一些大国政府已经越来越普遍绕过投资银行，通过互联网让购买者直接在网上购买债券。现在许多政府出售的大部分债券在网上竞价销售。通常是一次竞价销售大量债券。政府可能每年只进行为数不多的几次竞价销售。一些政府还将通过其他渠道不断地销售债券。

VI. Self-Testing.

1. A 2. B 3. A 4. B 5. D
6. C 7. D 8. D 9. A 10. D

VII. Writing.

Dear Sir,

We are pleased to inform you that we have approved your application for a RMB500,000 loan subject to the following terms and conditions:

(1) Purpose: construction financing

(2) Amount of loan：RMB500,000

(3) Method of loan：fund directly advanced in a lump sum to the borrower after the contract takes effect

(4) Maturity：10 years

(5) Interest rate：Prime plus 1% per annum

(6) Security：the borrower presents the security

If you agree with the above terms, please sign and return us the enclosed copy of this letter on and before January 30, 2013.

Yours sincerely,

×××

Unit 6

I. Reading Comprehension.

1. F 2. T 3. F 4. T 5. T

II. Vocabulary Building.

A. Match the term in column A with the definition in column B.

1. b 2. c 3. a 4. e 5. d

Reference Key for the Exercises in the Texts

6. g   7. h   8. f   9. j   10. i

B. Complete the following sentences with the words given in the box.

1. transparency   2. specified   3. fluctuate   4. termination   5. eliminate

6. negligible   7. forecast   8. predefined   9. perceive   10. dynamic

III. Cloze.

Passage 1

(1) B   (2) A   (3) C   (4) B   (5) D

Passage 2

(6) A   (7) B   (8) C   (9) A   (10) D

IV. Translate the following sentences into English.

1. The "new rules" will permit institutions to trade credit and commodity derivatives as well as encourage market-making activities.

2. The total trading volume for derivatives world-wide was around 600 trillion U.S. dollars, and China's trading volume accounts for less than 1/600.

3. China's derivatives market is disproportionately small, considering the size of its economy.

4. China Securities Regulatory Commission had already reached a consensus on reforms for the derivatives market and will open the derivatives market up to increased and broadened participation.

5. With the approval of new regulations and programs, China is taking another major step to rein in financial risks.

V. Translate the following paragraphs into Chinese.

1. 市场参与者面临不同的风险最终会导致系统性风险，这就是说，一方的失败会对其他的市场参与者带来负面影响，并会潜在地导致整个金融市场的不稳定。包括监管机构在内的所有利益相关者首要关注的应是最大限度地控制系统性风险。

2. 衍生品市场有一些减少衍生品交易产生的不必要的风险的措施。从现实的角度来说，这些措施已经被证明是成功的——衍生品市场中不必要的风险已被降低到一个可忍受的水平。即使市场中有的参与者失败，他们也不会严重影响到其他市场参与者。

VI. Self-Testing.

1. A   2. D   3. C   4. D   5. C

6. A   7. B   8. B   9. A   10. D

VII. Writing.

Dear Sir,

Check No. …for…

We are sending you herewith the captioned check drawn by your depositor Mr. Johnson on your Bank and request you to issue, in placement, a demand draft payable to our order in its equivalent U.S. Dollars and send it to us.

We confirm the correctness of the drawee's signature on the check and look forward to receiving your reply at an early date.

Yours faithfully,

×××

Unit 7

I. Reading Comprehension.

1. T   2. F   3. F   4. T   5. T

II. Vocabulary Building.

A. Match the term in Column A with the definition in Column B.

1. c   2. f   3. j   4. h   5. d
6. b   7. i   8. g   9. a   10. e

B. Complete the following sentences with the words given in the box.

(1) perform   (2) efficient   (3) facilitate   (4) raise   (5) mechanisms
(6) Diversification   (7) fulfill   (8) stake   (9) promotes   (10) coordinated

III. Cloze.

Passage 1
(1) B   (2) B   (3) A   (4) C   (5) D

Passage 2
(6) D   (7) A   (8) C   (9) D   (10) A

IV. Translate the following sentences into English.

1. Grace periods on credit cards may vary, usually ranging from 20 to 50 days.

2. Some experts hold that all financial institutions should be subject to strict regulation.

3. According to the agreement, the bank is entitled to decide whether or not to charge its customers fees.

4. China Development Bank is a policy bank specializing in financing important infrastructure projects.

5. The intellectual capital will replace the financial capital and will become the most important capital of knowledge-intensive enterprises.

V. Translate the following paragraphs into Chinese.

1. 金融机构目前正在经历着职能和形式上的翻天覆地的变化。事实上，这些正在影响着金融服务业的变化非常重要，以至于许多行业分析把这些变化趋势称为一场革命，一场很可能让下一代金融机构变得面目一新的革命。影响当前金融机构业绩的主要趋势包括服务项目日益增加、金融市场的全球化、金融机构间的竞争日益激烈、金融服务生产和提供方式的自动化程度日益提高。

2. 中国人民银行曾经同时行使中央银行的职能和权力及处理工商业信贷和储蓄业务。但是自从1978年改革开放以来，中国在银行体系中开展了一系列重大改革。因此，金融业取得了稳步的发展。中国目前已基本形成了在中央银行监管、控制和监督下，以国有银行为主体，政策性金融与商业性金融相分离，多种金融机构分工协作、功能互补的金融体系。

VI. Self-Testing.

1. D   2. C   3. B   4. D   5. C
6. C   7. A   8. A   9. C   10. D

VII. Writing.

Dear Sir or Madam,

    We would be grateful if you could provide us with the information regarding the capital composition, credit standing and business operation of XX Company. The information you provide will be kept strictly confidential, and there is no obligation on your part.

    Your assistance would be highly appreciated.

Yours faithfully,

×××

Unit 8

I. Reading Comprehension.

1. F   2. T   3. T   4. F   5. F

II. Vocabulary Building.

A. Match the term in Column A with the definition in Column B.

1. g   2. h   3. a   4. e   5. j
6. b   7. f   8. d   9. c   10. i

B. Complete the following sentences with the words given in the box.

1. hedge   2. previously   3. maintains   4. intent   5. flexibility
6. sufficient   7. critical   8. excess   9. generate   10. obligations

III. Cloze.

Passage 1

(1) D   (2) A   (3) C   (4) B   (5) A

Passage 2

(6) B   (7) D   (8) A   (9) B   (10) C

IV. Translate the following sentences into English.

1. Ancient records indicate that about 4,000 years ago the temples were acting as banks, because they offered money exchange and lending.

2. HSBC's credit card can be applied in branch, by phone, or online.

3. The famous bank tailors services to better meet the VIP customers' needs.

4. Participating commercial banks should use only its own account to conduct bond trading.

5. A bank's IT costs vary according to what type of services it provides.

V. Translate the following paragraphs into Chinese.

1. 银行对于经济至关重要。虽然资金可通过多种方式在经济中转移，但是银行在建立金融环境的过程中发挥了核心作用。银行在转移资金提供增长、稳定货币供给这两个重要职能中发挥了关键作用。银行贷款使得消费者和企业能够有资金购买他们原本可能无法购买的东西。此外，银行还协助进行信用评定，以保证资金不会损失在不良贷款上。

2. 城市商业银行在中国的经济发展中发挥了重要的作用，但是它们面临的风险远远高于大型国有银行。十几年前，城市商业银行从城市信用合作社中转型而来，它们通常面临着不良贷款率高、资本充足率低、市场渗透有限的问题。统计数据显示，在不断努力筹集资金之后，城市商业银行普遍经营业绩良好。

VI. Self-Testing.

| 1. D | 2. A | 3. C | 4. D | 5. A |
| 6. C | 7. B | 8. A | 9. B | 10. A |

VII. Writing.

Dear Mr. A,

Customers should return all the unused checks to the bank before closing the checking account. We would appreciate it if you could return the unused check No. 2854212 from your checking account No. 8976593 so that we could remit the balance to your Citibank account.

Thank you for your kind cooperation.

Yours faithfully,
×××

Unit 9

I. Reading Comprehension.

1. F   2. F   3. T   4. F   5. T

II. Vocabulary Building.

A. Match the term in Column A with the definition in Column B.

| 1. d | 2. g | 3. j | 4. f | 5. c |
| 6. a | 7. i | 8. b | 9. e | 10. h |

B. Complete the following sentences with the words given in the box.

1. separate   2. sponsor   3. opposed   4. accelerate   5. complements
6. dilute   7. served   8. allocate   9. concerned   10. substantially

III. Cloze.

Passage 1

(1) A   (2) C   (3) D   (4) B   (5) D

Passage 2

(6) A (7) C (8) A (9) B (10) D

IV. Translate the following sentences into English.

1. Investment banking is not confined to the provision of underwriting services.

2. Corporations engage in two types of primary market transactions: public offerings and private placements.

3. The results are in line with analysts' estimates.

4. The distinction between book and market values is important because book values can be so distinguished from true economic value.

5. Provided that there are sufficient investors that are ready to acquire freely all the information available, the market can be efficient.

V. Translate the following paragraphs into Chinese.

1. 投资银行在新证券发行中处于核心地位。它们提供建议、承销证券。投资银行家的成功取决于名誉。好的名誉可以为投资银行家留住老顾客，吸引新顾客。换句话说，金融经济学家认为每个投资银行家都拥有"名誉资本"的储备。

2. 传统的"并购数学"是一加一大于二：即在财务上，两家公司合并后形成的实体将大于这两家公司的总和。管理层向来最重视这一原则，所以往往专注于交易的财务架构。然而，"新"的并购数学包括了两个核心要素——经济协同效应和心理协同效应。

VI. Self-Testing.

1. D 2. B 3. C 4. C 5. A
6. A 7. B 8. D 9. D 10. D

VII. Writing.

Dear Madam or Sir,

Recently our company has decided to issue additional stock. Considering the good business relationship with Morgan Stanley, we sincerely invite you to support us.

The attached is our annual report last year for your reference. Please write to me if you are interested. We could have further discussion on the details.

Looking forward to your reply.

Best regards,
×××

Unit 10

I. Reading Comprehension.

1. T 2. F 3. F 4. T 5. T

II. Vocabulary Building.

A. Match the term in Column A with the definition in Column B.

1. d 2. j 3. e 4. a 5. g
6. i 7. h 8. c 9. f 10. b

B. Complete the following sentences with the words given in the box.

1. revealed 2. aided 3. qualified 4. extend 5. chartered
6. valuable 7. practice 8. options 9. dominated 10. execute

III. Cloze.

Passage 1
(1) C (2) B (3) C (4) D (5) D

Passage 2
(6) C (7) C (8) A (9) D (10) A

IV. Translate the following sentences into English.

1. The plan will usher in the digital age of consumer spending.

2. It is reported that the great losses from investment banks will lead to a restructuring of the business.

3. In 1933, President Roosevelt signed an act to deal with the crisis of banking industry in the United States.

4. A recent survey reveals that customers demand better credit card online services.

5. It is noted that the satellite town will be transformed into a new financial service park.

V. Translate the following paragraphs into Chinese.

1. 表外项目是指可能影响金融机构资产负债表未来状况的或有资产和或有负债。表外业务不太明显，财务报表的使用者通常无法看到表外业务，因为它们常常出现在账户的附注里。虽然现在表外业务是许多金融机构的重要的手续费收入来源，但是它们既有可能产生正的未来现金流量，也有可能产生负的未来现金流量。表外项目的有效管理是金融机构总风险控制的核心问题。

2. 提供国际业务的银行帮助它们的客户处理国际账户的议付、融资、转账和收账。国际金融和进出口业务专家帮助客户处理海量的文件。国际贸易融资方式有很多种。一些是向进口企业或其他国际企业提供简单的国内贷款。一些是通过政府银行或政府经营的行业向国外政府提供直接贷款。银行利用专业知识帮助公司评估其在国际商业活动中的前景和风险，帮助公司处理有关国际交易的文件。

VI. Self-Testing.

1. A 2. C 3. C 4. D 5. B
6. D 7. C 8. D 9. B 10. B

VII. Writing.

To whom it may concern,

Our London Office has sent us the credit advice No. K4638703 under the L/C No.120260-T-15. We have noticed that the account has been credited with GBP33230.00 which is GBP90.00 less than our T/T claim for GBP33320.00. We would appreciate it if you could look into the matter and pay GBP90.00 to our account under advice to us as soon as possible.

Thank you for your cooperation.

Yours faithfully,

× × ×

Unit 11

I. Reading Comprehension.

1. F   2. F   3. T   4. T   5. F

II. Vocabulary Building.

A. Match the term in Column A with the definition in Column B.

1. f   2. a   3. i   4. g   5. b
6. c   7. h   8. j   9. d   10. e

B. Complete the following sentences with the words given in the box.

1. facilitate   2. mortgage   3. covenant   4. withdrawal   5. redistribution
6. audit   7. guarantee   8. maintenance   9. monetary   10. maturity

III. Cloze.

Passage 1

(1) B   (2) A   (3) C   (4) B   (5) D

Passage 2

(6) C   (7) A   (8) B   (9) C   (10) D

IV. Translate the following sentences into English.

1. The subprime crisis has been blamed for steep declines in the stock market.

2. Medium and long-term loans are mainly used to assemble capital for infrastructure, based industries and pillar industries as well as technology upgrading projects.

3. These firms miscalculated the likelihood of defaults in a housing downturn; they're now holding a bunch of bad loans that no one wants to buy.

4. Many traditional forms of consumer credit have monthly payments-fixed repayment schedules from one to five years.

5. Credit unions have attained some importance in making personal loans at relatively low interest rates, and micro-credit programs and organizations, which offer small-scale loans, have been

proved useful, particularly in developing countries, in helping individuals to establish small business.

V. Translate the following paragraphs into Chinese.

1. 有抵押的贷款(相比之下，无抵押贷款仅以借款人的付款承诺为支持)是以贷方对财产权利的分配，私人财产或不动产担保物权的取得作为抵押。抵押借款人给予贷方被抵押财产的债权。工商业贷款可以以现金、存货清单、应收账款、可转让证券或其他可接受的担保物作为抵押。如果借款人未能根据原始信用证条款偿付，贷方可以采取合法行为回收或者出卖担保物。。

2. 供应商与进口商签订提供商品和服务的合同。合同的付款条件要求进口商以每半年一次的分期付款支付商品款项。供应商和进口商分别向各自的银行申请。进口方银行在接受申请之后签发一份以供应商为收款人的信用保证书。供应商银行与供应商签订贷款协定。贷款协定和合同在得到出口信用机构批准之后生效。

VI. Self-Testing.

1. A   2. C   3. C   4. D   5. B
6. C   7. C   8. C   9. D   10. A

VII. Writing.

Dear Madam or Sir,

We sincerely hope to establish business relationship with Standard Chartered Bank.

We would like to apply for loans to support the factory expansion and facility upgrading. The information of our company is attached for your reference. Please kindly provide the credit line, repayment period, interest rate and other necessary information. We wish to keep a long-term cooperation with you.

Looking forward to your reply.

Best regards,

×××

Unit 12

I. Reading Comprehension.

1. F   2. F   3. T   4. F   5. T

II. Vocabulary Building.

A. Match the term in Column A with the definition in Column B.

1. b   2. d   3. e   4. a   5. i
6. f   7. h   8. c   9. g   10. j

B. Complete the following sentences with the words given in the box.

1. encountered   2. evolved   3. unconditional   4. carriage   5. insuring
6. worthiness   7. tenor   8. request   9. undertaking 10. assume

III. Cloze.

Passage 1

(1) A   (2) B   (3) C   (4) A   (5) C

Reference Key for the Exercises in the Texts

Passage 2
(6) B (7) A (8) C (9) B (10) A

IV. Translate the following sentences into English.

1. The confirming bank effectively assumes the same obligations as the issuing bank and must pay, accept the usance draft, or negotiate without recourse to the beneficiary, provided all the documents stipulated in the documentary credit are presented in order and that the terms and conditions of the L/C are complied with.

2. Normally, title to the goods does not pass on to the buyer until the draft is paid or accepted by the buyer.

3. In effect, all the parties to the letter of credit transaction, i.e., the issuing bank, the buyer and the seller, must agree to any amendment to or cancellation of the letter of credit.

4. By negotiating the beneficiary's draft, the negotiating bank becomes an "endorser and bona fide holder" of the draft, and is protected by the issuing bank's undertaking to pay under the credit.

5. The collecting bank takes up the role of ensuring that the buyer pays or accepts to pay for the goods before shipping documents are released to him.

V. Translate the following paragraphs into Chinese.

1. 只有进口商的银行可以满足他的特殊需求，这些特殊需求包括：直到进口商确信买方履行了合同义务后才付款；进口商有可能得到银行贷款去支付货款，直到收回销售收入时才归还以及获得有关贸易流程与外汇交易活动的建议与帮助。

2. 信用证是依据于单据而非事实。没能及时提供符合规定的单据会导致信用证无效。作为一个卖方/出口商/受益人应当将各种单据与公司内的不同部门、人员进行对照以检查是否存在不符问题。如果出现不符情况，应在货物装运前修改信用证。

VI. Self-Testing.

1. A   2. C   3. B   4. C   5. D
6. C   7. B   8. A   9. C   10. A

VII. Writing.

Dear Madam or Sir,

It is our sincere hope that we could provide our tea to Bill Company and establish a long-term cooperation with you. Our company has a good reputation for exporting Chinese tea.

We invite you to be our agent in the United States and use the L/C issued by the local bank for settlement. The enclosed is the latest catalogue of our products.

Looking forward to your reply.

Best regards,

×××

Unit 13

I. Reading Comprehension.

1. T 2. F 3. T 4. T 5. F

II. Vocabulary Building.

A. Match the term in column A with the definition in column B.

1. d 2. a 3. e 4. c 5. g
6. i 7. b 8. f 9. j 10. h

B. Complete the following sentences with the words given in the box.

1. sound   2. granted   3. impaired   4. benchmarks   5. subject
6. deregulation   7. susceptible   8. optimize   9. comprises   10. pose

III. Cloze.

Passage 1

(1) C   (2) A   (3) B   (4) C   (5) D

Passage 2

(6) C   (7) B   (8) A   (9) A   (10) D

IV. Translate the following sentences into English.

1. Online merchant banking entails the same level of risks as other types of banking.

2. Bank supervision involves monitoring and examining the condition of banks and their compliance with laws and regulations.

3. It is argued that bank inefficiency mainly arises from bad loans, most often due to bad management of the bank.

4. When bank regulators assess the adequacy of a bank's capital to handle losses from its loans, investments, and other assets, they take into account the riskiness of those assets.

5. Banks in market economies play a major role in the allocation of financial resources, intermediating between depositors of surplus funds and would-be borrowers, on the basis of active judgments as to the latter's ability to repay.

V. Translate the following paragraphs into Chinese.

1. 在一个越来越相互联系的世界中，全球金融灾难会影响几乎每个人的生计。金融监管的主要目标包括保护存款人的资金，保持货币体系的稳定，促进一个高效、有竞争力的银行体系，保护消费者与银行关系和交易相关的权益。

2. 根据原则3，审批发牌的过程，至少应该包括评估银行所有权结构，银行的管理，以及更广的人员，包括董事会成员和银行高管的身体健康和行为规范，银行的战略和运营规划，内部控制和风险管理，以及其预计的金融条件，包括其资本金基础。如果银行的所有人或是母公司是一家外国银行，必须先获得其本国监管机构的审核批准。

Reference Key for the Exercises in the Texts

VI. Self-Testing.

1. B	2. B	3. D	4. C	5.B
6. C	7. D	8. C	9. A	10. B

VII. Writing.

Dear Sir/Madam,

An Invitation to a Regional Policy Forum
on Financial Stability and Macropredential Supervision

The Financial Stability Institute, the Bank of International Settlements and the China Banking Regulatory Commission will host a Regional Policy Forum on Financial Stability and Macropredential Supervision in Beijing from May 29 to May 31, 20 ××. We wish to express our pleasure of inviting you to attend the forum.

Since the participants are mainly governors of the central banks of the countries in East Asia and the Pacific Region as well as senior officials of the countries' banking regulatory commission, it is a great opportunity for the participants to exchange views and seek cooperation.

You are welcome to make a speech at the forum. The abstract of your speech should be submitted to us before March 15. If you need more information, please contact Mr. Wang Qiming and his email address is wangqiming@cbrc.gov.cn。

We look forward to meeting you at the forum.

Yours sincerely,

×××

Unit 14

I. Reading Comprehension.

1. T	2. F	3. F	4. T	5. T

II. Vocabulary Building.

A. Match the term in column A with the definition in column B.

1. c	2. e	3. b	4. d	5. a
6. h	7. j	8. f	9. g	10. i

B. Complete the following sentences with the words given in the box.

1. claim	2. subject	3. assume	4. hazards	5. submitted
6. indemnify	7.exceed	8. chances	9. inception	10. catastrophic

III. Cloze.

Passage 1

(1) C   (2) C   (3) A   (4) D   (5) B

Passage 2
(6) C   (7) B   (8) A   (9) C   (10) C

IV. Translate the following sentences into English.

1. In accordance with the contracted insurance obligations, the insurer is liable for indemnification when an insured peril occurs.

2. The CIRC's shift to solvency-based supervision will increase the insurer's focus on adequacy of capital and policy reserves.

3. The insurer is obligated to keep confidential all information obtained in the course of conducting insurance business regarding financial position and individual privacy of the applicant, the insured or the beneficiary.

4. In the investment of the insurance company funds, the overall aim is to enable the company to meet liabilities when they fall due while earning the highest possible yield without incurring too great a risk.

5. If the contract stipulates that the premium is to be paid by installments, the applicant shall pay the first installment at the inception of the contract and the other installments as scheduled.

V. Translate the following paragraphs into Chinese.

1. 核保是评估所承保的风险的过程。在此过程中，承保人确定损失发生的概率有多少，损失的金额会是多少，然后用这些信息来决定所投保的保险费。承保的过程能使承保人确定什么样的投保人符合他们批准的标准。例如，保险公司可能只接受那些他们估计其实际发生的损失与保险公司计算进保险费的预计损失相当的投保人的投保。

2. 共保和分保根本上是不同的。在共保中，保单持有人和共保人之间存在一种契约关系，一旦损失发生，每一方都直接、分别负责向保单持有人支付其负责的那部分损失。另一方面，分保合同是分保公司和分保人之间签署的合同，原保单持有人不是该合同的签约方。根据合同相对性原则，在分保合同中，原保单持有人既不享有任何利益，也不承担任何责任。

VI. Self-Testing.

1. A   2. A   3. B   4. B   5. C
6. A   7. B   8. C   9. C   10. D

VII. Writing.

Dear Sir,

Inquiry for Insurance Rate

We shall shortly have a shipment of 120 cases of leather shoes, valued at 5,050 pounds CIF London to be shipped by s.s. Dongfeng from Shanghai. Would you please be kind enough to quote us your most favorable rate for Marine Insurance, ICC(B), including War Risk?

As the ship will sail from Shanghai on or about August 4, please give us a reply as soon as possible.

Yours sincerely,

×××

Unit 15

I. Reading Comprehension.
1. T 2. T 3. F 4. F 5. T

II. Vocabulary Building.
A. Match the term in Column A with the definition in Column B.
1. j 2. e 3. a 4. f 5. h
6. b 7. d 8. c 9. i 10. g

B. Complete the following sentences with the words given in the box.
1. crucial 2. assumed 3. concern 4. sorted 5. evaluate
6. assessed 7. involves 8. ensure 9. authorities 10. focuses

III. Cloze.

Passage 1
(1) B (2) A (3) B (4) C (5) D

Passage 1
(6) A (7) C (8) B (9) D (10) A

IV. Translate the following sentences into English.

1. Fair value accounting can better reflect the economic environment and improve the relevance of the accounting information.

2. Securities and Exchange Commission has the authority to prescribe accounting principles for listed companies.

3. The consistency principle implies that accounting methods should be consistent period after period and should not be arbitrarily changed.

4. Those who render tax consulting services should have an extensive knowledge of tax laws.

5. According to the double entry rule, each transaction affects at least two accounts.

V. Translate the following paragraphs into Chinese.

1. 权责发生制在实现收入时确认收入，发生费用时确认费用。会计期末需要编制调整分录记录应计和预付项目，以便确定这一会计期间的净利润。收付实现制在收到现金时确认收入，付出现金时确认费用。这意味着收付实现制下一个会计期间的净利润相当于现金收入和现金支出的差额。收付实现制与公认会计原则不一致。人们通常认为，与收付实现制相比，权责发生制更好地反映了企业的业绩。

2. 账户是对某一特定资产、负债、所有者权益、收入或费用项目的增减变化的记录。账户的左边称为借方，通常缩写为 Dr。右边称为贷方，缩写为 Cr。借方或贷方用于记录增加还是减少取决于账户的性质。账户借贷双方包括期初余额在内的差额称为账户余额。复式记账法规定，每一个会计事项至少影响两个账户，并被记录在至少两个账户内。这也意味着每一个会计事项的借方金额之和必须等于贷方金额之和。

VI. Self-Testing.

1. A   2. C   3. B   4. B   5. B
6. C   7. A   8. D   9. C   10. D

VII. Writing.

To whom it may concern,

Your statement of account ending October 31, 20×× does not indicate particulars for USD10,350 of October 220×× and USD5680 of October 17 on the debit side and we are not able to trace them in our records. We would appreciate it if you could inform us of the nature and numbers of these transactions so that we can do the needful.

Thank you for your kind cooperation.

Yours faithfully,

×××